Weaving

Step-by-Step

Sue Muldoon

This book is dedicated to
Roberta Muldoon, my mother
who sowed creative seeds,
to Garland Reedy, my
seatweaving instructor
who helped me evolve,
and to my grandchildren
who make life bloom.

TABLE OF CONTENTS

SUE MULDOON

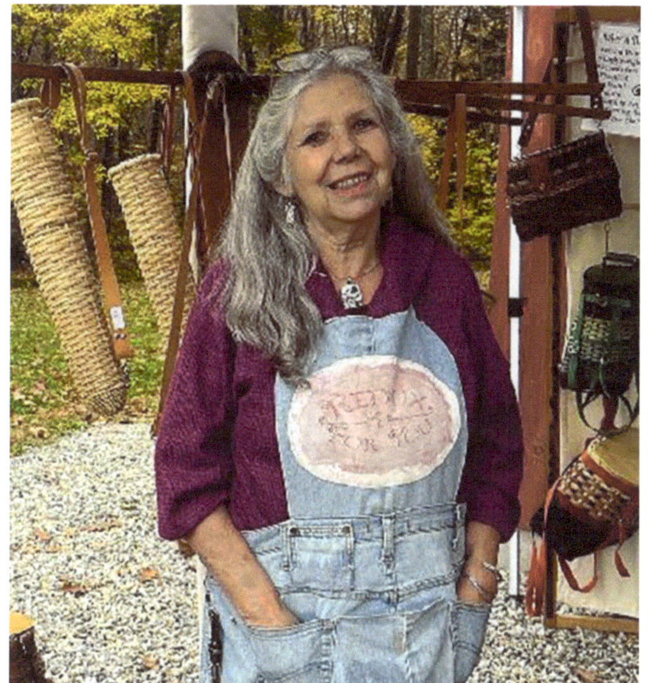

Sue Muldoon   Photo: Jean Cardinale Nelson

I am an artist by nature. Just like nature, I fluctuate with the seasons. My youth was full of adventure as I took off cross-country at 21 and became an interior painter and wallpaper hanger in Oklahoma City. Following my wanderlust, I landed in Seattle, Washington, ultimately returning to my home state, CT.

When my kids were young, I took adult-ed classes in caning and woodcarving. The seatweaving hooked me. I had a small business for a few years repairing woven chairs.

My love of the floral industry began in my first supermarket job as a teen and prompted me to return in my 30's as a young Mom.

twenty eight years in retail and wholesale in the floral industry were fascinating and fulfilling. As a designer, merchandiser, Mass Market sales professional, graphic designer, and trade show organizer, I traveled around the country and spent time immersed in flowers.

In 2014, I incurred a broken ankle, and was housebound for months. I started working on my own delayed projects in the basement that had been left orphaned. Down time became my friend. I started caning and posting pictures on Facebook. Requests for seatweaving began pouring in. While looking up a special pattern online I discovered The Seatweavers' Guild and joined. I now have about 160 contacts across the country in the industry. My focus changed, as did my job description. Seatweaving is a practical and in-demand profession.

Then I discovered basket weaving, which was my next step in creativity. I enjoy weaving functional items and wearable art.

My focus now is teaching and basketry, while still repairing chairs. Teaching at many venues across the country in-person and virtually, I am reaching hundreds of people each year. This book is to help aid in your creative journey.

Top it off with an invitation to be on "J Schwankes Life in Bloom" with my friend of 20+ years...and I'll call it a happy life.

I had a "lucky break" that brought me back full circle to a creative lifestyle.

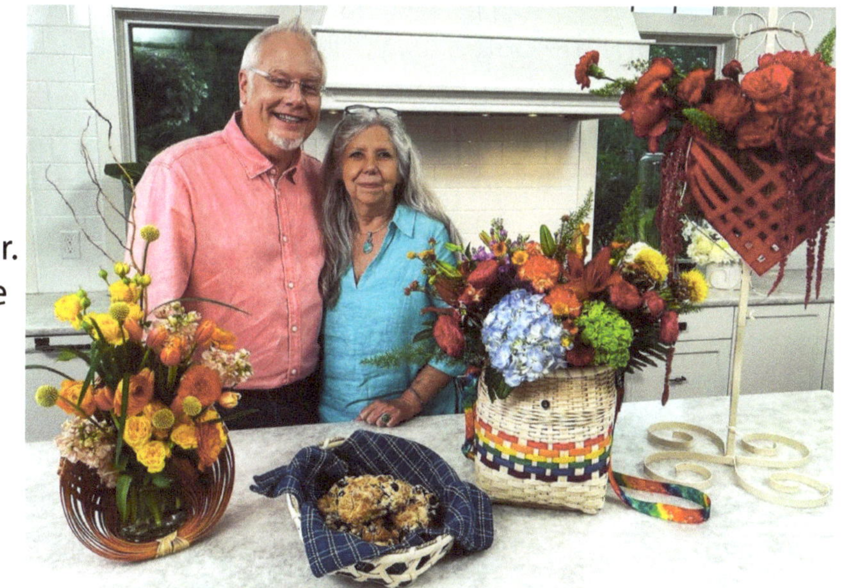

J Schwanke and Sue...Photo: Kelly James Blank

CRAFT

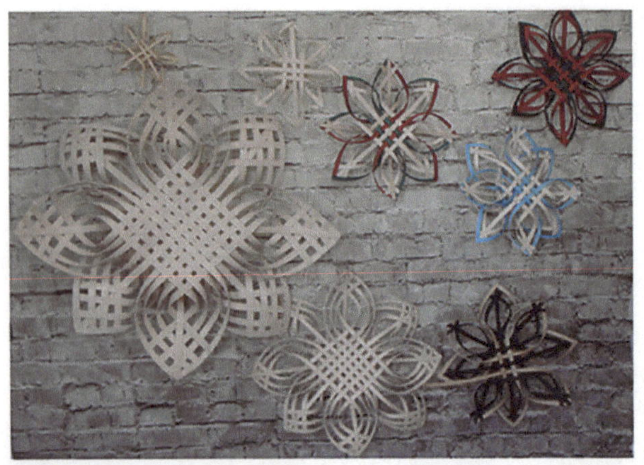
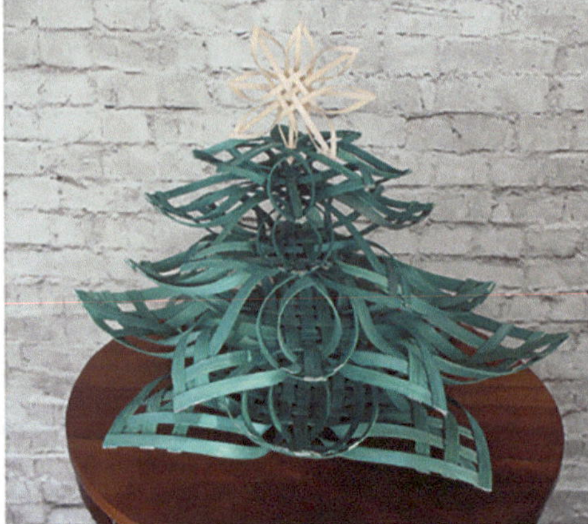
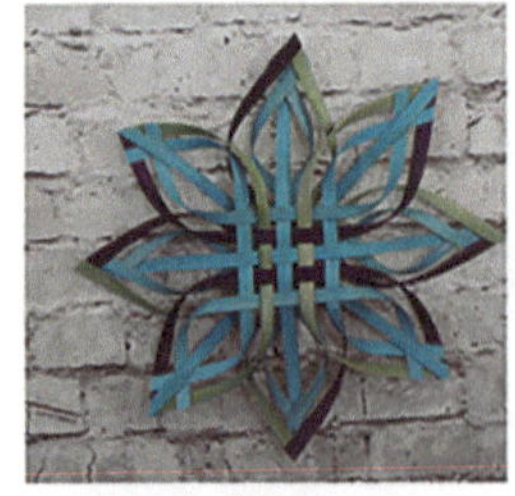
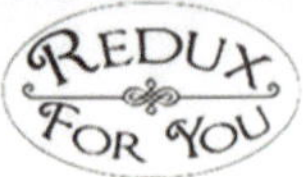

REED HEARTS & SNOWFLAKES

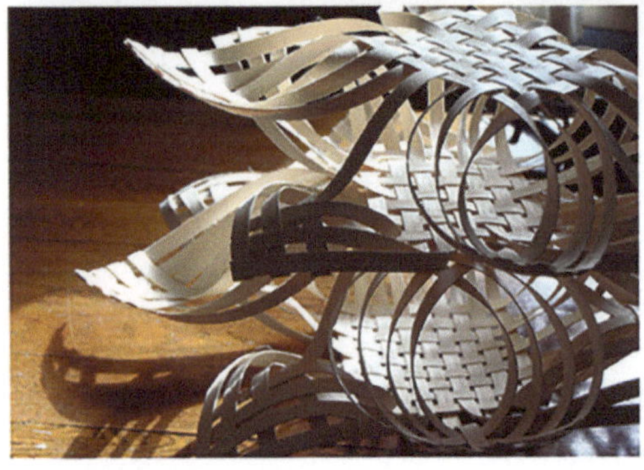
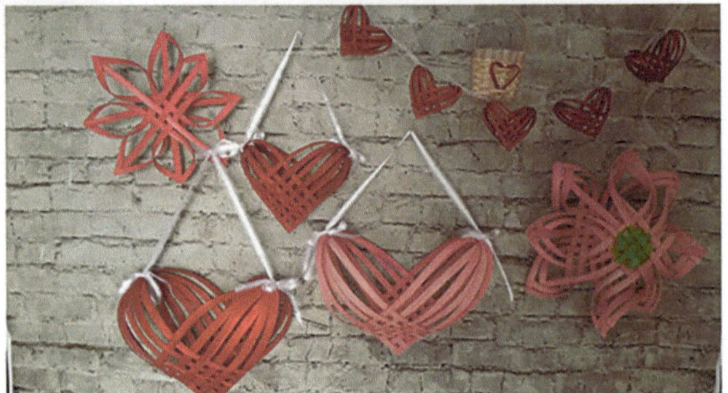
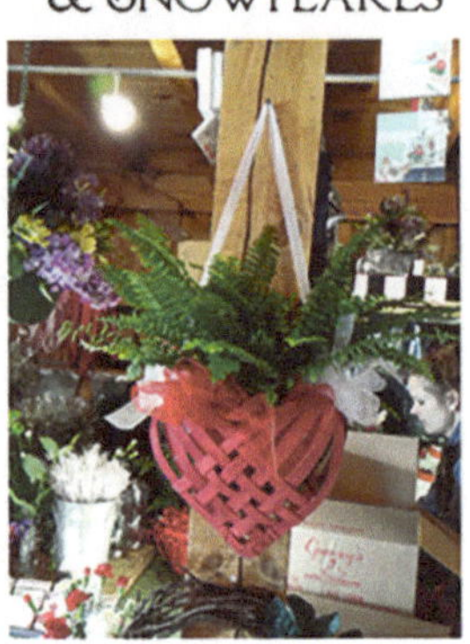

Grab your scissors and glue and get ready to create! These crafts are great for individuals or groups of all ages. The hearts and snowflakes can be made with paper and glue sticks for young crafters. Adults can use reed and superglue. Don't use hot glue. The reed is porous and will draw moisture from the air, and the crafts might loosen. A tip for using superglue: wrap your non-dominant fingers in adhesive bandages or painter's tape to avoid gluing them. Small 2" clamps work best for reed and clothes pins are sufficient for paper and glue sticks.

Once you learn the patterns, you can explore making different colors, sizes, and styles using various sizes of reed and colors. The hearts make a wonderful way to carry gifts, display plants or even floral designs! Different sizes can nest together. A row of small hearts can be strung together for decoration. Twinkle lights look great in them, as well as behind a large snowflake for your front door.

Make gradating sizes of green snowflakes and stack them on a dowel embedded in foam in a basket, to make a Christmas tree! Top off with a small natural snowflake. Celebrating St Patrick's Day? Make 3 green hearts, glue them together, and add a stem.

Patterns are designated as beginner, intermediate or advanced. This is only a suggestion. I have had beginners with no experience begin with a backpack and weave like a pro!

Reed (or paper) Snowflake

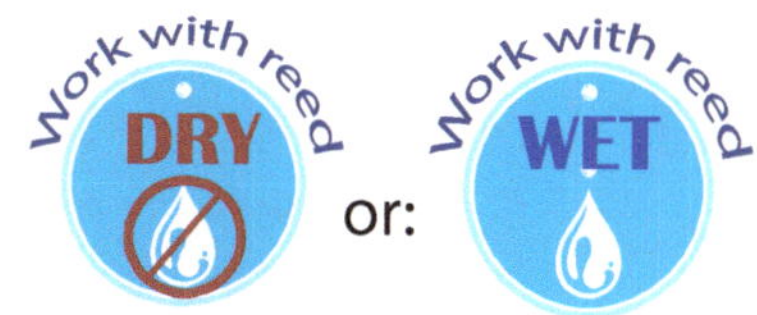

 Cut 12 strips of reed or card stock
3/8"-1/2" wide, 11 " long
(4 center color, 8 outside)
Superglue (adults) glue stick (children)
Clothespins or small clips

Arrange
vertical
pieces

Weave center strip
Under / Over / Under

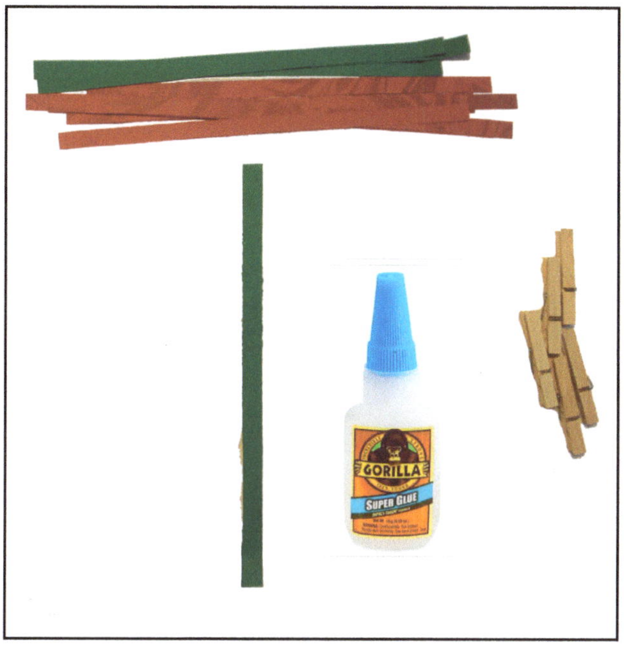

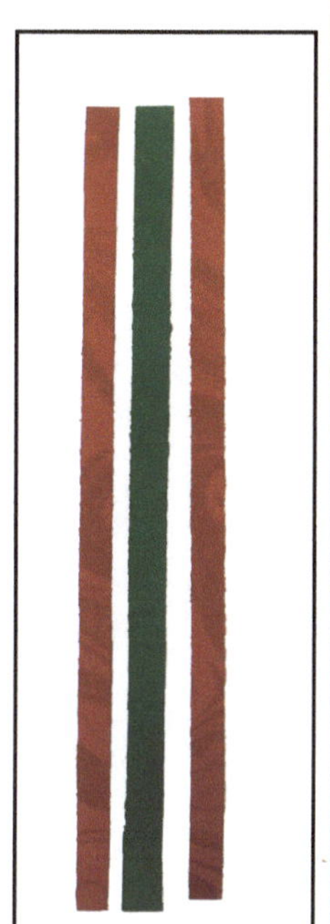

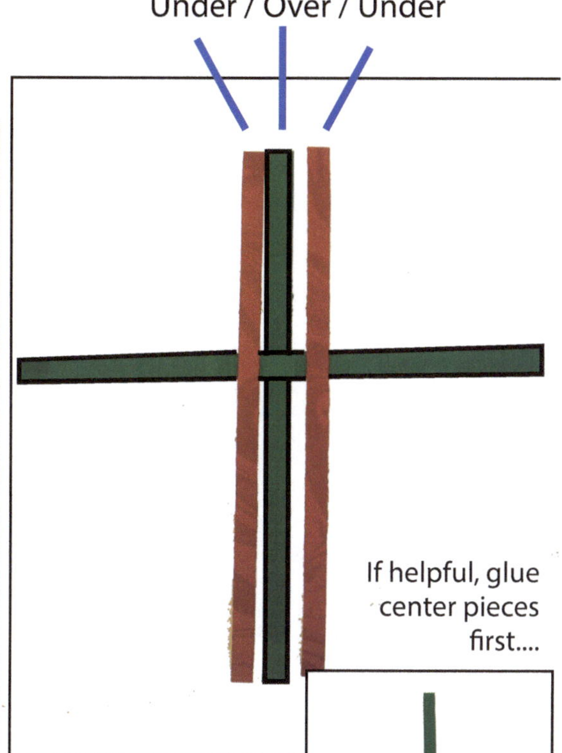

If helpful, glue
center pieces
first....

Weave outside strips
Over / Under / Over

Add a dot of glue between
pieces and clamp together.

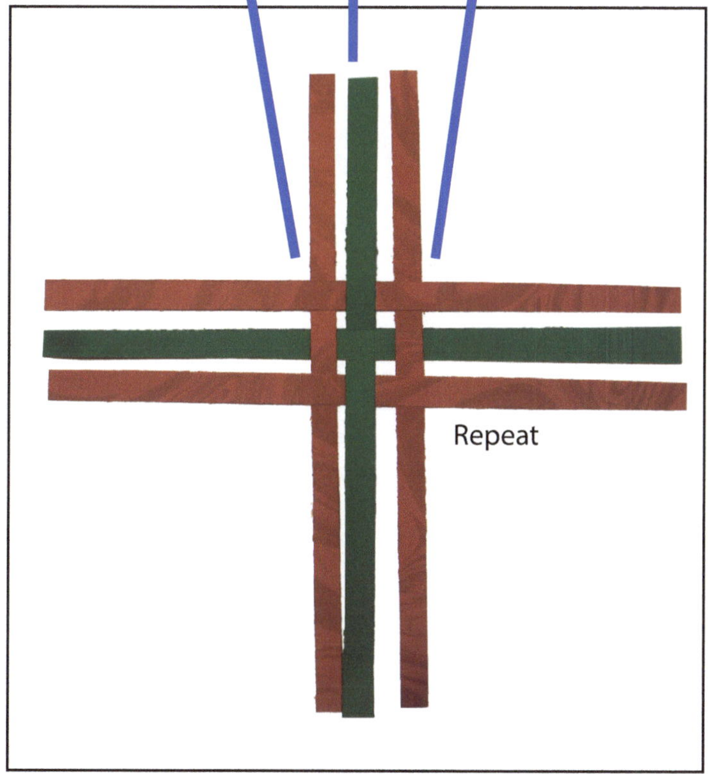

Repeat

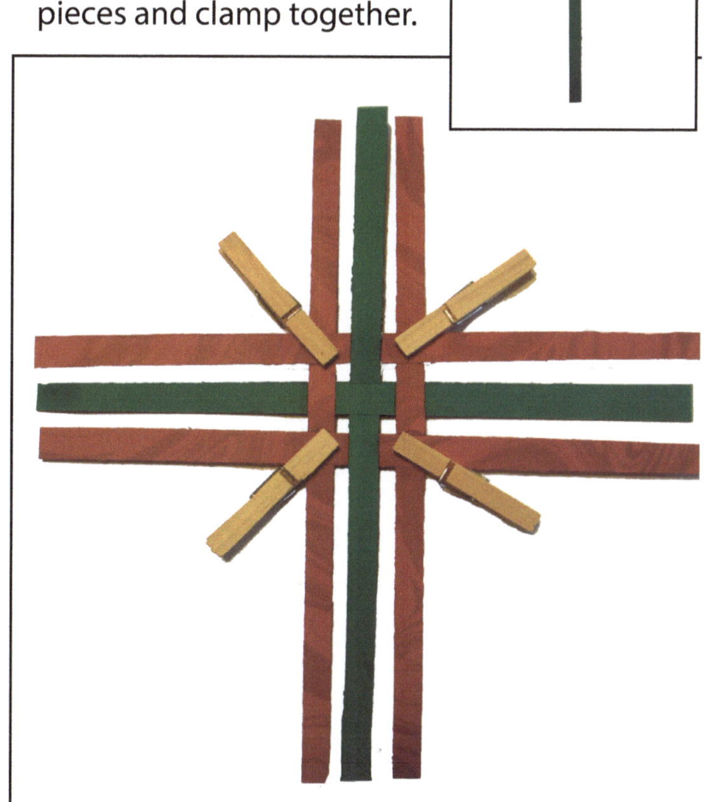

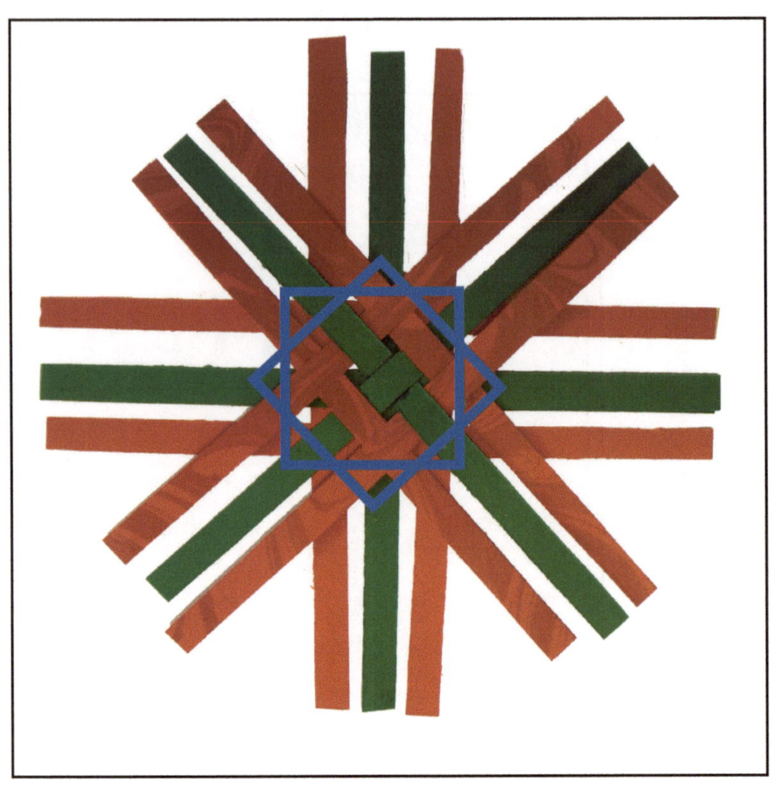

With wrong sides to inside, lay piece #1
90 degrees over piece # 2.

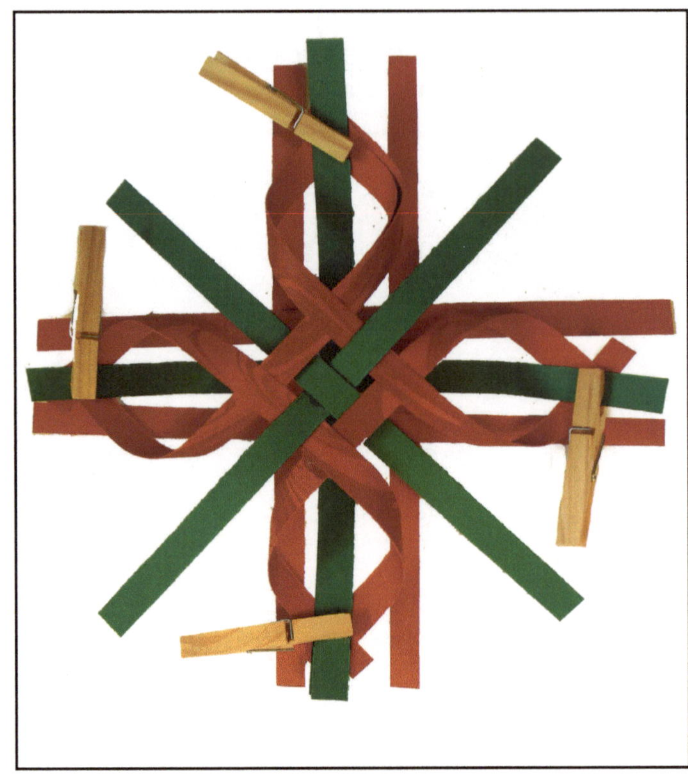

Bring outside (red) strips behind center green
strips. Dot glue on green strip, overlalp with red.
Dot red strip, overlap with second red strip.
Clamp together. Do all 4 sides.

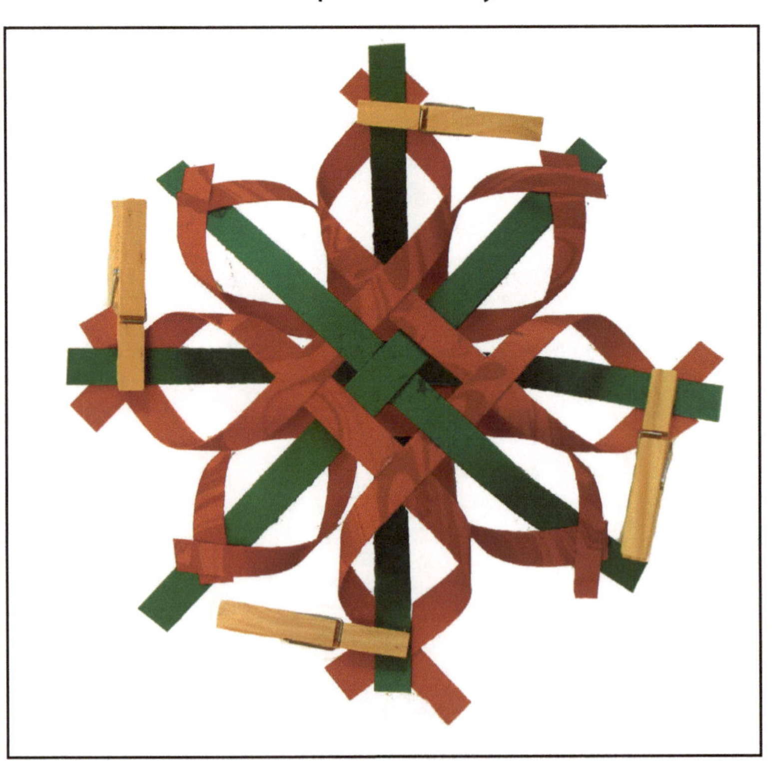

Flip snowflake over and repeat on other side.
Clamp and let dry.

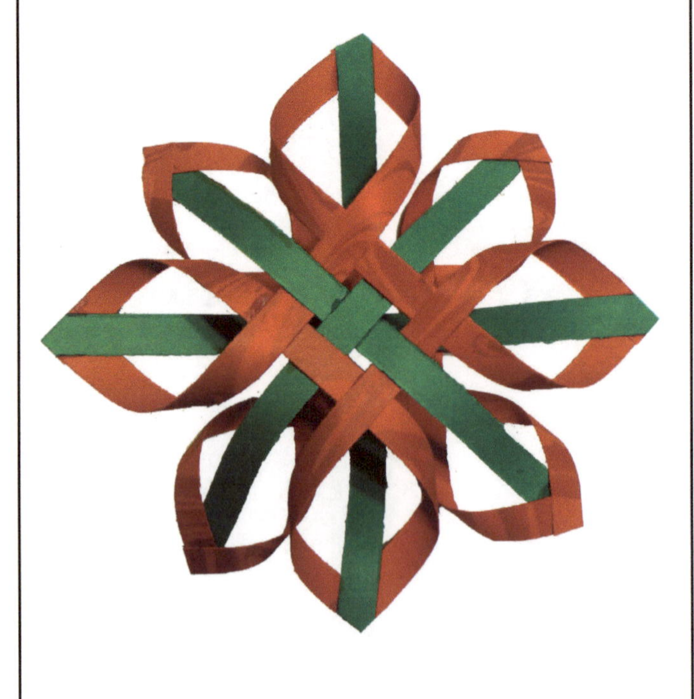

Trim the ends...and enjoy!

Reed Snowflake 5 x 5

20 - 16" 3/8" flat reed for 12" snowflake

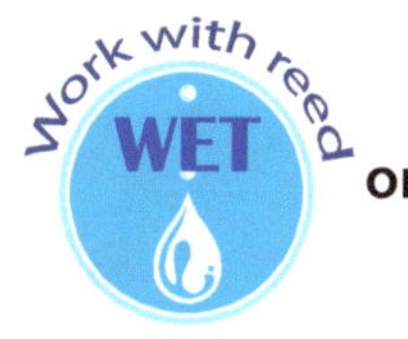

or:

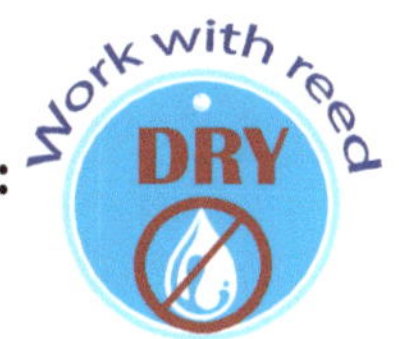

Glue using Superglue (not hot glue)

Helpful hint: put bandaids or painters tape on left hand to avoid glue on fingers.

May be woven with paper and glue sticks for children.

o - over, u- under

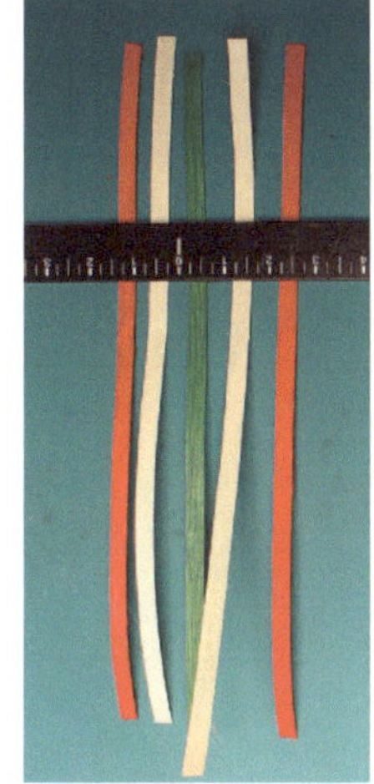

4 spine
8 middle color
8 outside color
(point weaver)

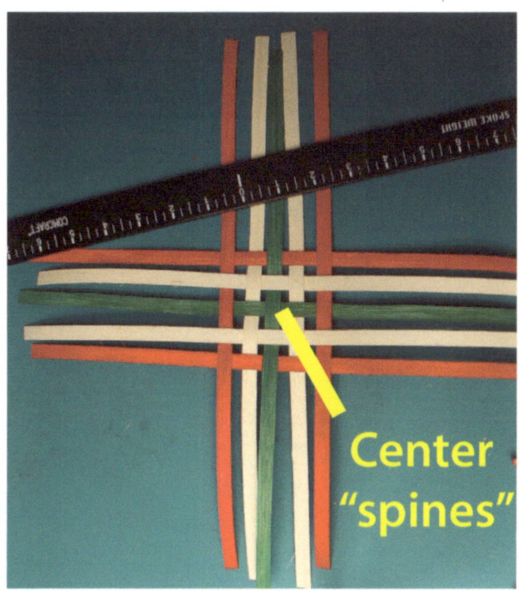

Mark centers of reed.
Lay out colors vertically.
Weave center spine first horizontally (u,o,u,o,u)
Alternate next weaving patterns (see grid)

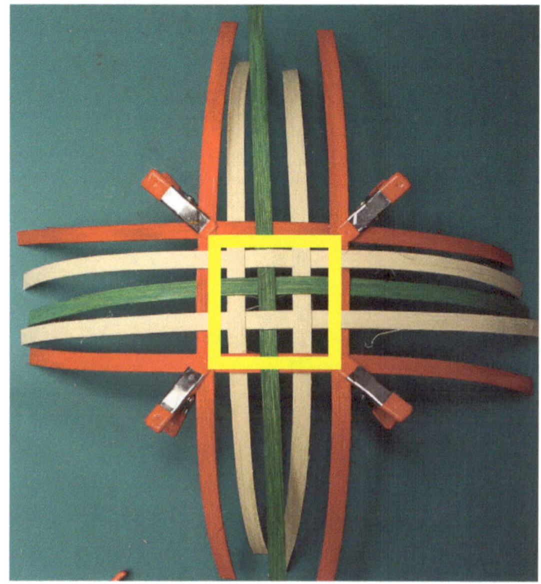

Make spacing even to make
a square. Glue 4 "points"
with Super Glue.
Clamp and repeat.

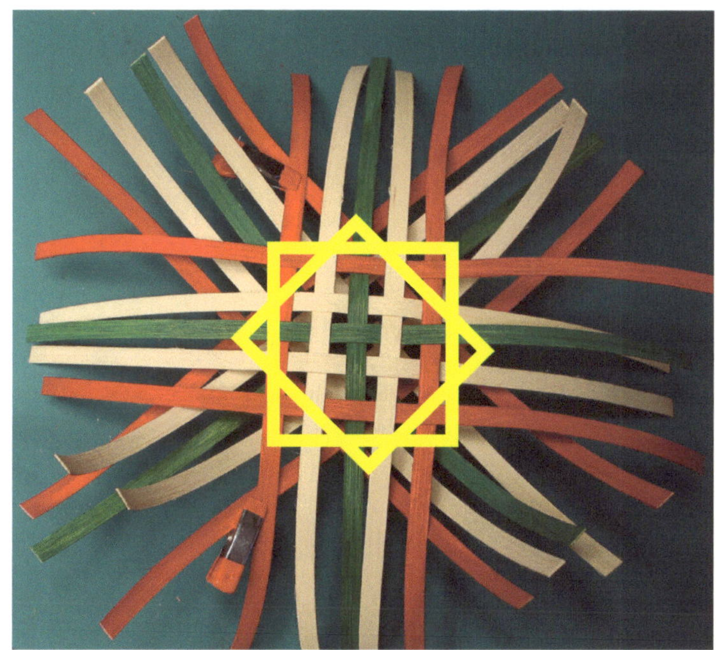

Lay weave 1 on top of weave 2
turning top one 45 degrees so point is at top.

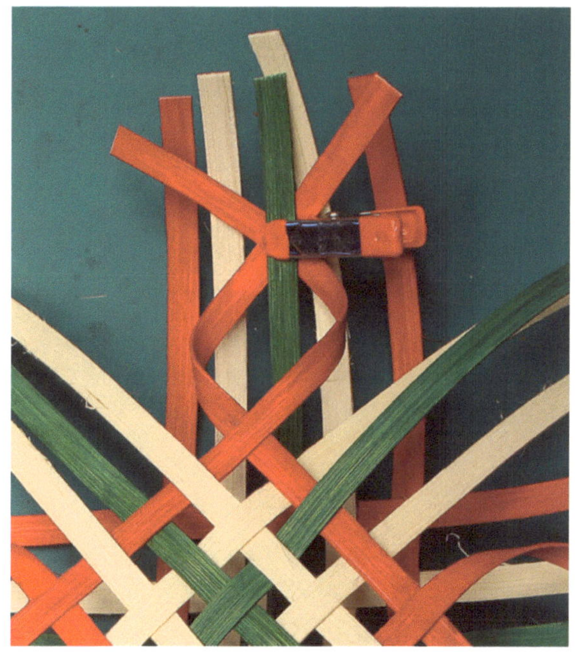

Find point and point weavers.
See next diagram.

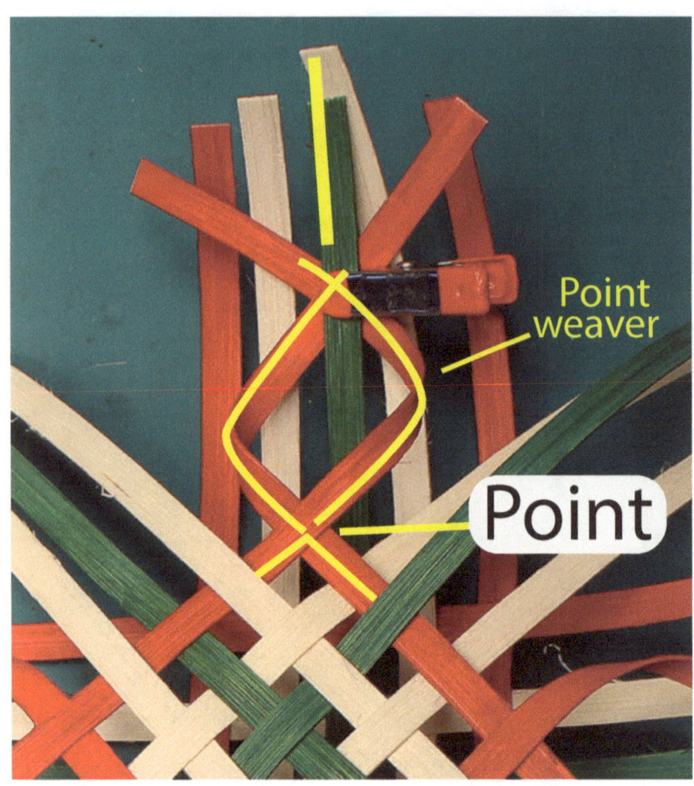

Find the top point. Bring the point weavers about 2/3 the way up spine. Glue left, then right weaver behind spine. Clamp.

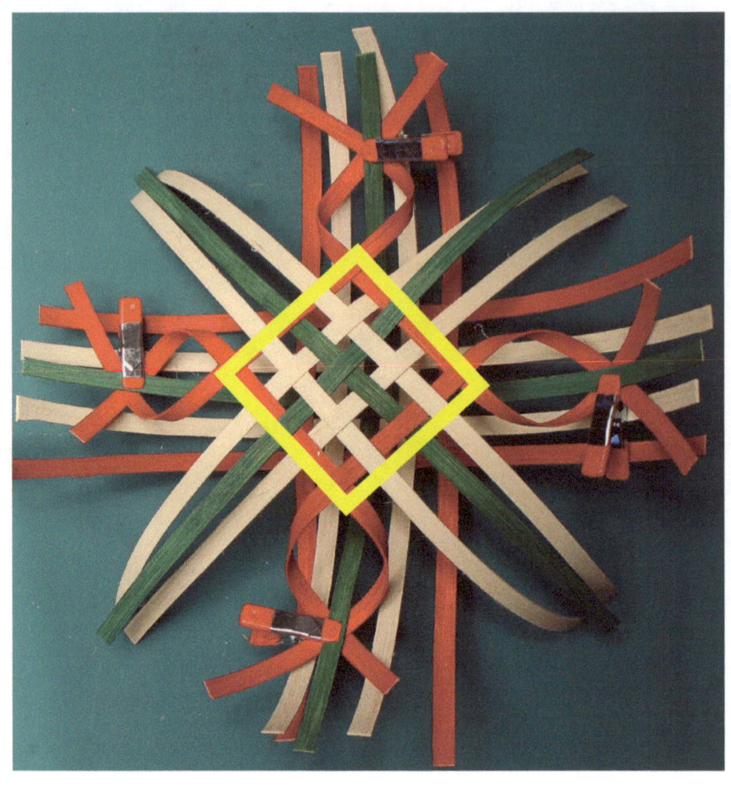

Do on all 4 points of first side.

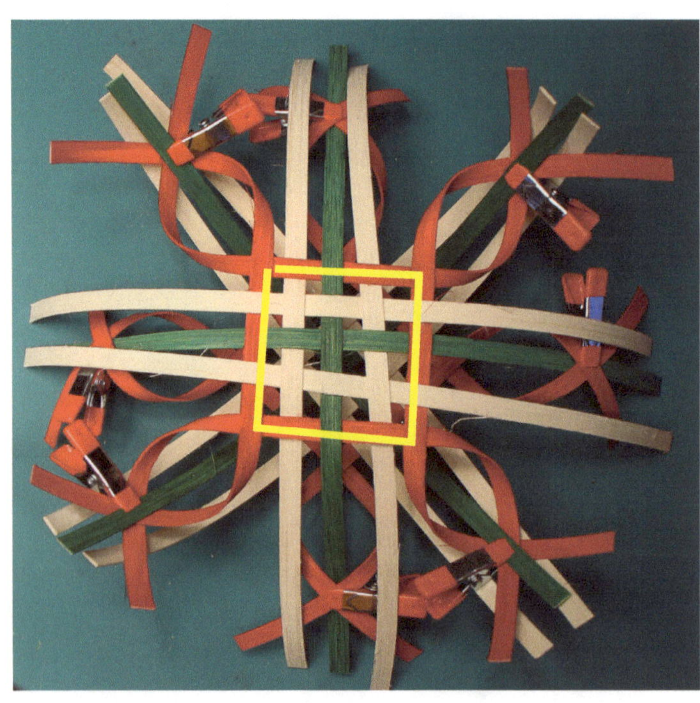

Flip, then do all 4 points on opposite side.

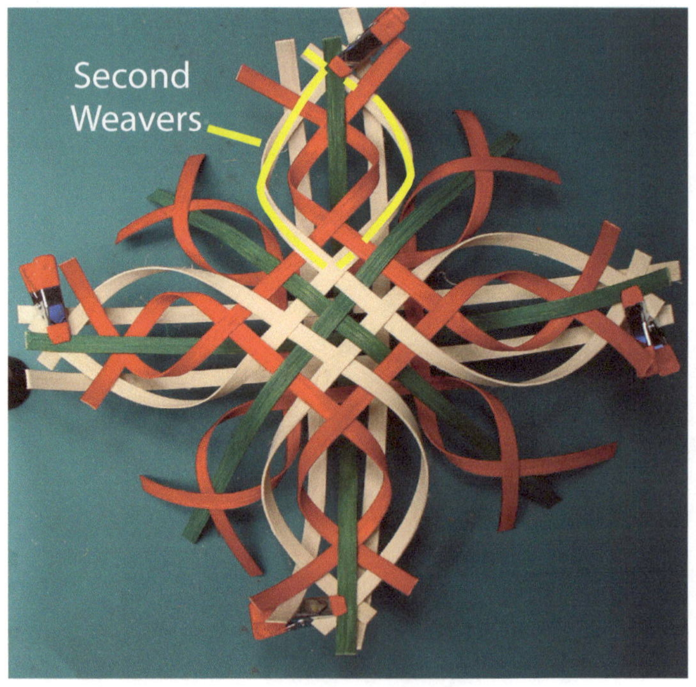

Find second weavers and glue closer to top of spine (behind spine). Leave room to trim ends after gluing.

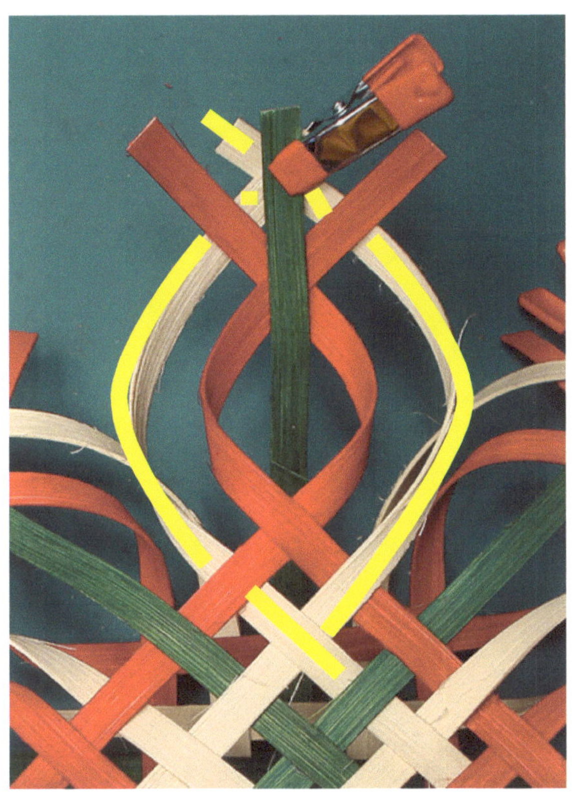 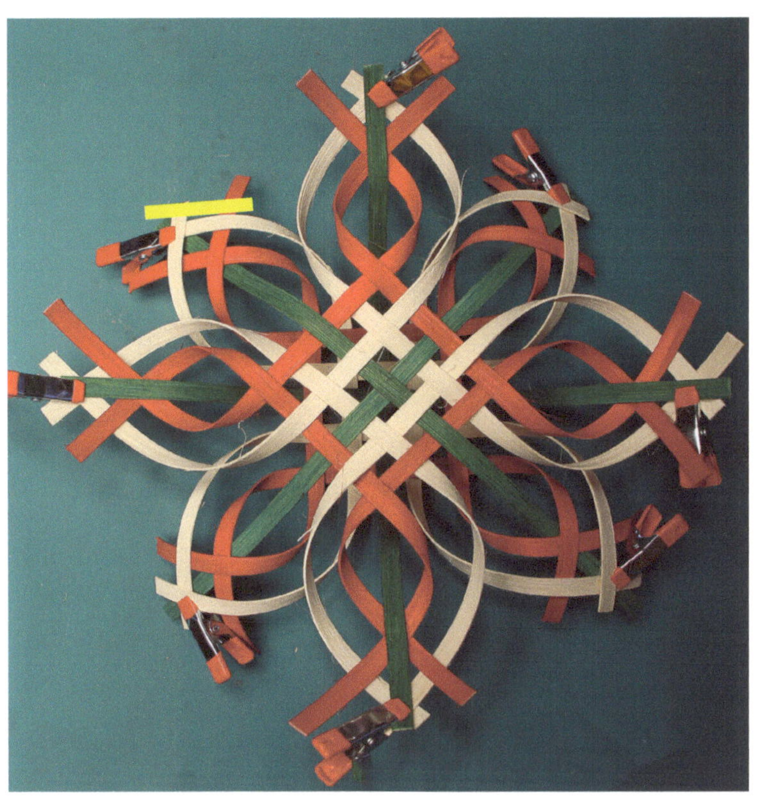

Glue second weavers above point
weavers and below top of spine.

Flip and repeat on other side.
Cut ends flush to weavers.

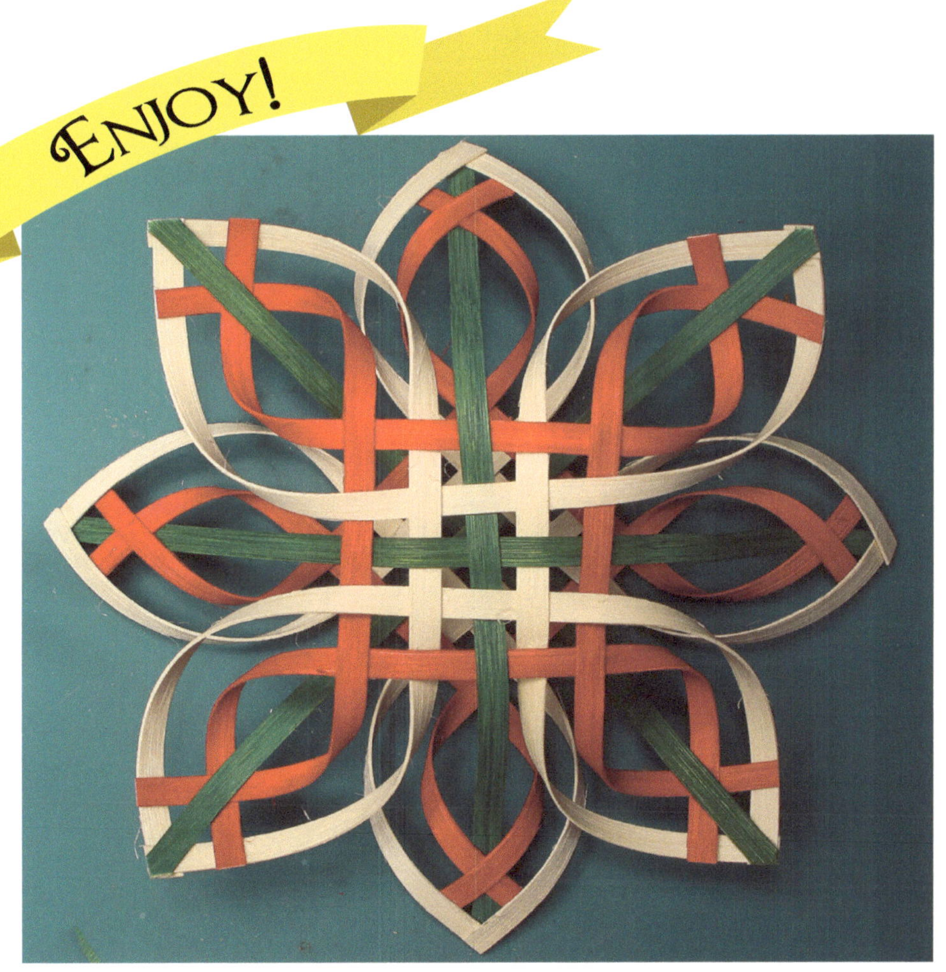

1" snowflake grid

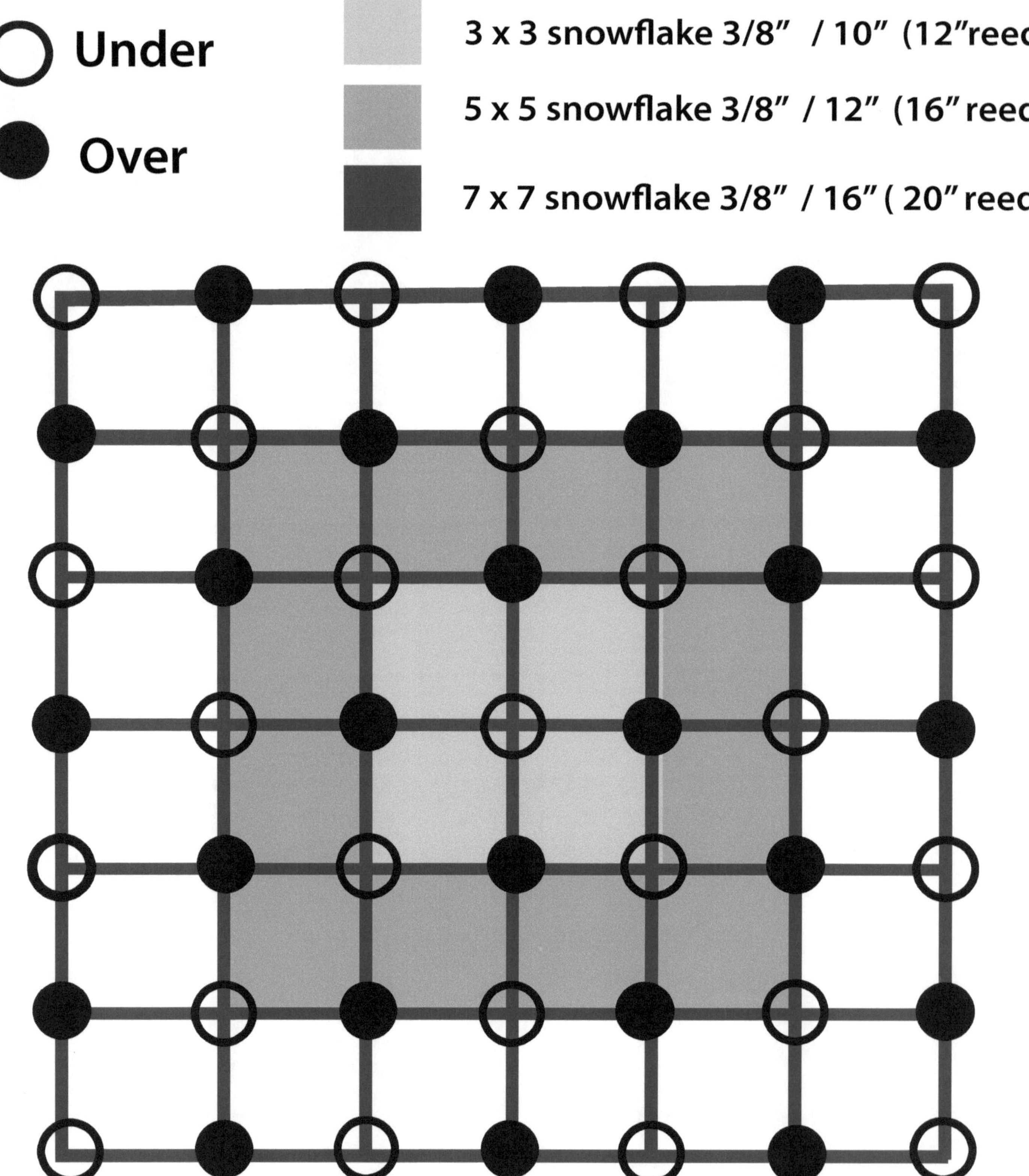

3x3 is actual size. 5x5 and 7x7 is for pattern layout (over/under)
Adjust closer for tighter pattern.

Reed Heart

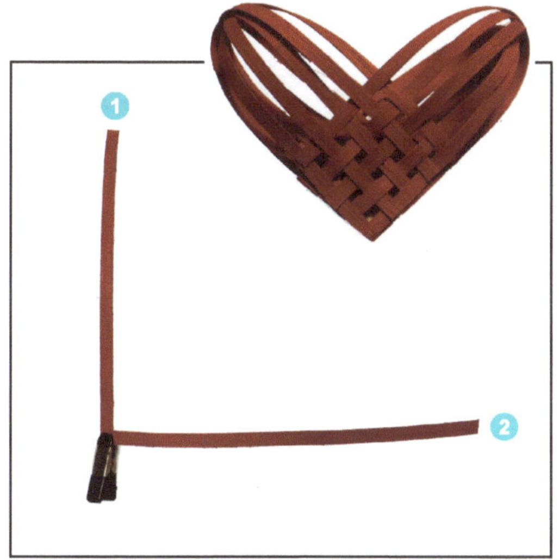

Cut 10 strips of reed
Glue #1 and #2 at 90°
angle

Glue & clamp 3-5, keeping
a uniform distance
(width of reed)
Alternate Over (O)
Under (U)

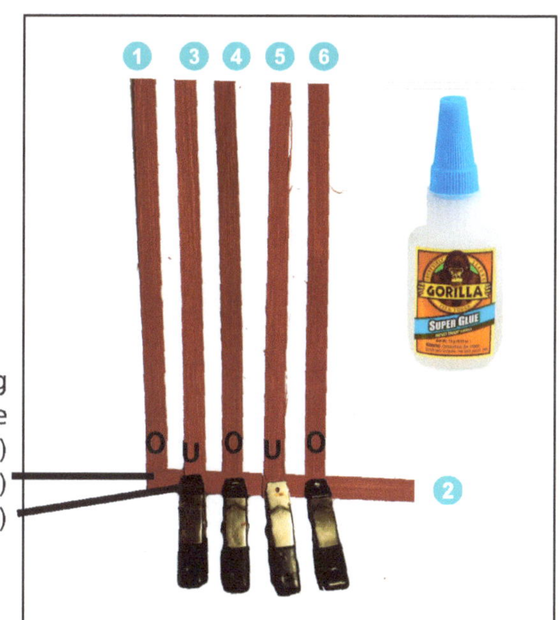

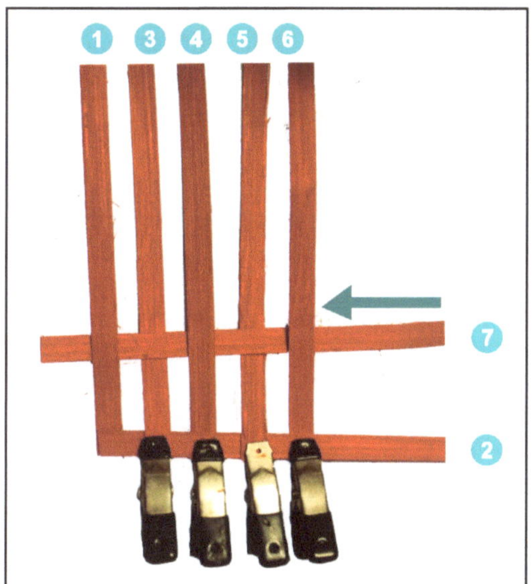

Begin the first
weave #7
U,O,U,O,U

Continue weave,
alternating rows

O,U,O,U,O

U,O,U,O,U

O,U,O,U,O

U,O,U,O,U

Glue and clamp
(aim for a SQUARE)

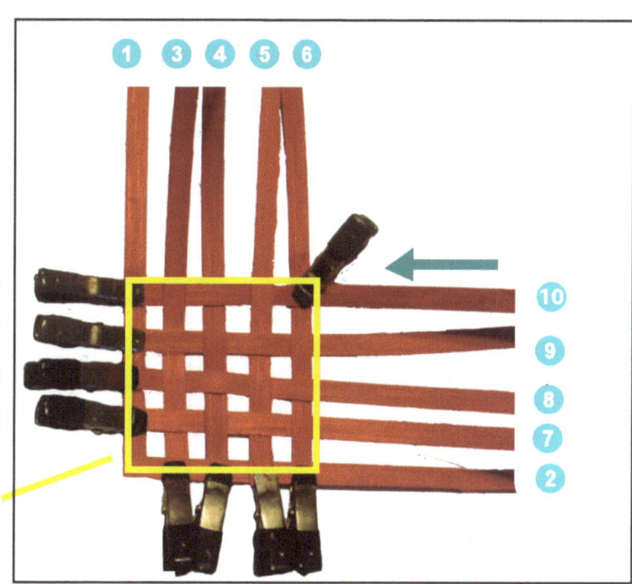

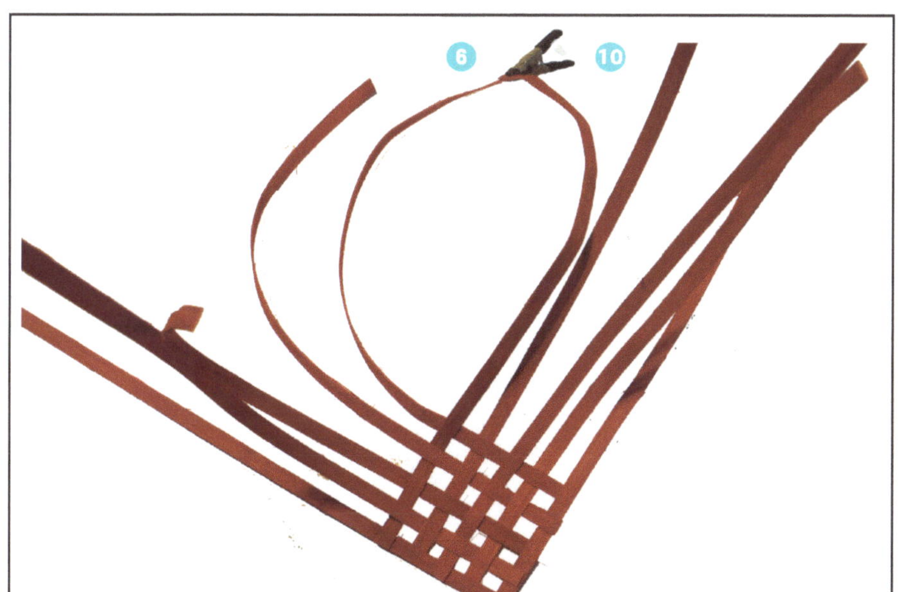

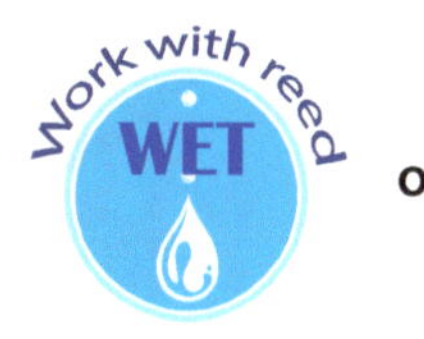

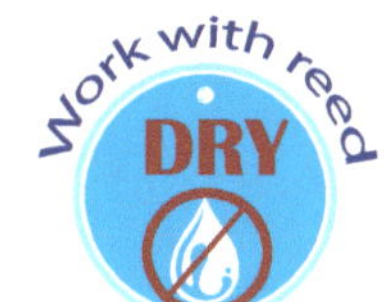

Glue the 2 pieces at the top of the
square (diamond)
#'s 6 and 10
Clamp

10" Heart 10: 20" 3/8" fla-t reed
8" Heart: 10: 16" 1/4" flat reed

SL

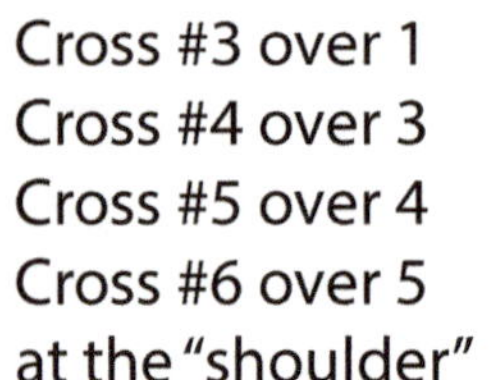

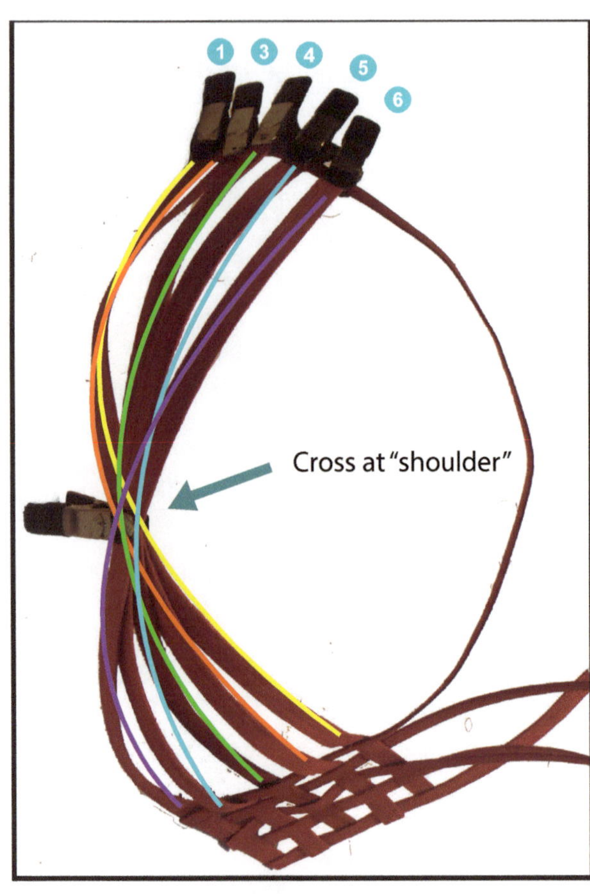

Cross #3 over 1
Cross #4 over 3
Cross #5 over 4
Cross #6 over 5
at the "shoulder"

Keep spaces even
like in front
(1 reed width apart)

Glue and clamp.

Clamp at shoulder
NO GLUE

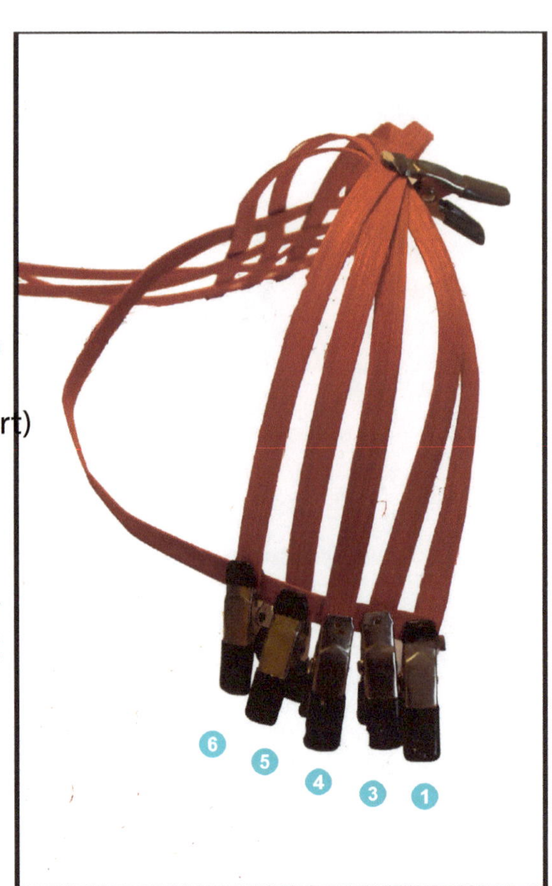

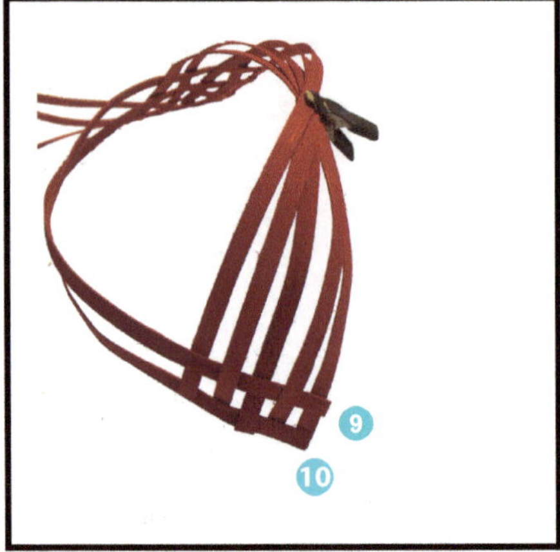

Begin 9 weaving as in front,
alternating Over/ Under

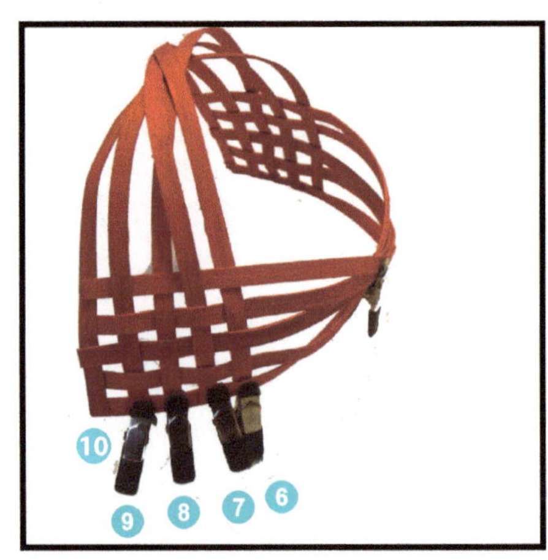

Weave 8, 7, 6 , alternating rows
Glue and clamp

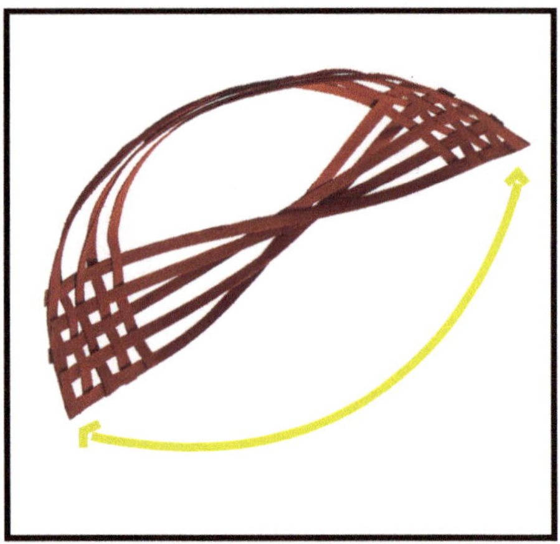

Bring points together,
gently folding

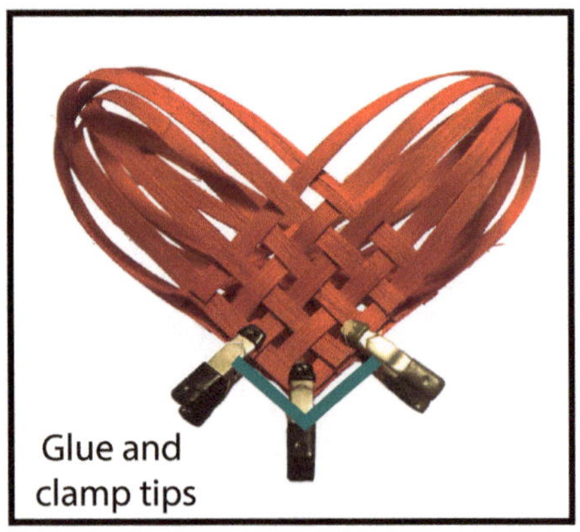

Glue and
clamp tips

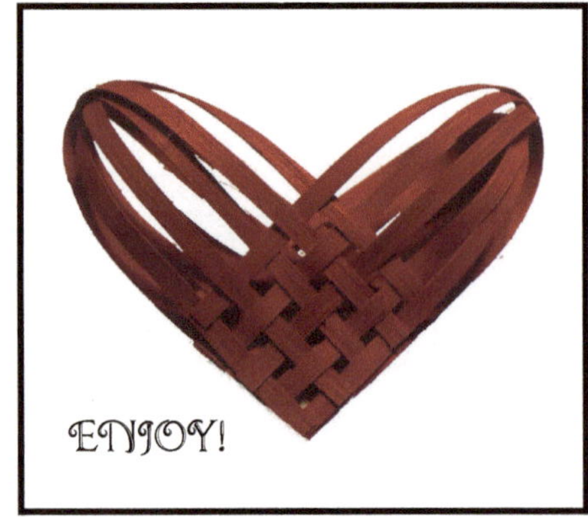

Seatweaving...

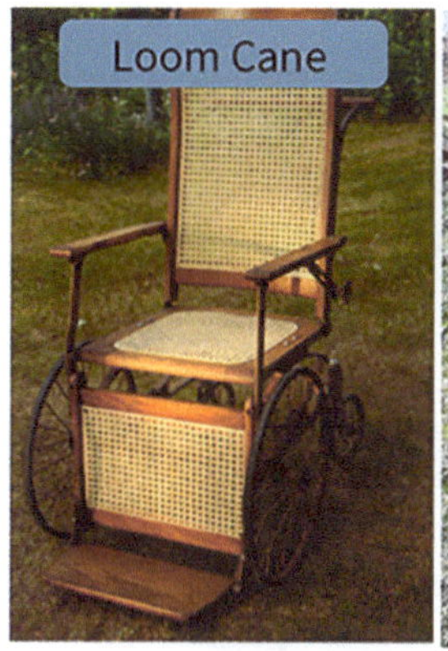

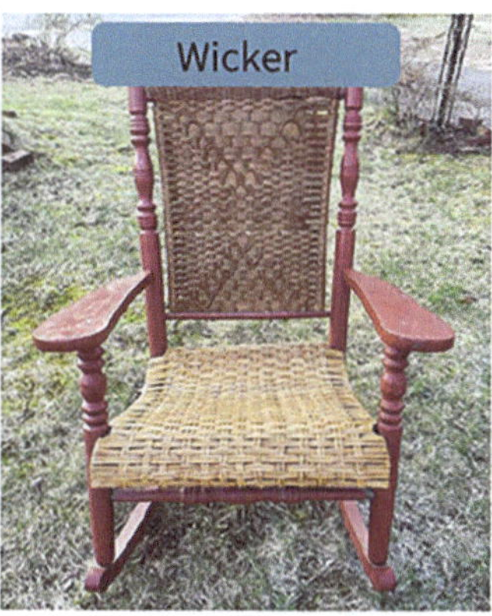

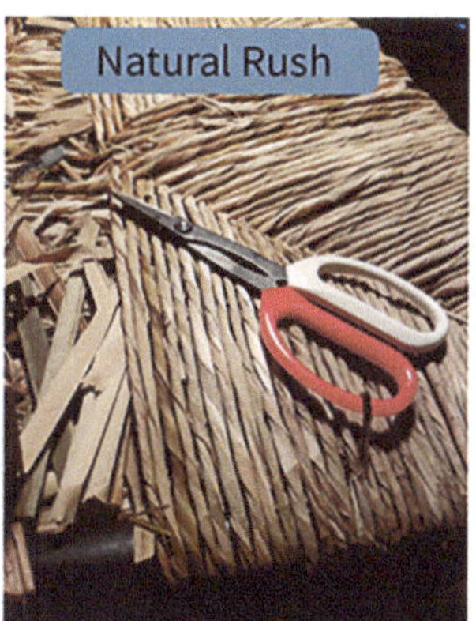

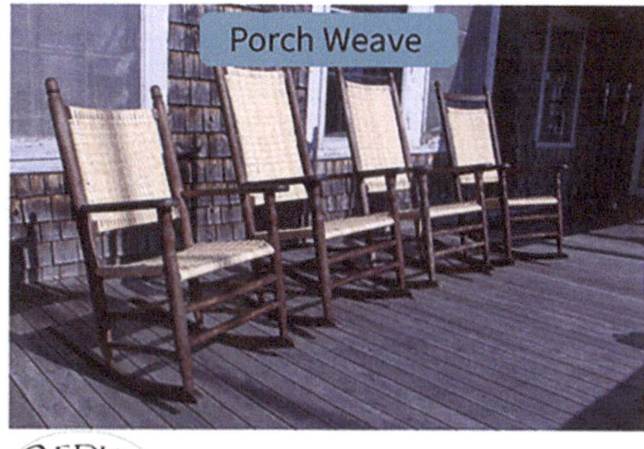

TRADITIONAL MATERIALS

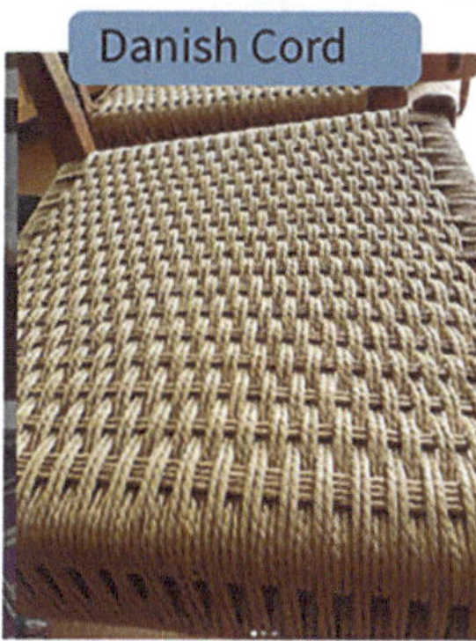

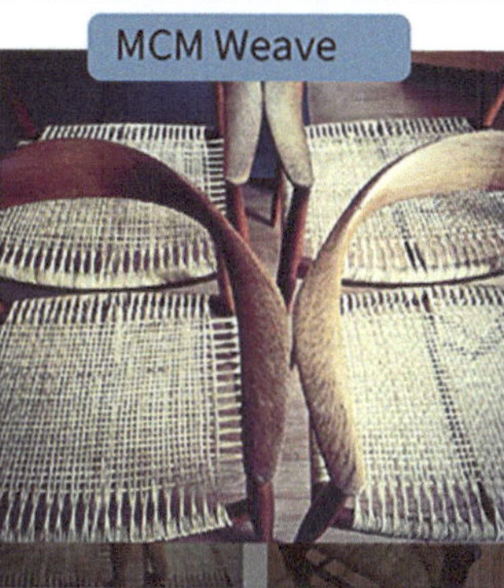

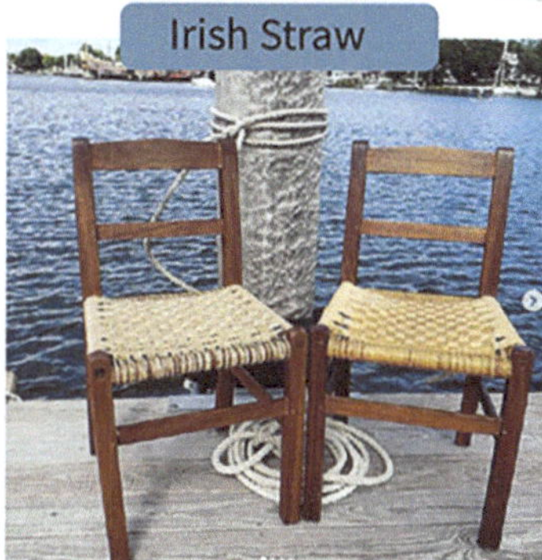

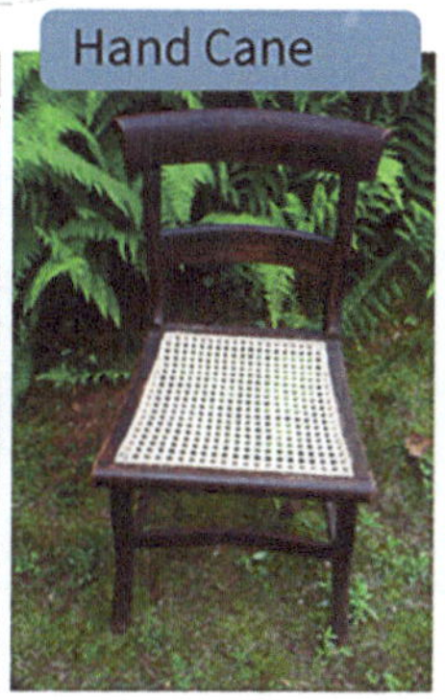

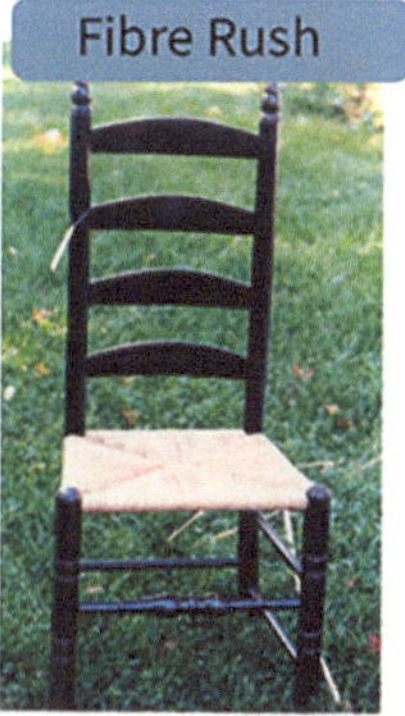

Seatweaving has been called a "lost art" by many. Once you are aware of it, you'll discover many seatweavers all over the country. As a member of The Seatweavers' Guild, Inc ®, it is my pleasure to promote the art of seatweaving through as many venues as I can.

I have been seatweaving since my 30's, and repaired hundreds of chairs. It is repairing memories, not chairs. Restored family pieces bring joy to my customers.

Once you have started to weave stools and seats, you may be on the lookout for chairs orphaned on the side of the road or calling to you from a tag sale or auction. Be careful!

When friends know you can repair seats you'll get many requests, or find chairs left in your yard like kittens at a farm. It may even lead to a career in seatweaving. Be careful or your collection will overwhelm you and your storage areas.

While I haven't covered caning in this book, I have sources for learning on the resource page.

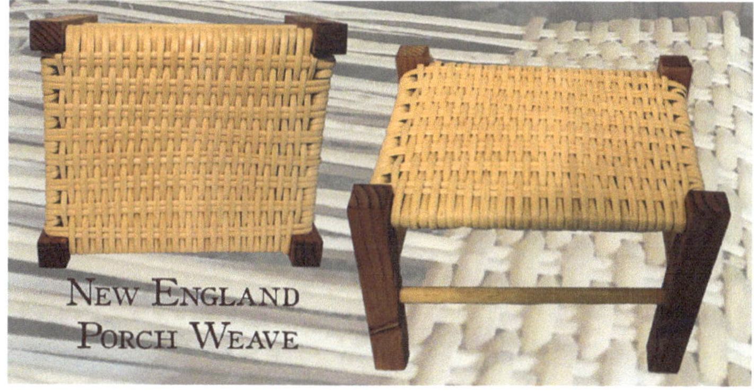

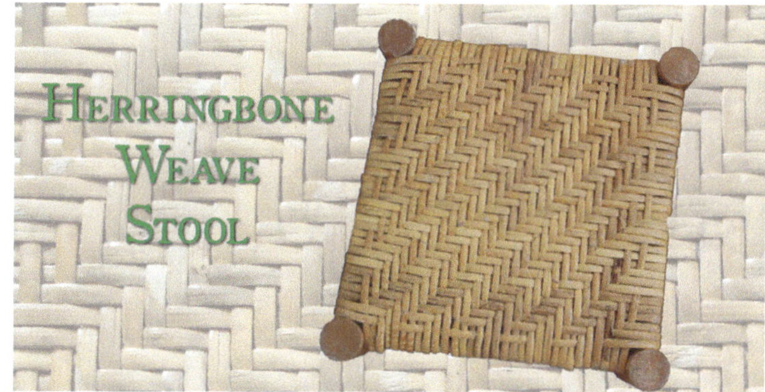

WITH TRADITIONAL AND UNIQUE MATERIALS

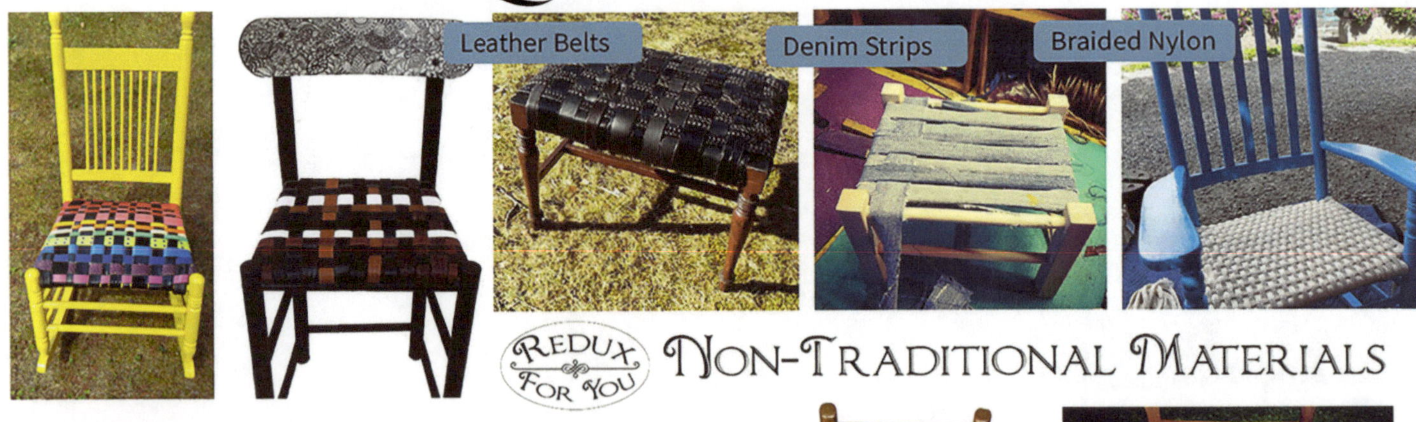

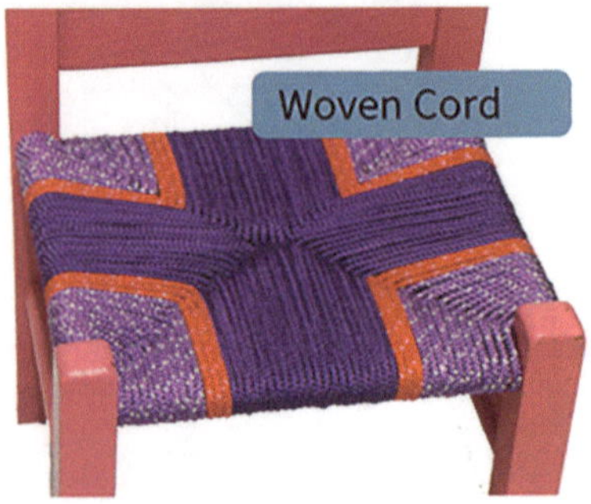

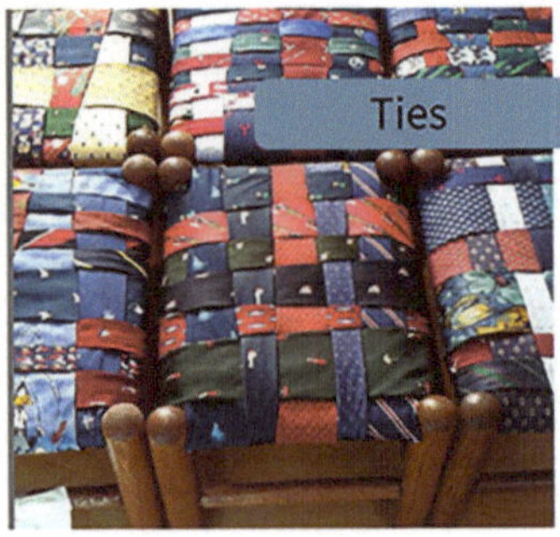

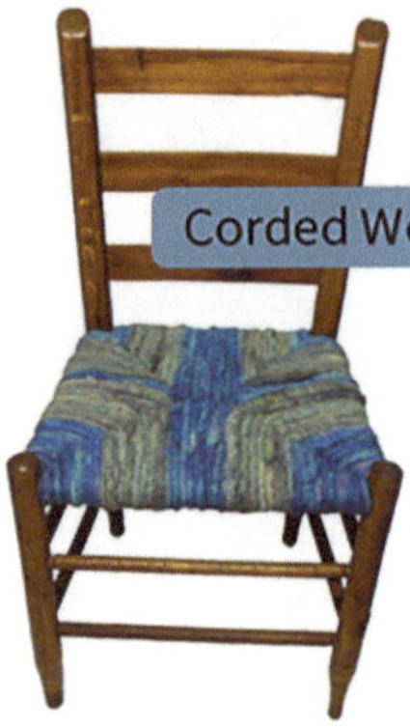

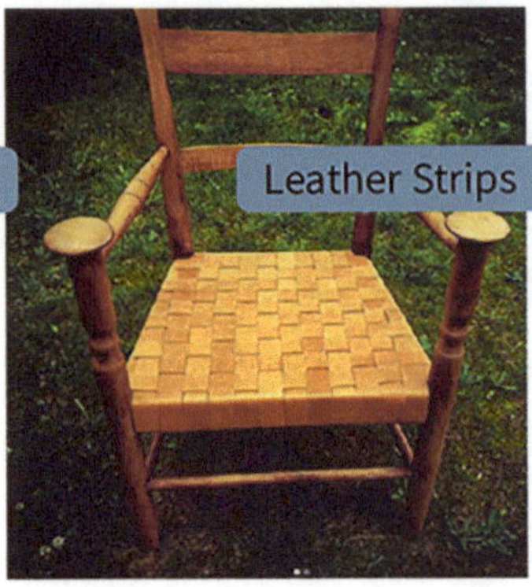

I was lucky to have many influences on upcycling, repurposing, and working with unique materials. My Mom taught me at a young age to sew, reupholster, and refinish. Seatweaving was an extension of this, and using non-traditional materials was the next step. I was influenced by her love of quilting, and using whatever was available, with creativity.

Corded or core-spun wool (referred to as a bump) is luxurious to work with, and a perfect material for wool fans. It is a great project for younger students or weavers that may have issues with hand strength. It is tactile, luscious and forgiving as it nestles into the row before it. The rush pattern can be used with other materials such as fibre rush, natural rush or any type of cord, which require more tension.

Ties woven on a stool make a wonderful gift (think memorial or retirement). Belts are amazing and torn strips of denim lend themselves to weaving.

The second edition of this book is in the works and will include more information on upcycled materials. Reed, cane, Shaker tape and corded wool are included in this book.

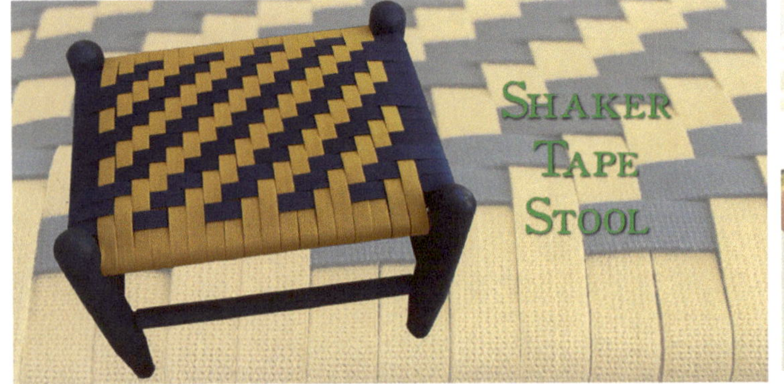

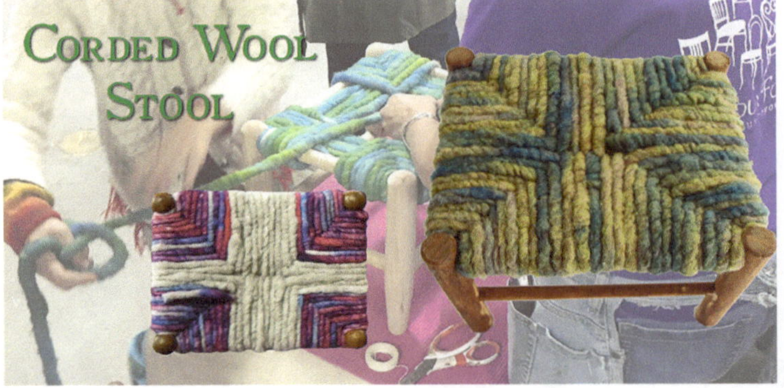

New England Porch Weave

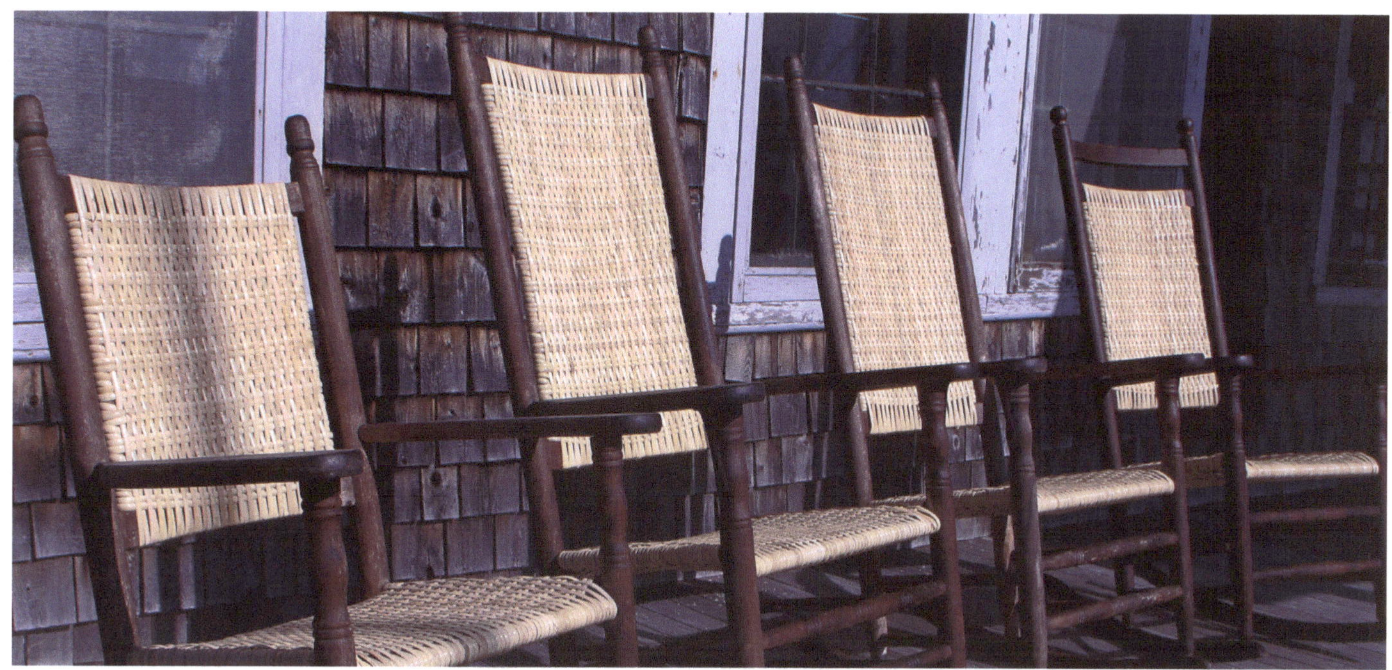

There's nothing like a big ol' rocker to spend time in! They are my favorites as they seem to have a solitary purpose...relaxing and watching the world go by.

While other chairs are functional for dining or working, rocking chairs stand out as an invitation to relax.

New England had many factories in the 1800's, especially in New Hampshire, where chairs were produced by the hundreds. They were woven by locals and shipped around the country. If you're lucky enough to find a rocker to restore and reweave, you will enjoy it for years to come.

The chairs in the photo above belonged to a family for over 50 years. I was instructed to reweave them "to last another 50". We chose 6 mm binder cane which has the shiny bark of the rattan palm. s

Before taking on a large rocker start by weaving a stool. The stool is woven with 7 mm flat-oval reed, and sealed with shellac on completion. The reed is porous and needs to be sealed to avoid stains or mold.The dimensions are 12" wide by 9" deep and 9" high for all stools pictured, unless noted.

I chose the rectangular stool kit because it's a great start to learning how to weave, and easy to ship. I have taught this in-person, and virtually to at least a couple of hundred people over the past few years. It is a wonderful introduction to seatweaving.

You will need a bucket to soak the reed in warm water for about 5 minutes.You will also need masking tape, scissors or clippers, and a stapler. You may want to use a butter knife to feed pieces in near the end, when the weaving gets tighter.

Seatweaving is often called a "lost art". If you begin now you will join the many seatweavers around the country I call friends. Help keep it from being called lost.

Porch Weave Stool

Stool, 7 mm flat oval reed (FO)

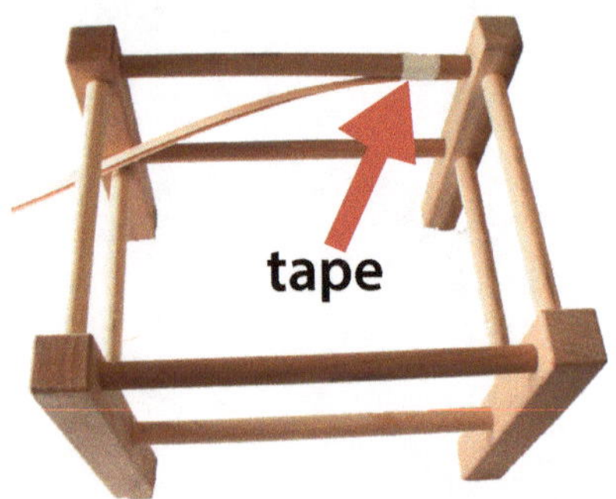

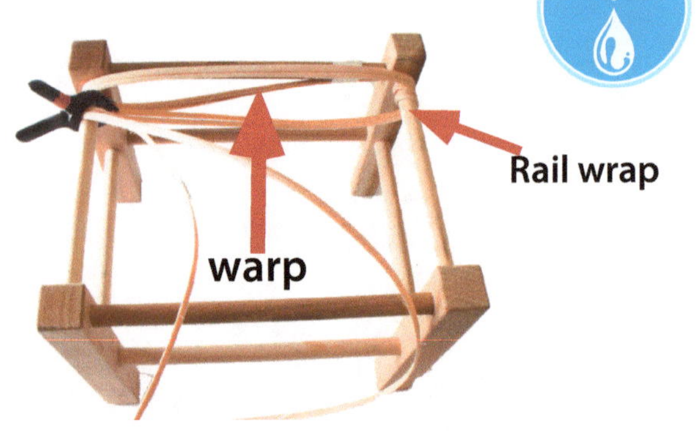

Tape 2 pieces of FO on long side of rail, underneath, weaving two at a time. Flat side towards rail, oval side up.

Bring warp over rail, across, wrap around rail once, go under and across, add rail wrap.

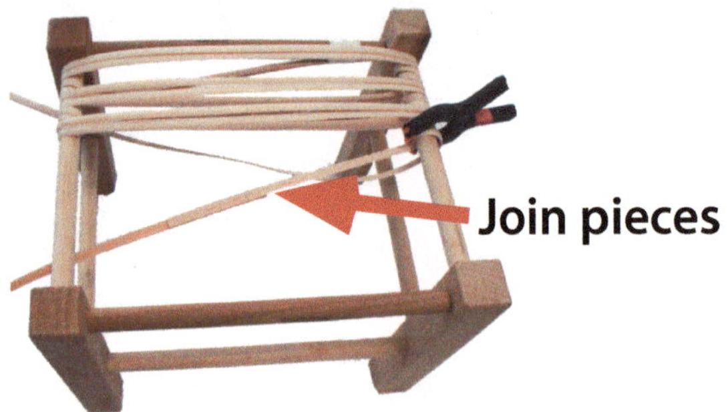

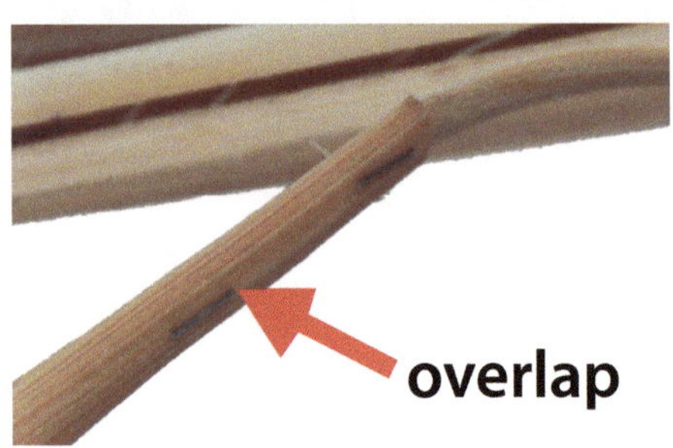

Continue pattern of 1 warp, and 1 rail wrap on each side. Join pieces as needed . (underneath, never on top).

Overlap about 1.5" and staple twice with smooth side of staple on oval side.

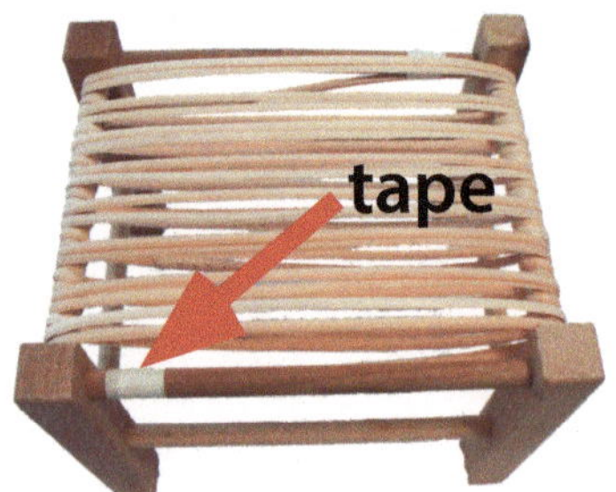

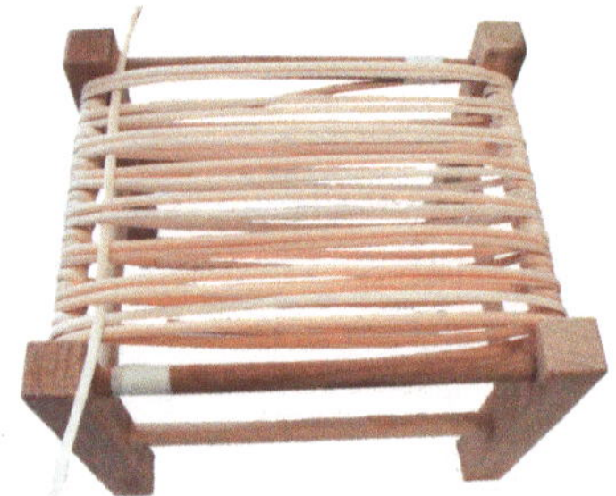

Finish with warp (adjust on sides as needed to fit) and tape at far end of rail.

Begin weave: over/under each double set of warps with single pieces of FO.

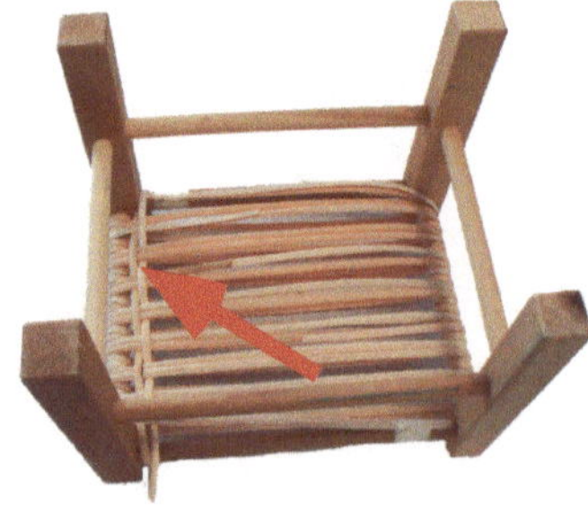

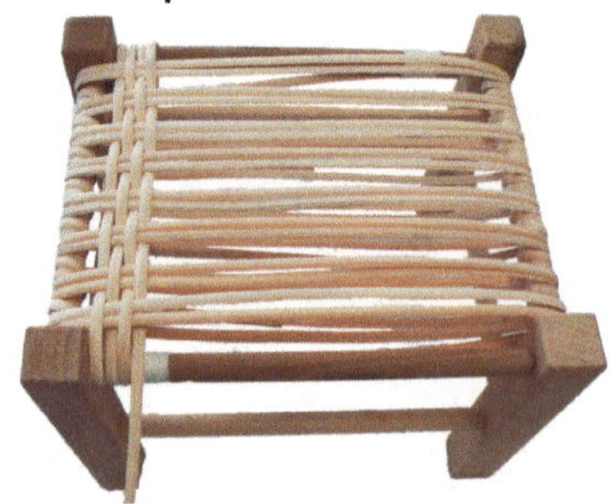

Weave one over/under on bottom, begin weaving opposite with next piece.

Continue alternating over/under weaves until stool is completed. Fill in space at ends with small pieces.

Stool Kit Assembly

1.)

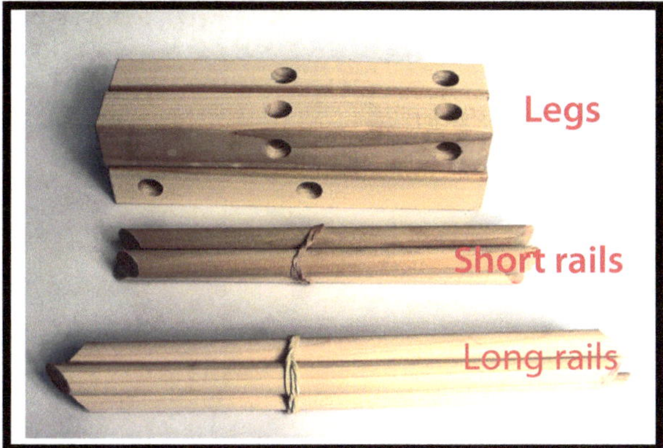

Kit contains: 4 legs, 4 short rails, 4 long rails
You will need wood glue. I prefer Titebond*
(pictured below) but any wood glue should do.

2.)

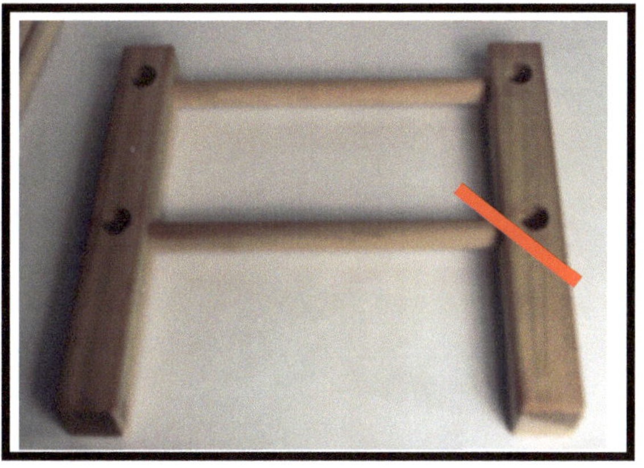

Glue short rails into legs as pictured.
be sure 45 degree cut is facing UP in hole.
Long rail will meet up at 45˚ inside leg.
Do both sets of short rails

3.)

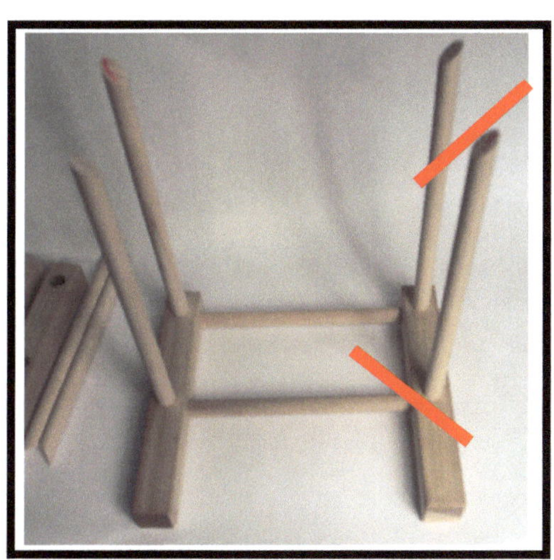

**Glue long rails into legs, be sure 45˚
angle is placed as shown to match up
with short rail cut.**

4.)

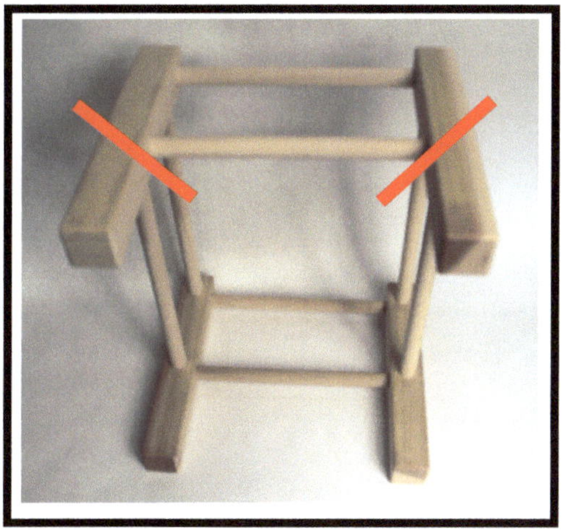

Glue second set of legs/ short rails on
to long rails.

*****

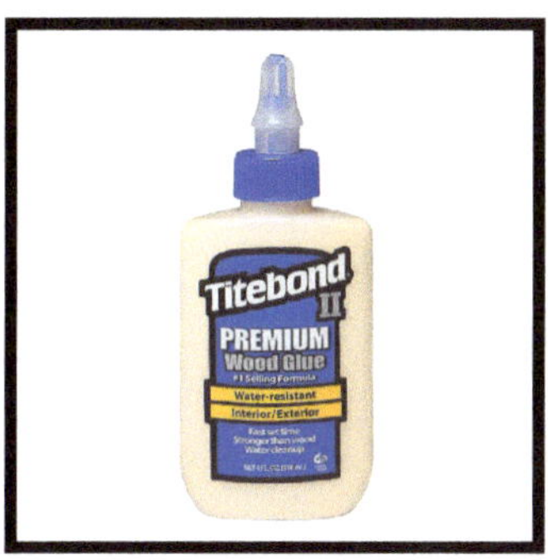

5.)

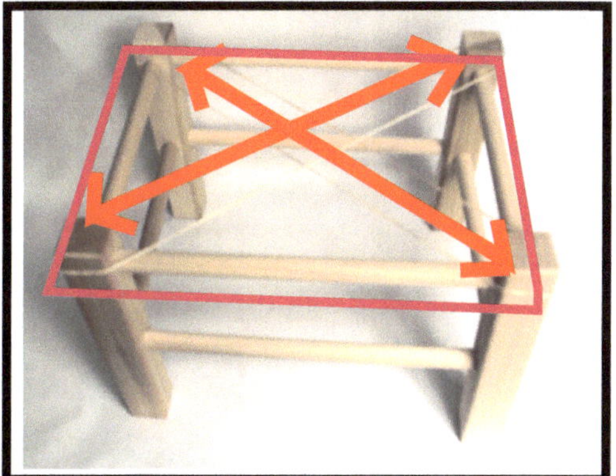

Use elastics to hold stool together until dried, either between corners or around all
4 legs (depends on size of your elastics) Finish stool as desired when dry (paint, oil, stain)

Herringbone Binder Cane Stool

5 mm or 6 mm binder cane.

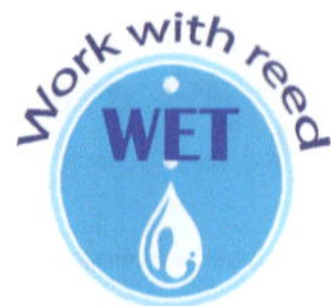

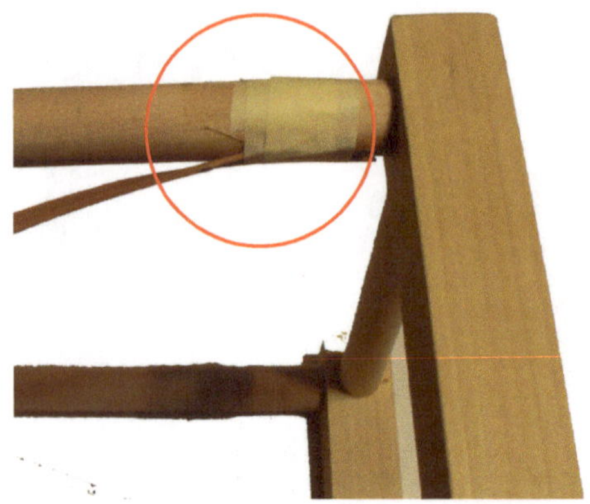

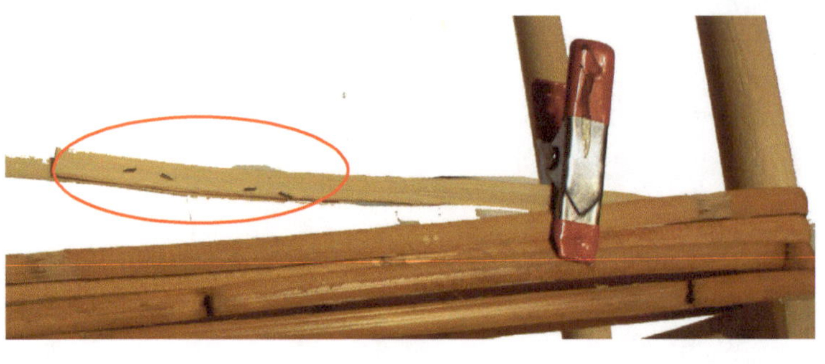

Tape cane under rail, flat side to rail. Wrap under and over rails, adding new pieces by stapling (2" overlap) Smooth sides of staples on cane bark side. ONLY connect pieces on bottom of stool.

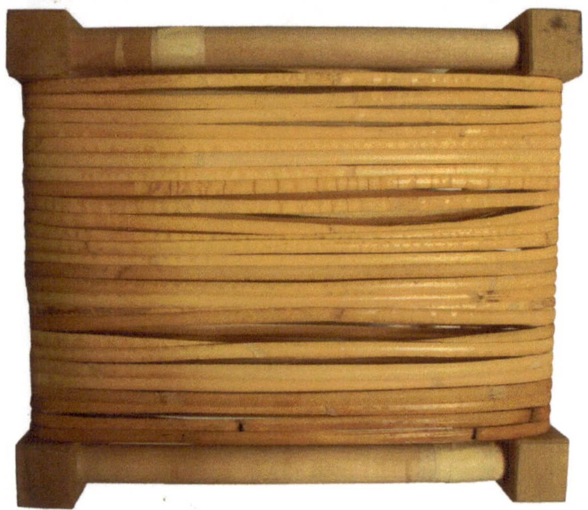

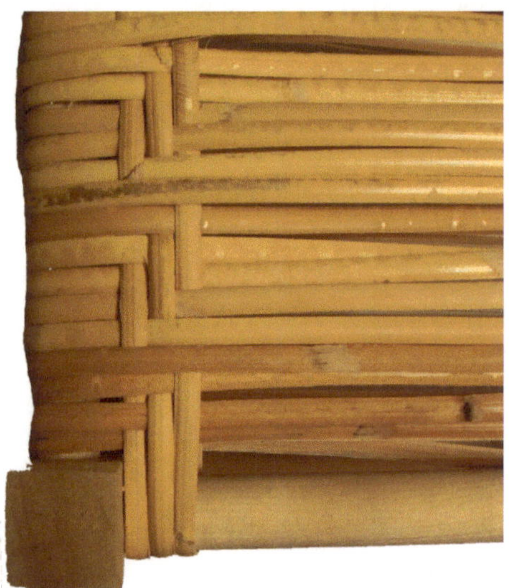

Wrap until warps are completed. Secure with masking tape at opposite corner you started.
Tape under rail. Begin weaving following pattern (top and bottom) Weave top first,
leave a tail and begin weave on bottom. Flip over and weave next sequence.

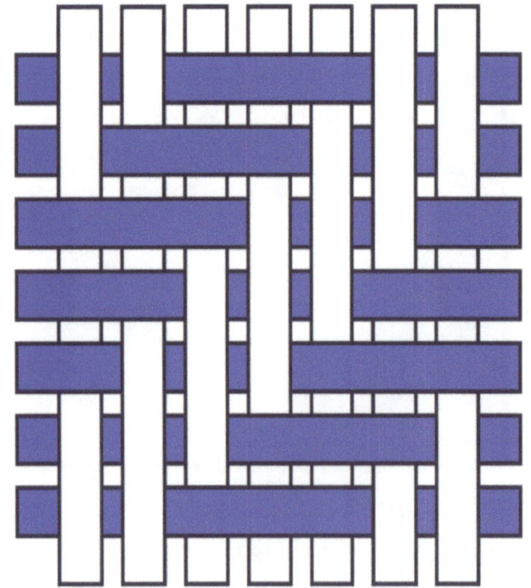

Follow 3 over 3 twill Pattern

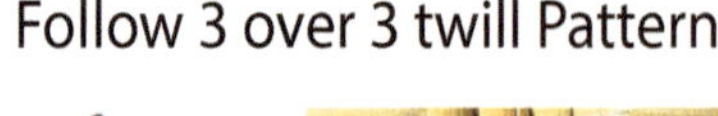

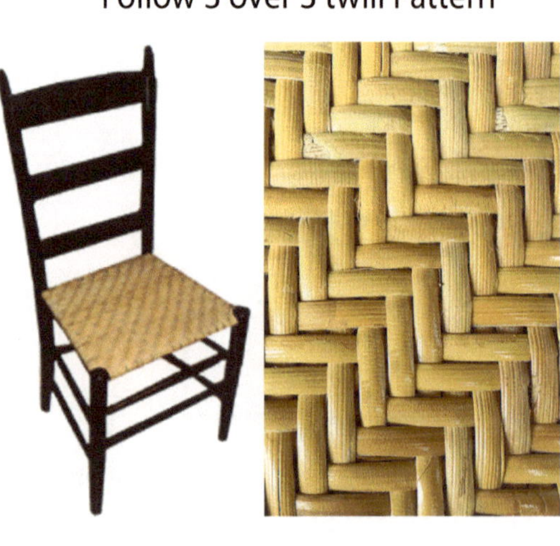

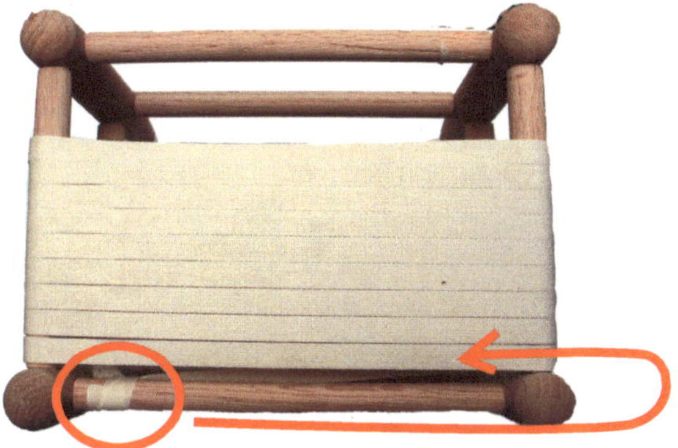

Shaker Tape Stool

To determine the quantity of 5/8" width tape needed
per chair seat, just multiply the widest width
by the widest length and divide by 5.3
Stool shown is Colonial Stool 10 1/2" x 13" x 10 1/2"

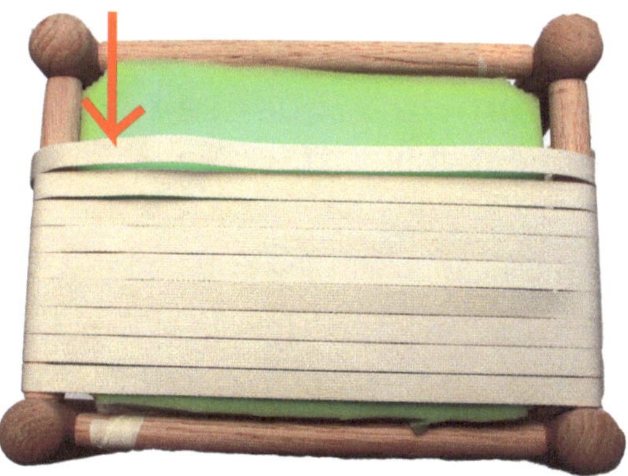

Tape under the rail with masking tape.
Wrap continuously around rails.
Stop 2/3 way through.

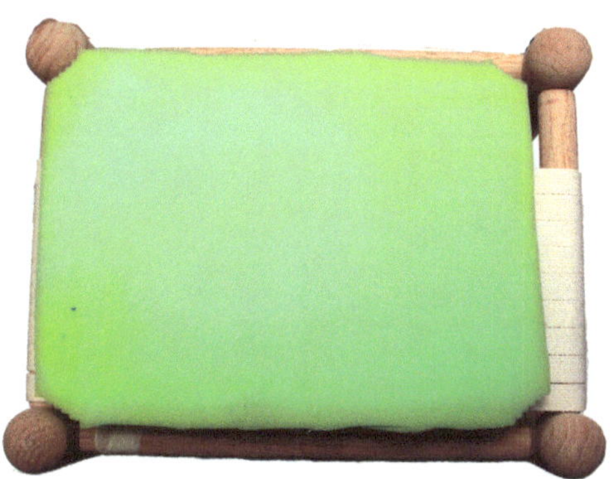

Cut a piece of 1" foam the size
of the stool top. Cut corners of
foam so it doesn't show when done.

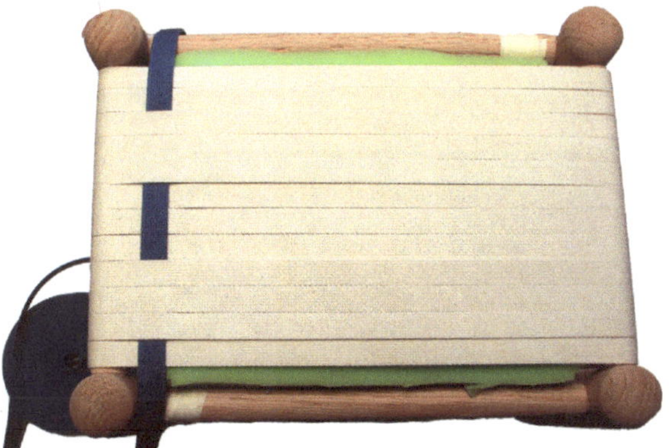

Slide the foam in between the wraps.

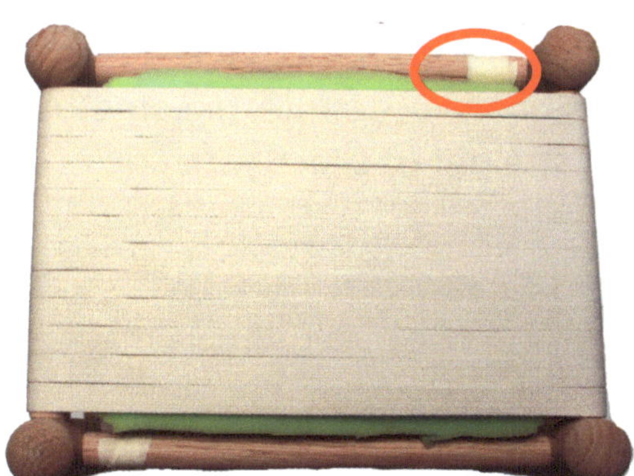

Continue wrapping. End by
taping under rail

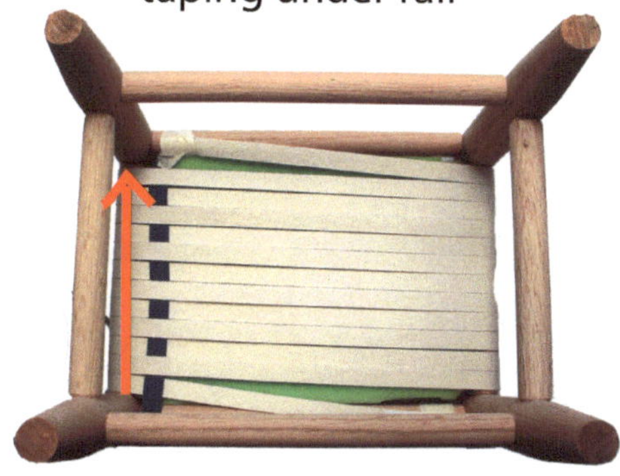

Begin weaving on top. O1, U3,O3,U3,O2
Leave a tail to begin bottom.

Pattern will vary
depending on
size of stool.
Keep the O3 (Over 3)
U3 (Under 3) pattern
consistent. First and
last rows will vary.

With tail weave "checkerboard" on bottom.
O1, U1. End first piece BEHIND leg.

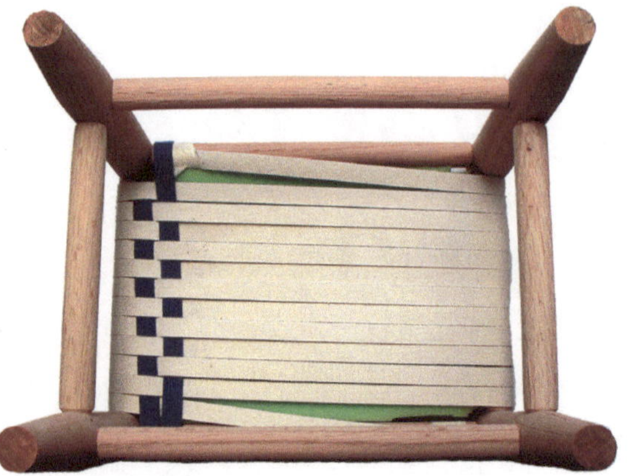

Alternate weave on bottom also
known as checkerboard.

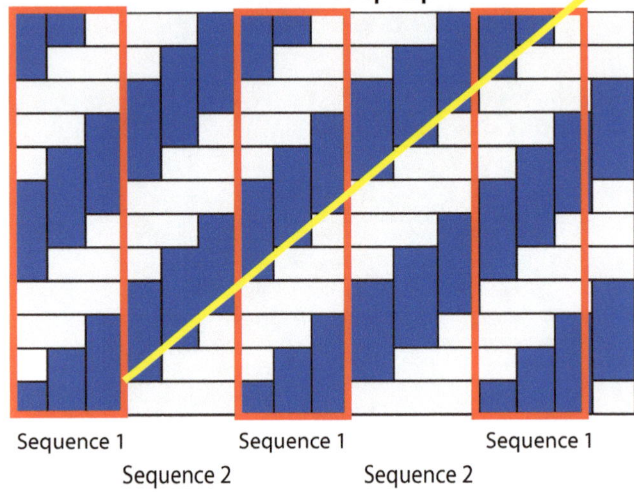

Begin sequence 1
You will be weaving from the top.
The most important thing to look for
is the "step up"

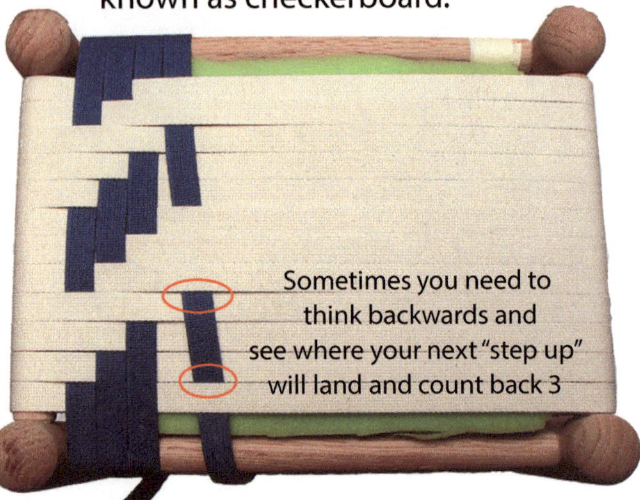

Begin Sequence 2
Occasionally use a ruler or something
straight to check your lines

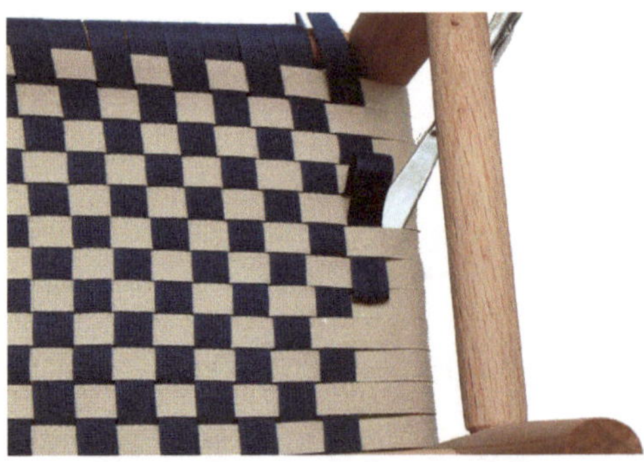

Alternate Sequence 1, 2
or continue to follow the "step up" pattern

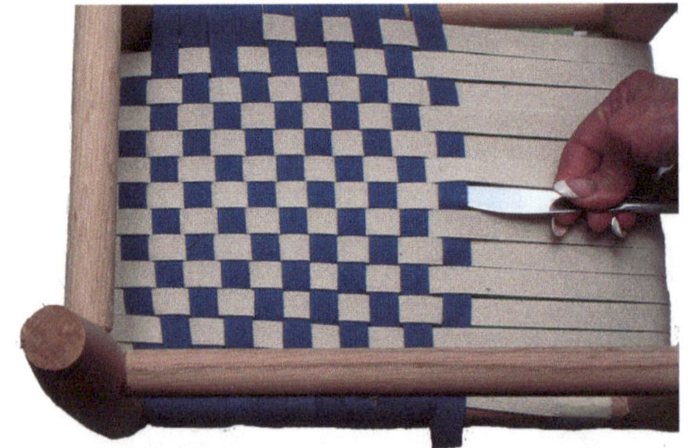

Use a Weaverite tool or butterknife to compact your weaving, or to nudge the last pieces through

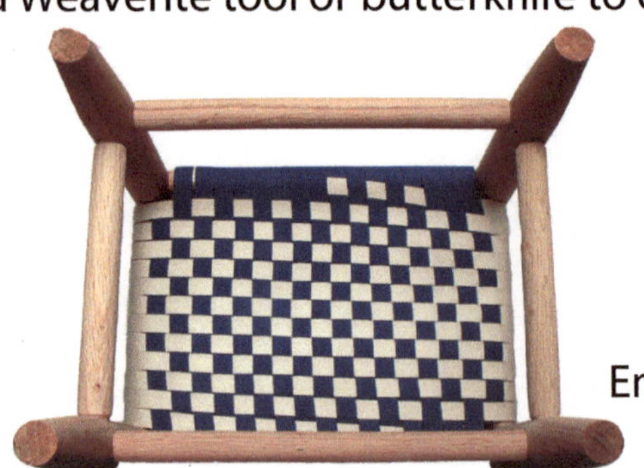

The beginning
and end pieces
will be behind
the legs.

Enjoy your new stool!

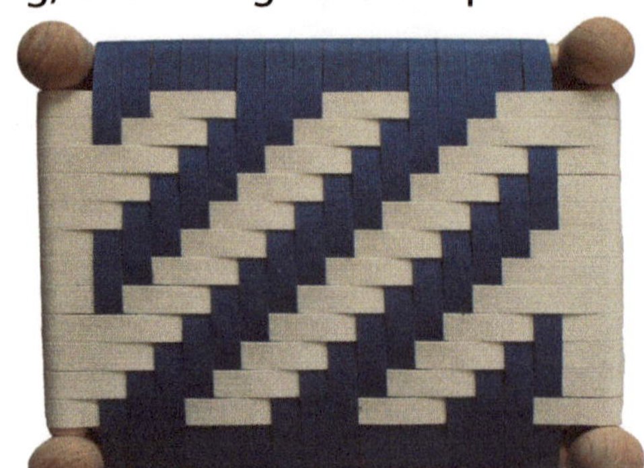

4 x 4 Twill (herringbone) pattern 

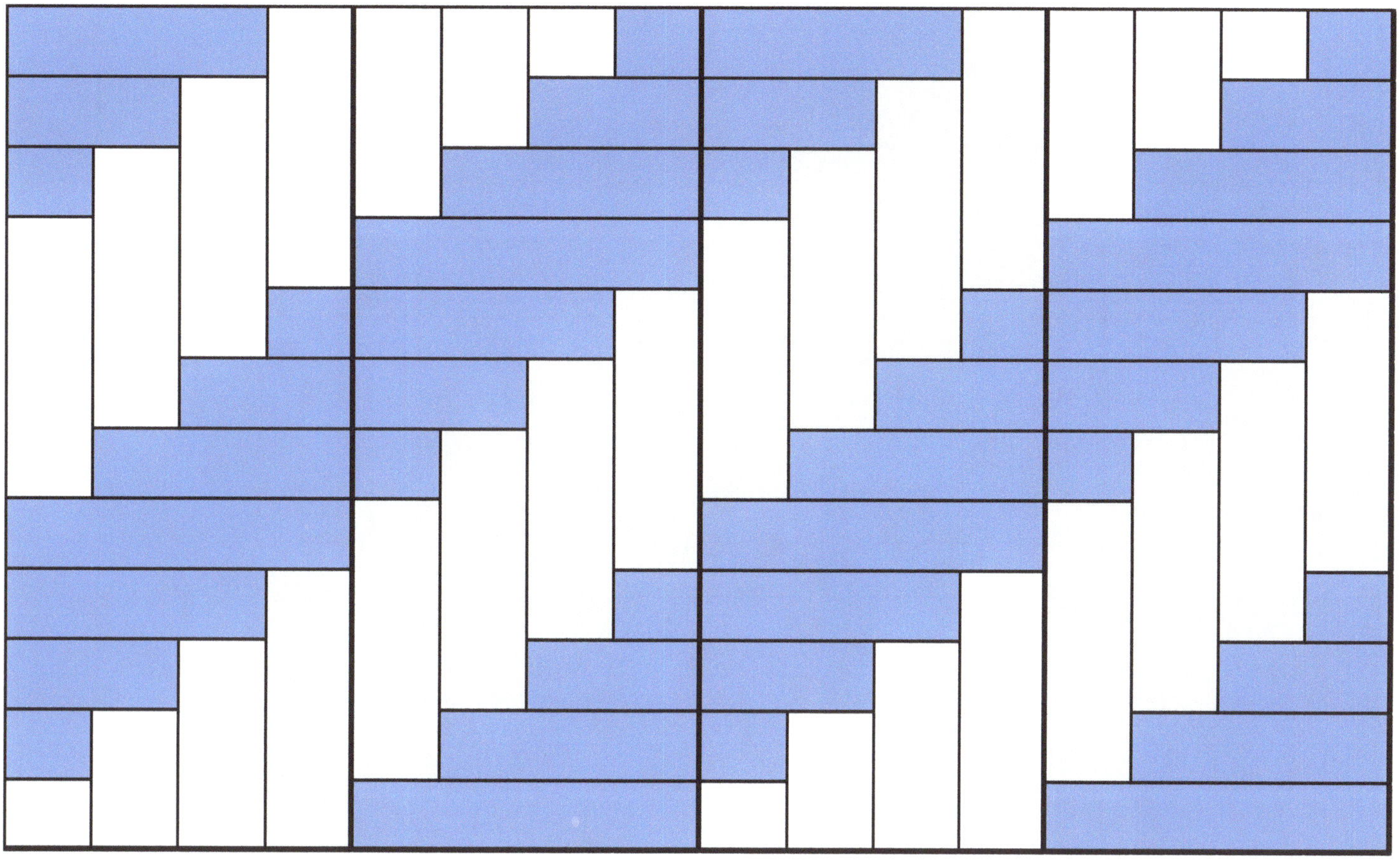

The weave repeats in a pattern. Once you have completed sequence (pattern) one, shift to sequence 2. Repeat.

Stool Top
Repeat on bottom

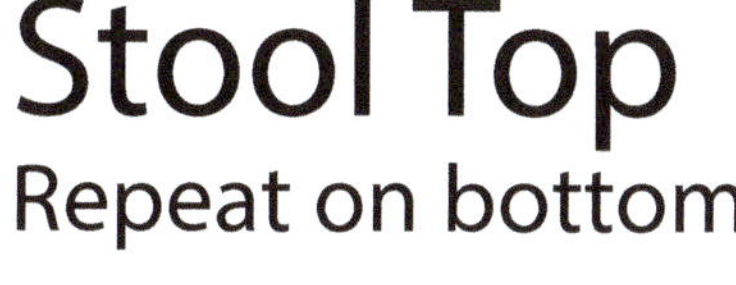 Over

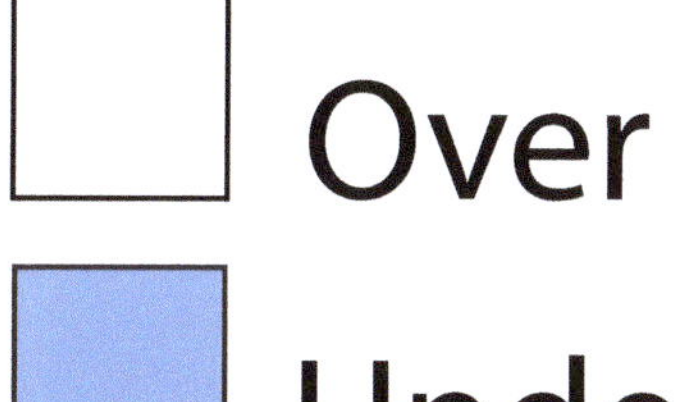 Under

Pattern is suitable for binder cane, reed, Ash splint, Shaker Tape, Macrame cord, Polypropylene cord, belts, woven cord, denim strips, etc. Use your imagination!

Advanced Patterns

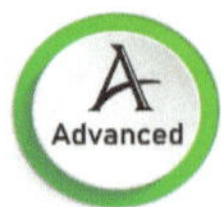

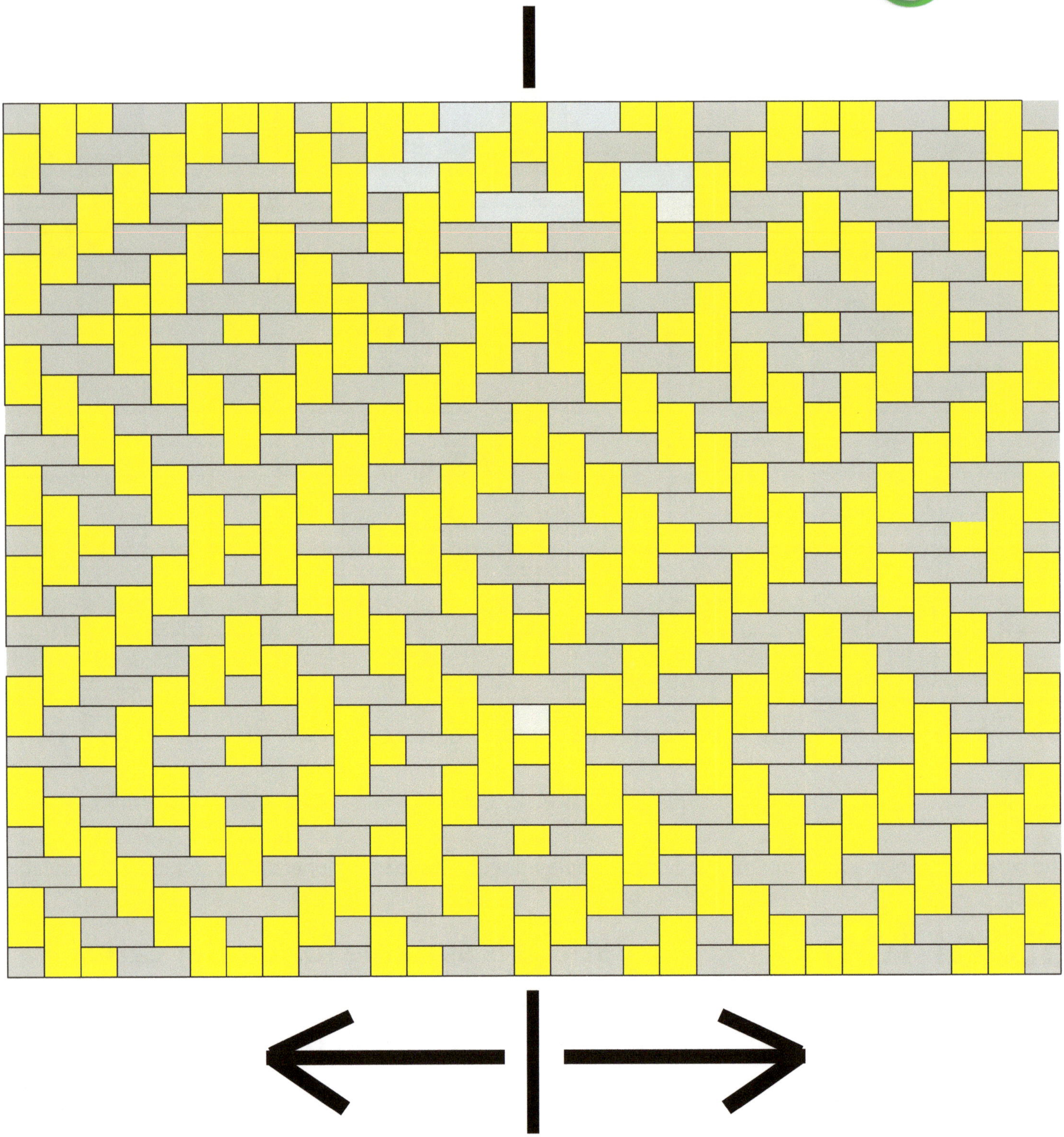

Repeating diamond pattern.
Find the center of your weaving and start in center.
Work left and right sides out from center.
Can be used with Shaker tape, binder cane or reed

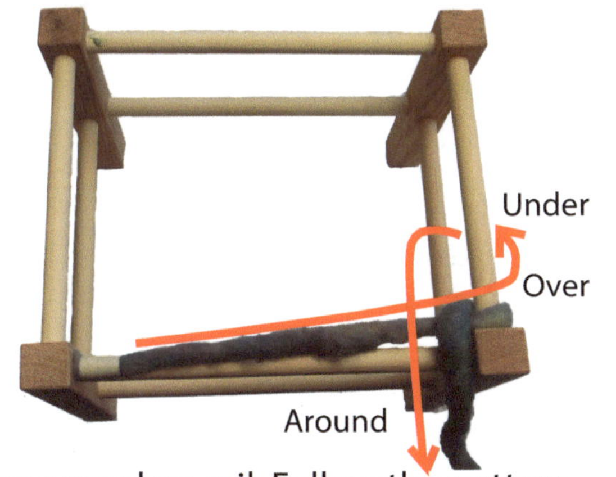

Corded Wool Stool

Corded wool is spun with a cord in the center for strength. Referred to as a "bump". Besides being luxurious, it's a great project for children or people that have limited strength in their hands. It is tactile, soft, and forgiving as a weave. It nestles into the next row,

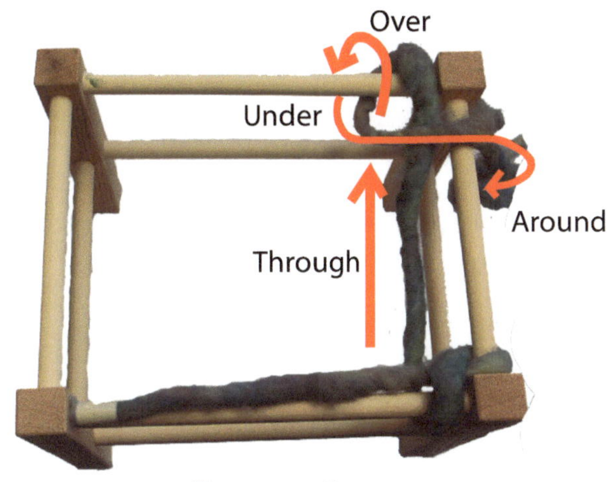

Corner 2

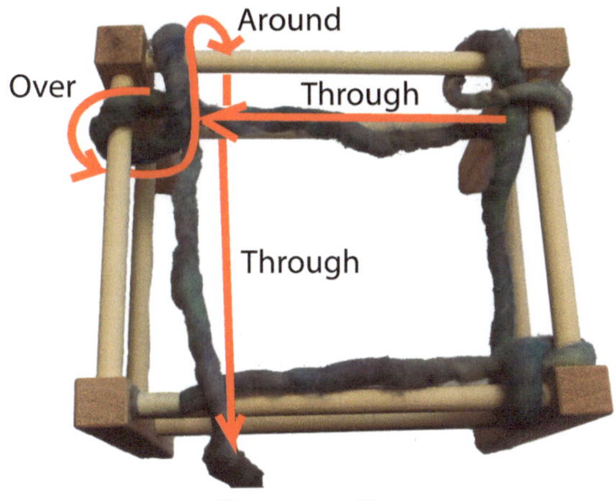

Tape wool on rail. Follow the pattern "over, under, around and through" Always end on TOP of the rail

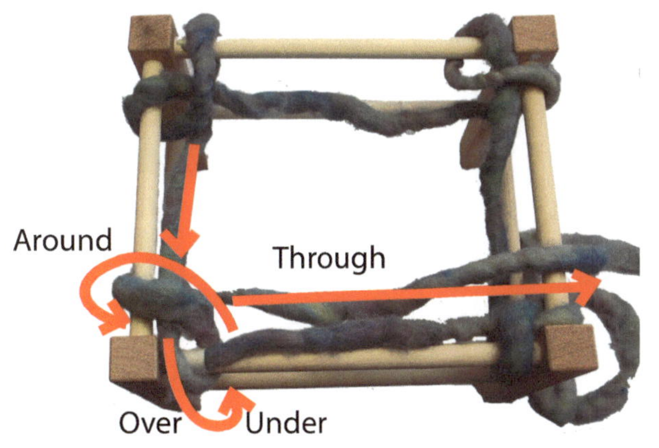

Corner 3

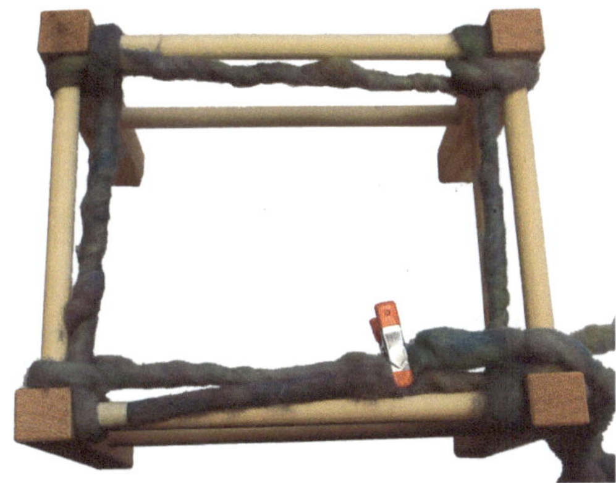

Corner 4

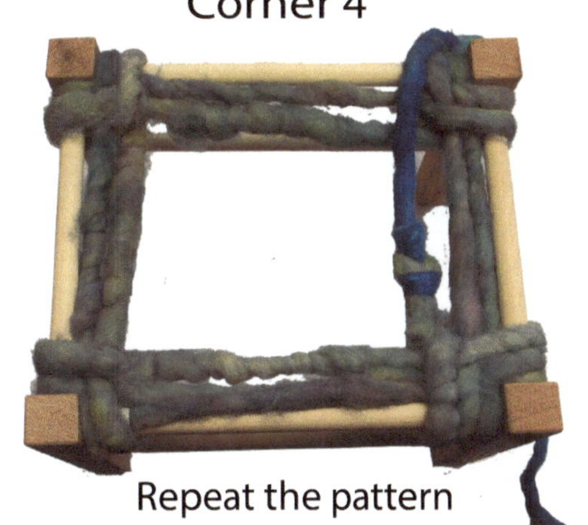

Go back and tighten your weave

Repeat the pattern
Add new pieces using
a square knot in the middle

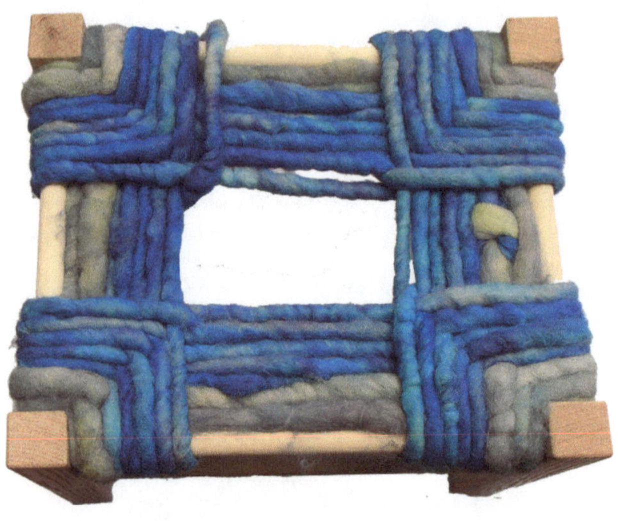

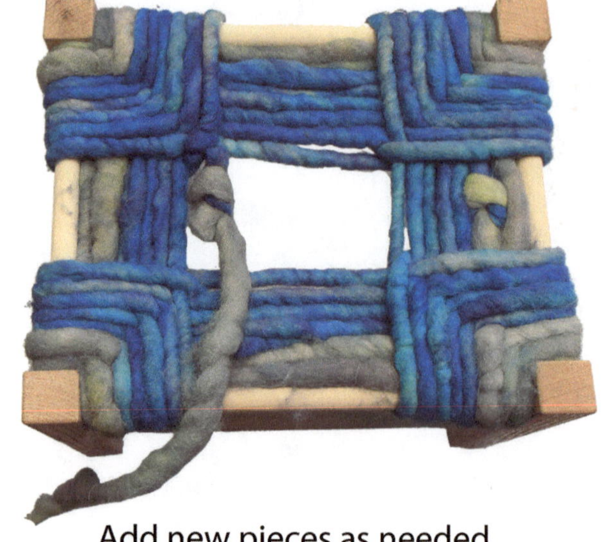

Keep repeating your 4 corners pattern "over, under, around, through"

Add new pieces as needed. Make knots in middle, they will be hidden,

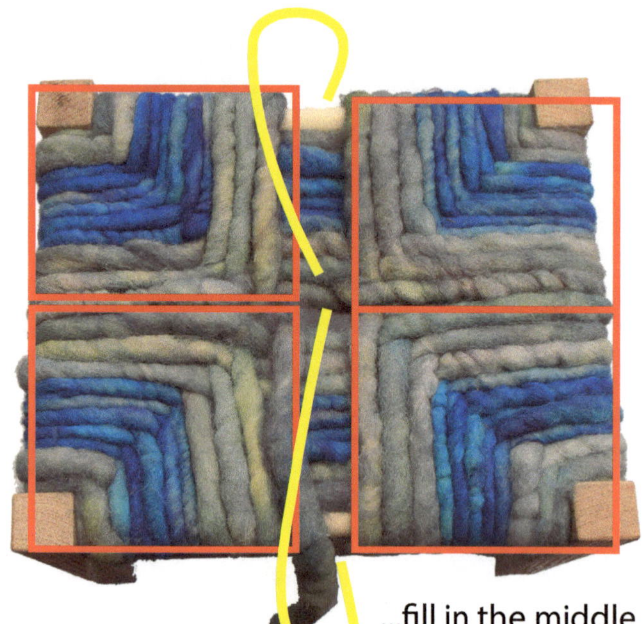

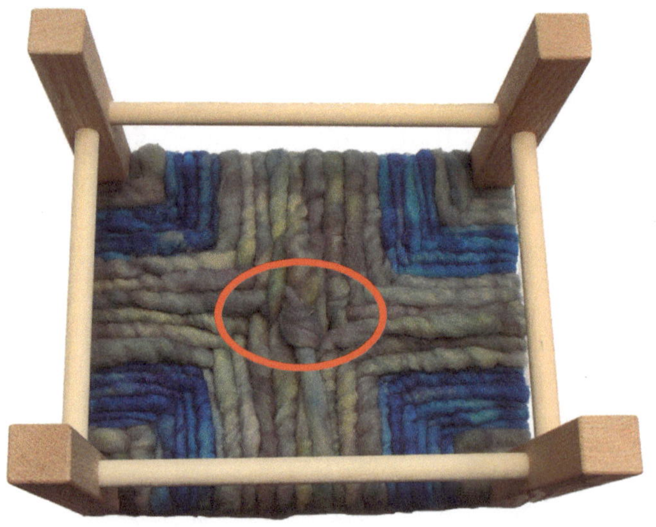

After the 4 corners are done...

...fill in the middle going back and forth in a "figure 8"

Tie the last piece on the bottom.. pick up a couple strands from the other side. Tie a knot and cut end.

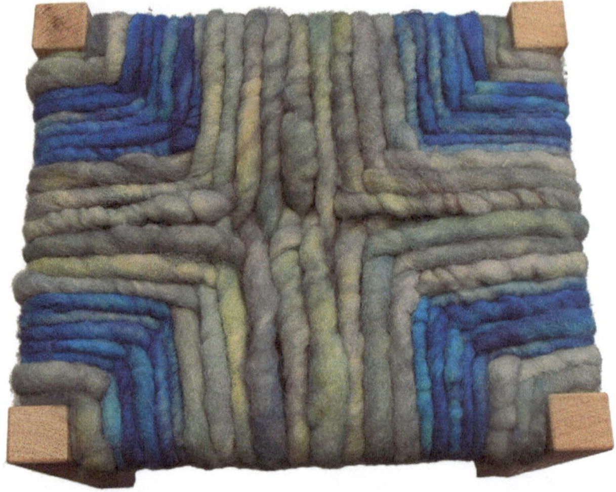

Enjoy your new comfy stool!

BASKETS

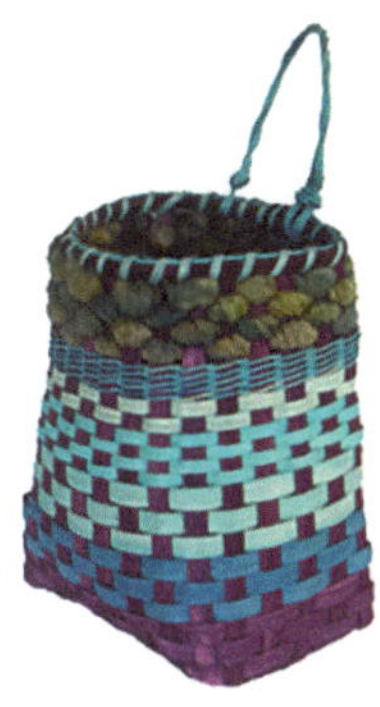 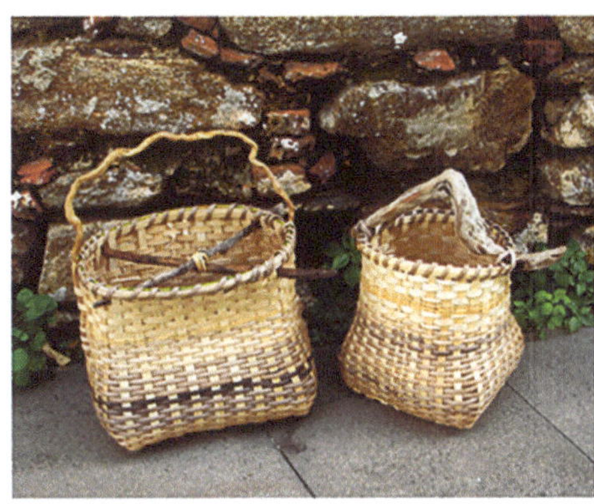 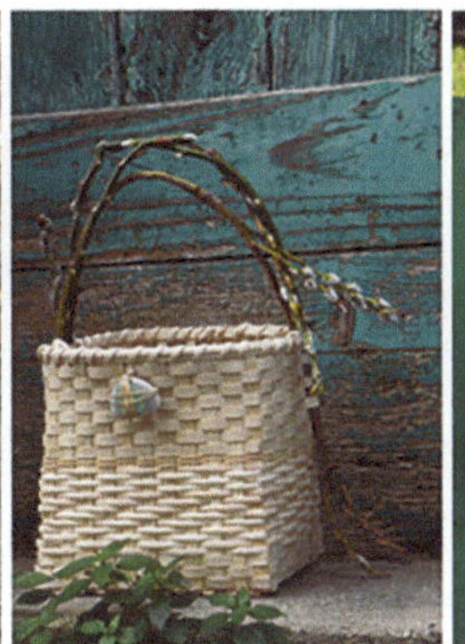 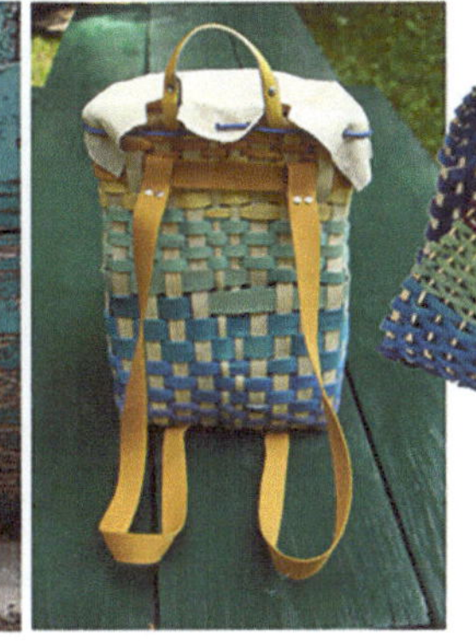 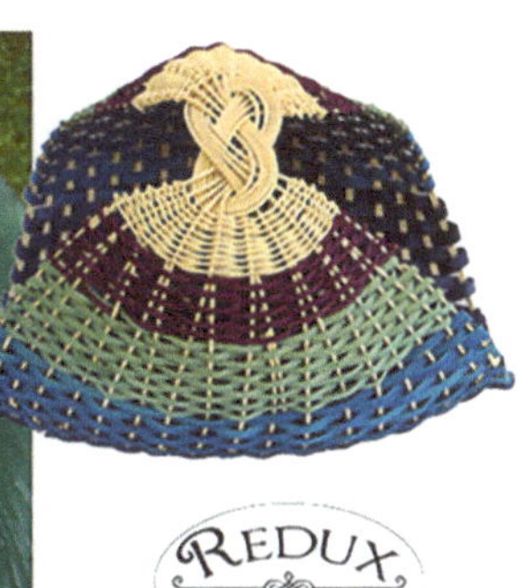

BASKETRY

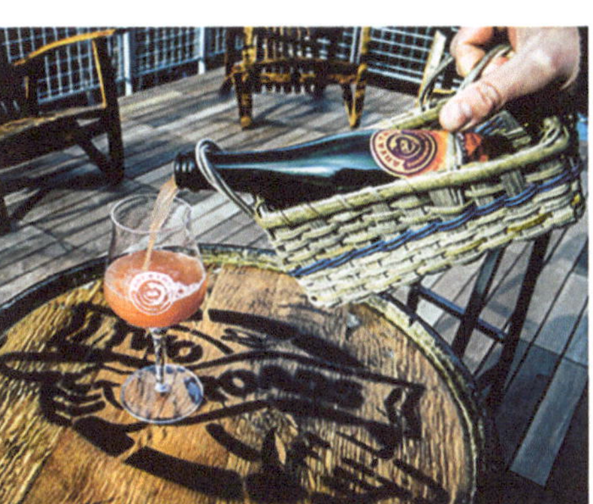 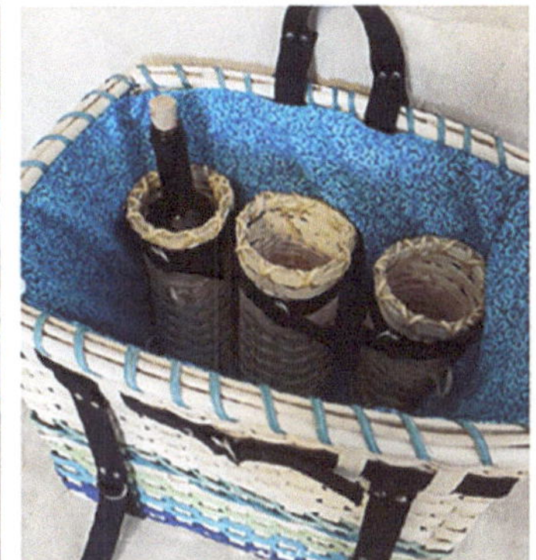 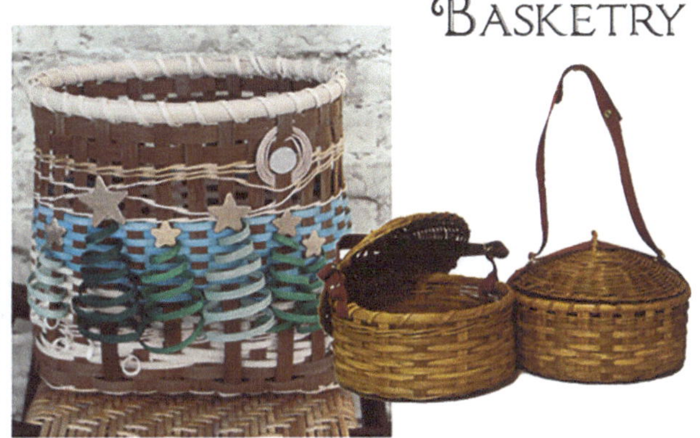

INTRODUCTION TO BASKETWEAVING

Basket weaving is a wonderful pastime, whether it is a hobby, a passion, or an occupation. All the weaving in this book is done with varying sizes of reed or cane. Reed is a rattan vine that grows in humid environments in Southeast Asia. The bark is harvested as cane and the pithy inside of the vine is cut into different shapes of reed. Round, Flat, Flat Oval and Half Round. The sizes vary from narrow 3mm (1/8") to 1" wide.

Reeds need to be wet to work with. Soak them in warm water for different lengths of time depending on the thickness of the reed. Don't soak it too long! Minerals in water vary and can lead to the reed discoloring to a gray/green tint. It is best to soak reed a couple of minutes before you need it and replenish your supply as you weave. Never soak overnight.

Because reed is porous, it should be sealed after the baskets are dry, so they don't stain. Finishes may be Tung oil, Danish oil, oil-base stain for a natural look. Specialized painted finishes or dyed reed may bleed. I use a UV Archival Varnish that is commonly used on photographs and paintings for these bright colors. Preserving or conditioning your basket is important to its long life. Instructions for dyeing reed are on pages 56 and 57.

The baskets in this book are good for a beginner, intermediate, or advanced weaver. Joining a guild will give you many opportunities to learn. I am a member of the Northeast Basketmakers Guild and the National Basketry Organization. Links are in references. There is a list of Guilds around the country on the National Basketry Organization website, along with a wealth of informaton and galleries.

  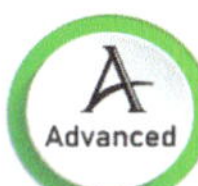

24

TERMINOLOGY

Staves or Warps: The sides of the basket that are the foundation that you weave on. The smooth side of reed is outside of basket. The rough side is inside.

Twining: A lockstitch with narrow round reed using two pieces to secure a base, or add a decorative weave to a basket.

Weavers: Reed used to weave the body of the basket using either a stop and start or continuous weave. Keep smooth side of reed to outside.

Cut and Tuck: Cutting staves flush to the top of the basket alternating with longer staves left long to fold over and tuck into inside weavers. This holds the basket to the rim.

Lashing: Using a narrow reed to "sew" or "lash" an outside and inside rim to top of basket.

Rim filler: seagrass or round reed filler between the tops of the rims to cover the folded staves.

Over/ Under weave: Woven over and under staves. When woven on uneven number of staves it is a continuous weave. On even number of staves weavers overlap on 3 staves, and are done row-by-row.

Twill Weave: A pattern of weave using a sequence that "steps up" one warp at a time.

Scarf: To thin down the ends of overlapping reed to make overlap less bulky.

BASKET PATTERNS IN THIS BOOK:

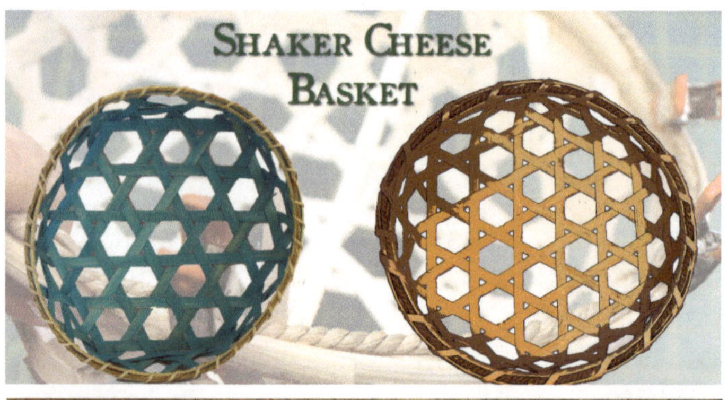

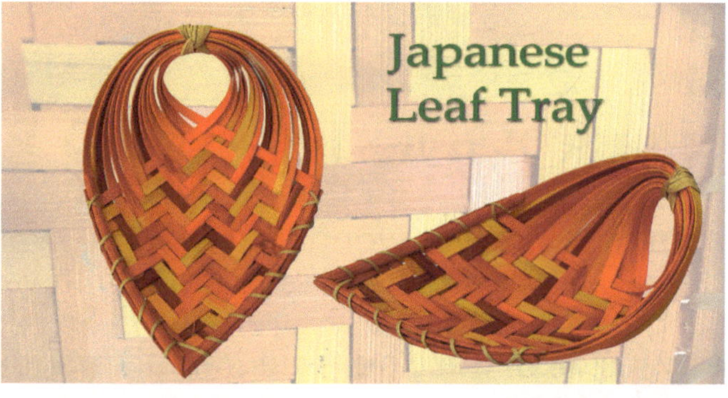

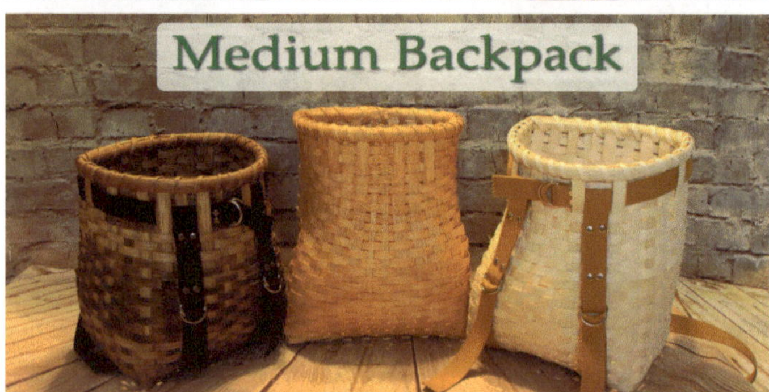

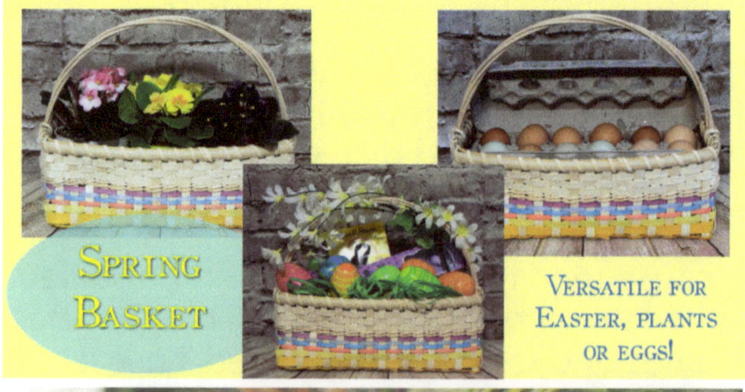

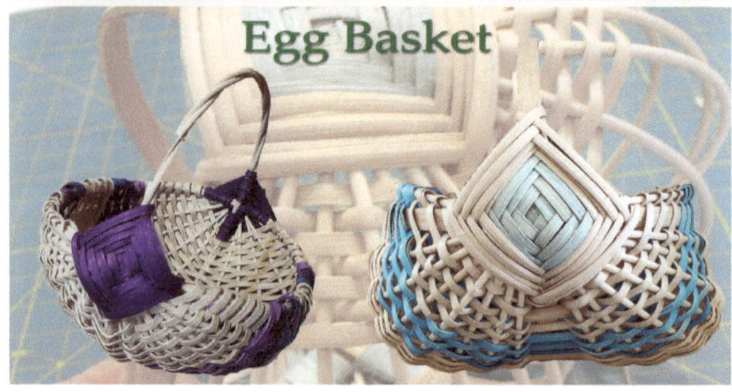

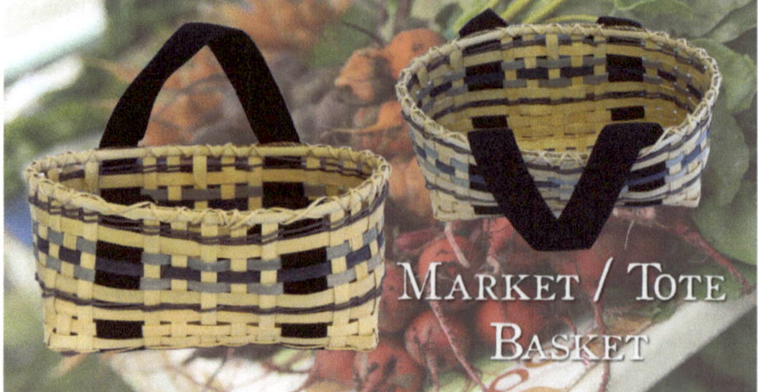

Shaker Cheese Basket

The Shaker cheese basket is traditionally lined with cheese cloth and used to drain the whey from the curds. Learn how to weave this hexagonal pattern and add your own creativity by using color, or adding rows. This pattern is for the traditional 2 row weave used for cheese. Make your staves longer and add more rows of weavers for a taller basket.

3/8" reed: (18) 21" (base) / (3) approx 45" (weaver and false rim)
(2)1/2 " flat oval reed approximately 45" long for rim
Seagrass : (1) approximately 45" long (rim filler) 120" 1/4" flat reed (lashing)

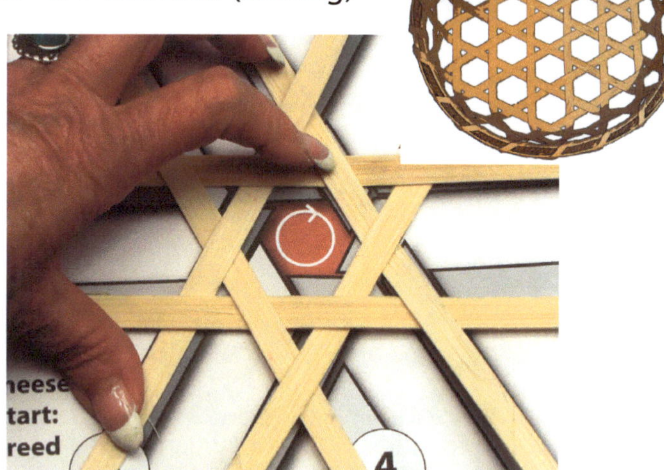

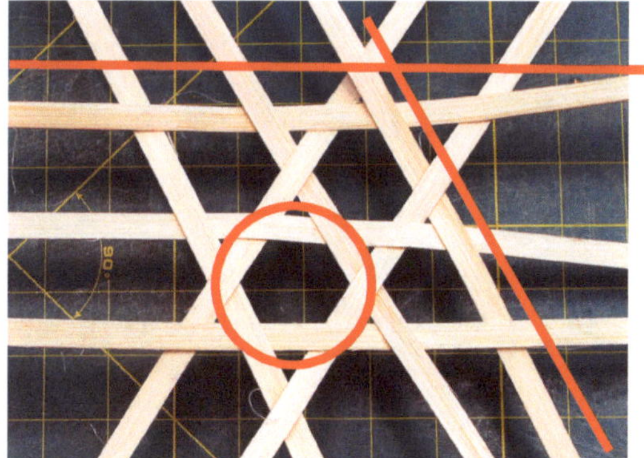

Use the grid to start laying out the center of the basket. Follow the over/under pattern on the diagram.

Complete the pattern and remember to "flip and lock" the last weave.

Begin adding rows around the center. Turn to the right and continue to add rows to the pattern.

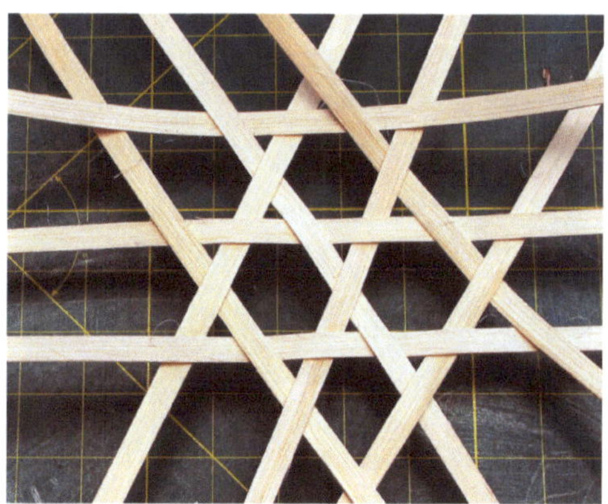

Keep turning clockwise right and adding.

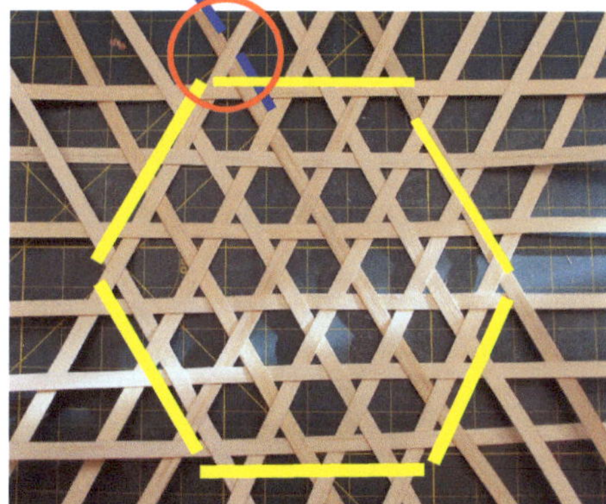

"Flip and lock" each row after weaving. Each side will have 3 hexagons.

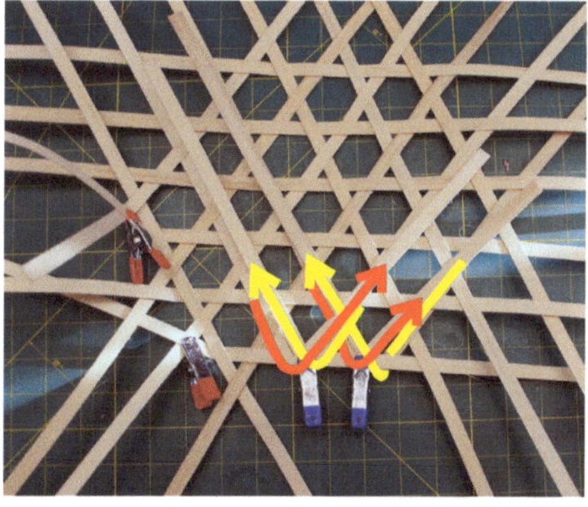

Wet the reed and then bend the staves to follow the hexagon pattern.

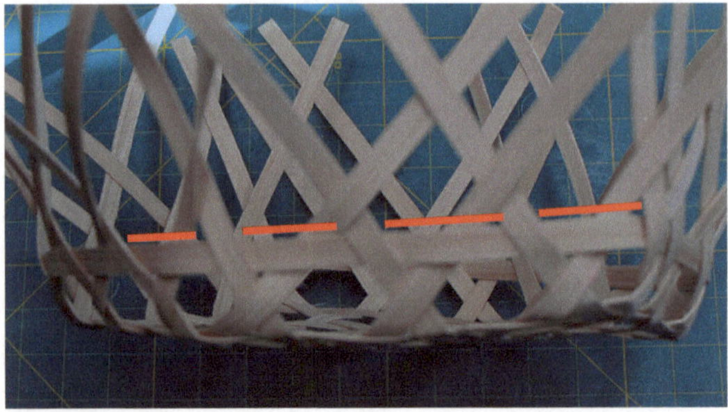

Upright staves and weave following the over/under pattern.

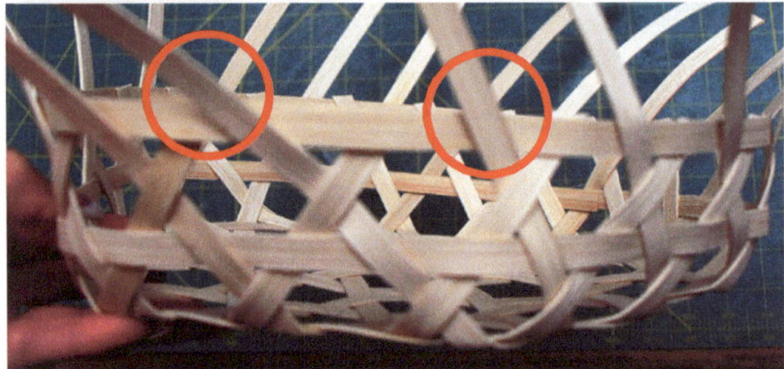

Be sure to "flip and lock" at every juncture. (these aren't locked yet) Tuck the right stave behind the left.

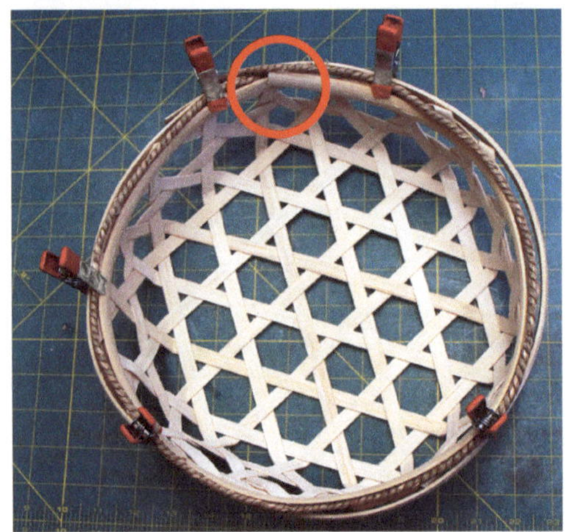

Add rim (outside and inside) overlapping scarfed joints. Add seagrass (or 6 mm round reed) rim filler and clamp.

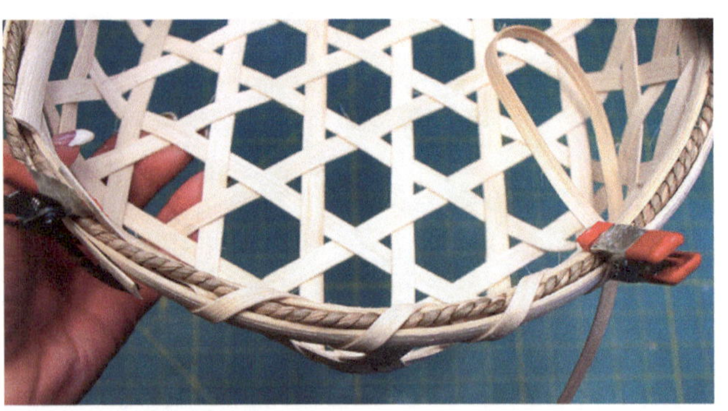

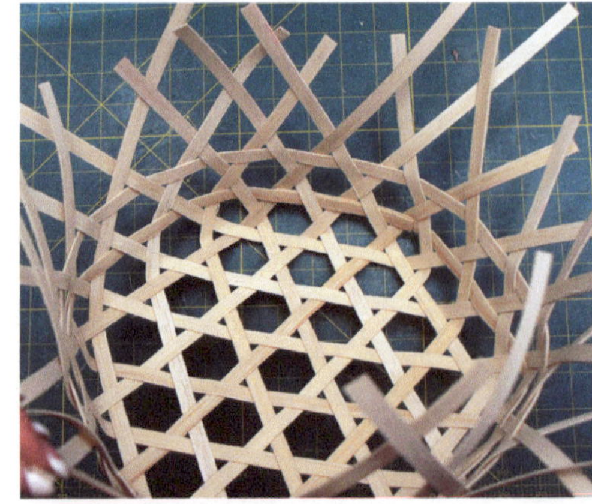

Weave a second row .

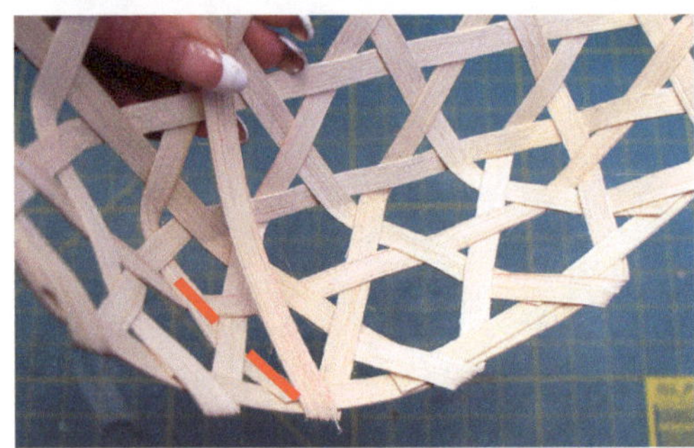

Fold over and tuck in under weave to hold in place.

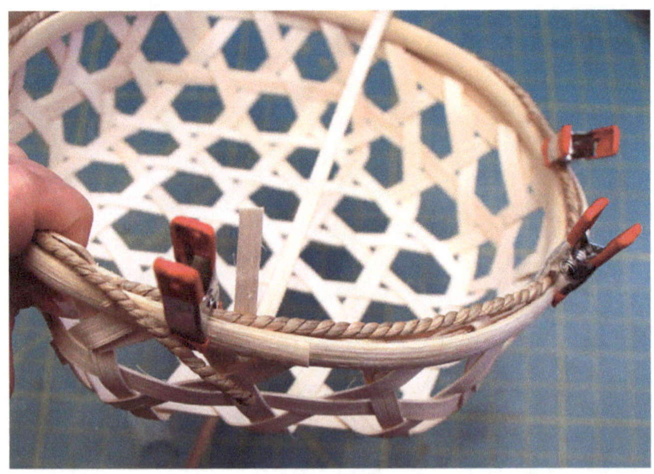

Insert lashing (right side facing center) between inside rim and rim filler.

"Sew" the lashing going through each large weaving space. Pull the lashing between rims and tuck into last lashing wrap. Trim beginning and ending of lashing.

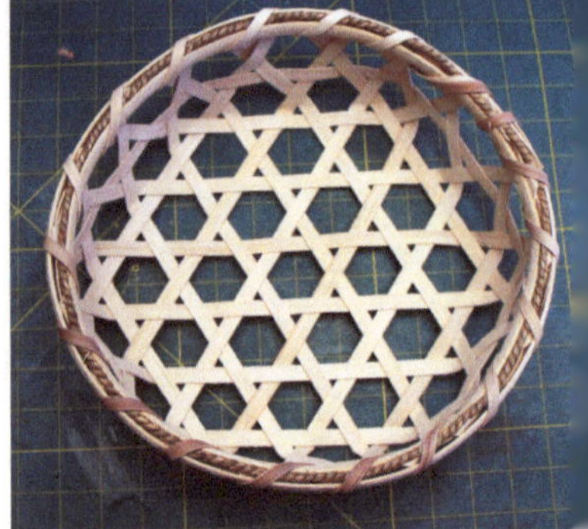

Enjoy your new basket.

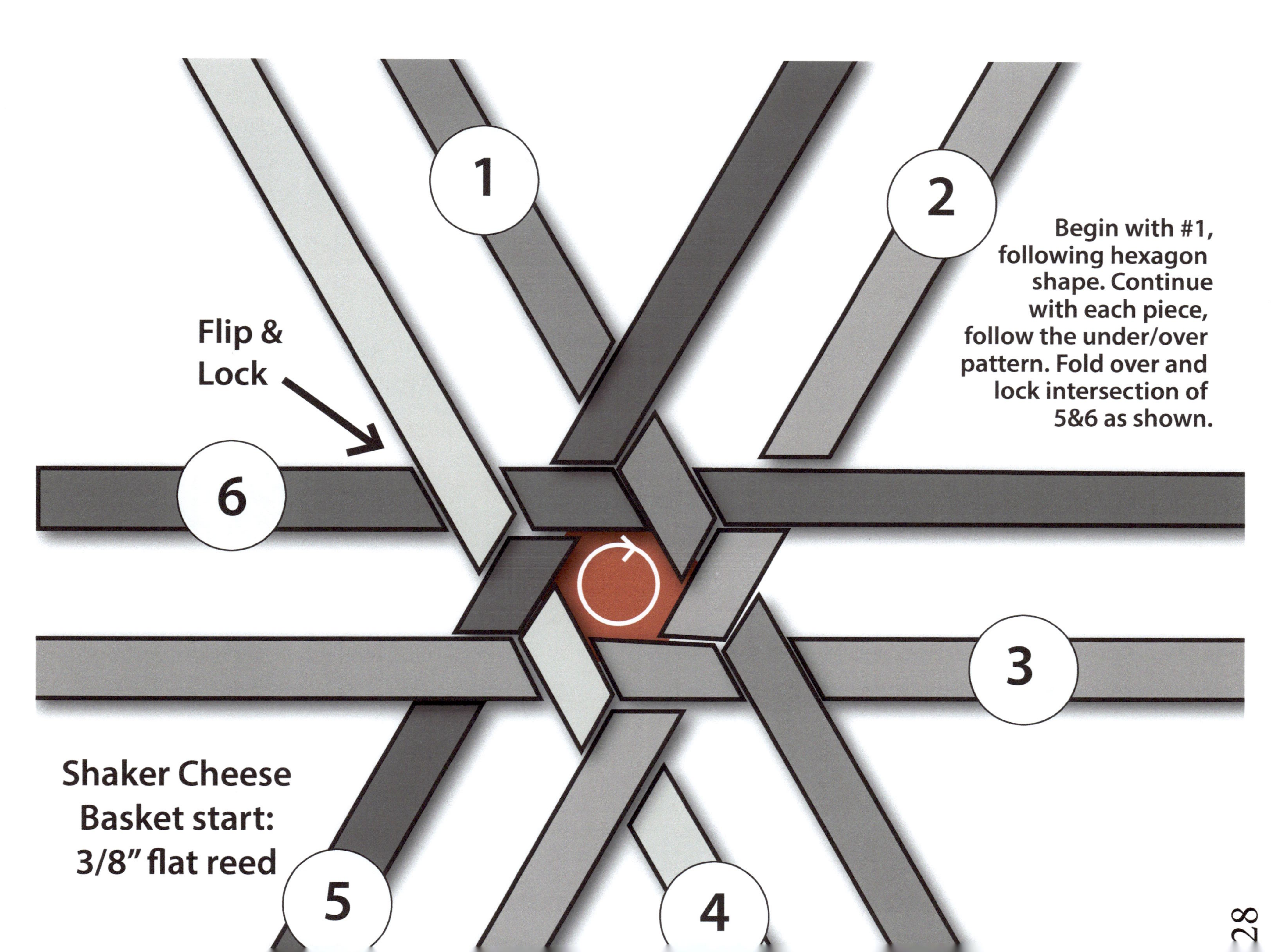

1
2
Begin with #1, following hexagon shape. Continue with each piece, follow the under/over pattern. Fold over and lock intersection of 5&6 as shown.
Flip & Lock
6
3
Shaker Cheese Basket start: 3/8" flat reed
5
4

SIDE
SIDE
SIDE
SIDE
SIDE
SIDE
SIDE
BEND
BEND
BOTTOM
BOTTOM
BOTTOM
BOTTOM
BOTTOM
BOTTOM
BEND
90"
BEND
90"
BEND LINE
BEND LINE
BEND LINE
REDUX
FOR YOU

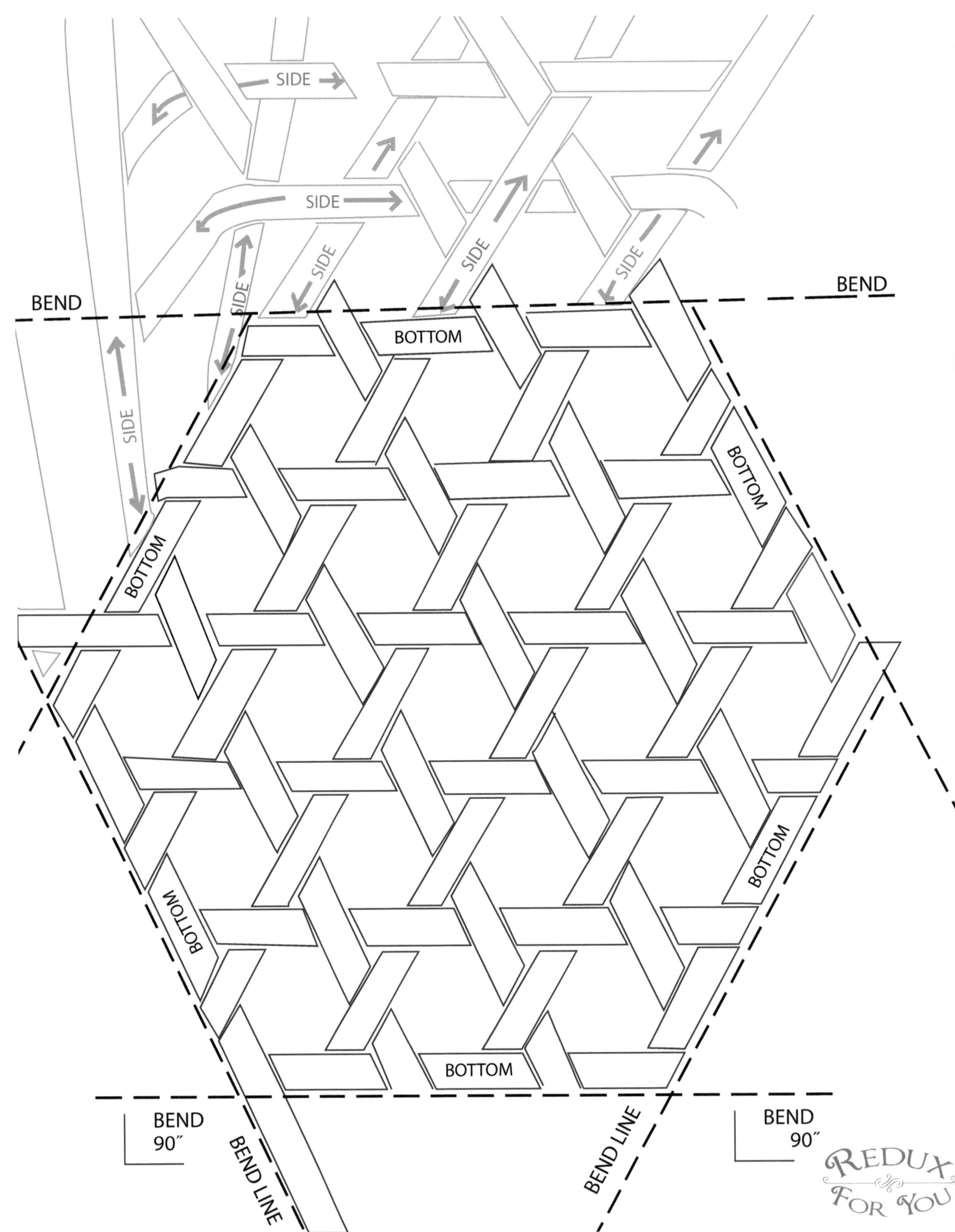

29

Japanese Leaf Tray 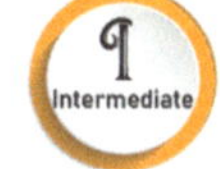

3/8" flat reed
4 mm binder cane

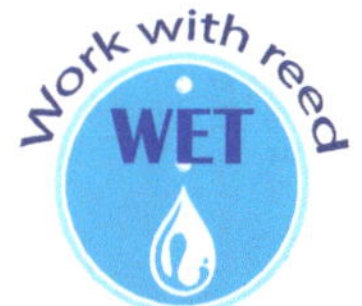
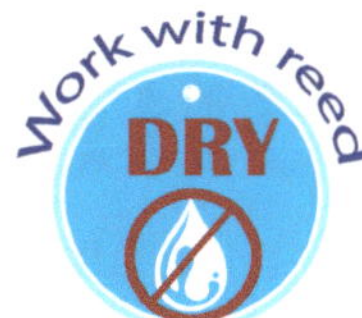

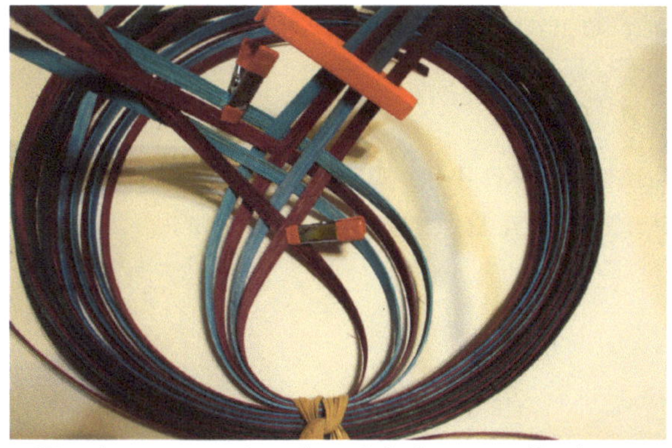

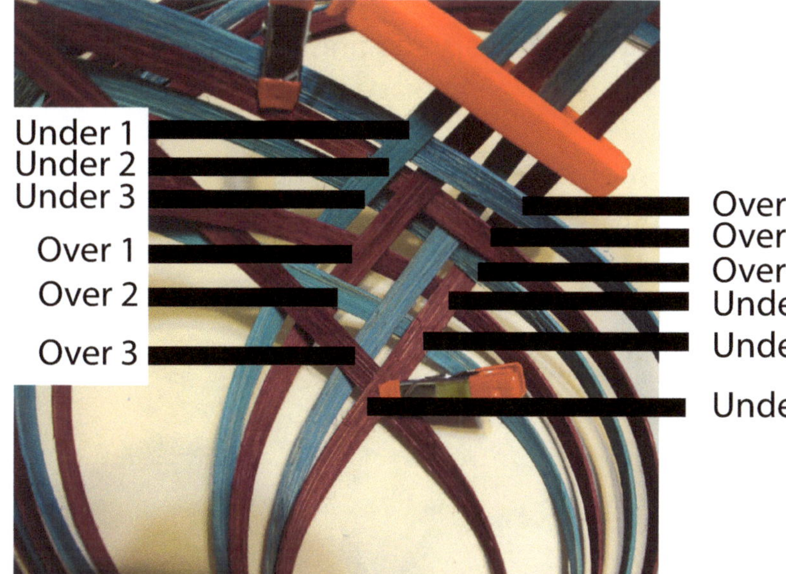

Find center. Lash with butterfly knot.
Establish your herringbone pattern
 (3 over 3)
Use 2" clip and bag holder clip to
hold in place while weaving.

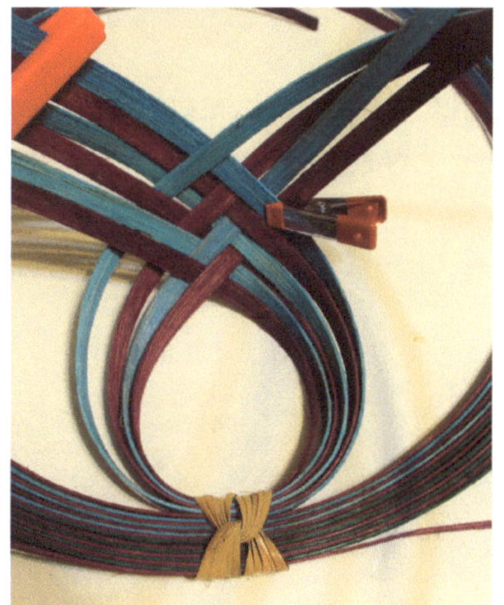
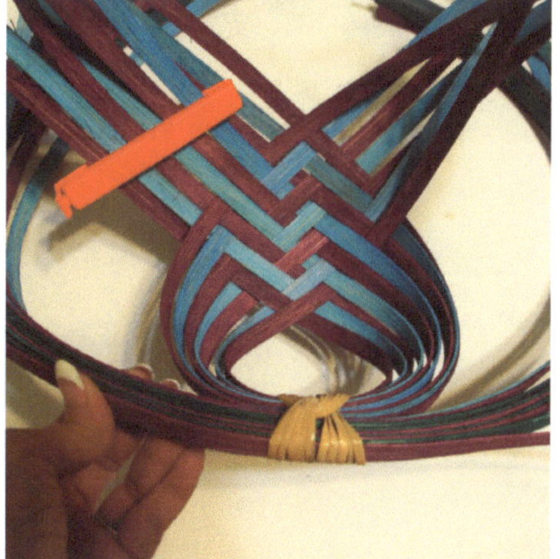
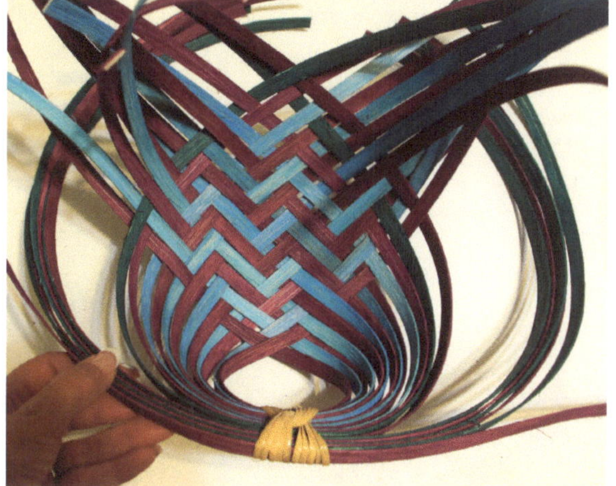

Tighten your weave. Add more weavers from each side, following the pattern.

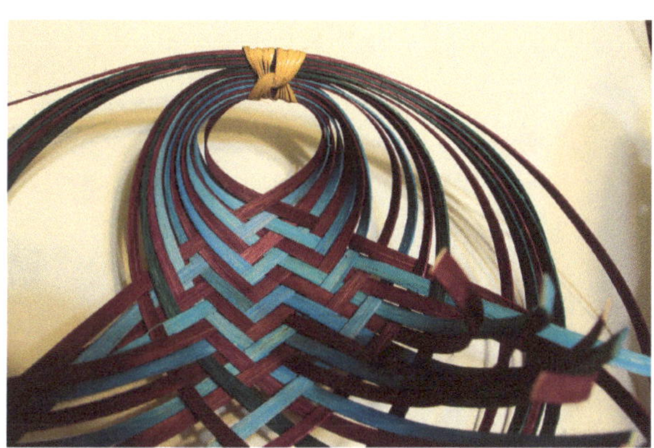
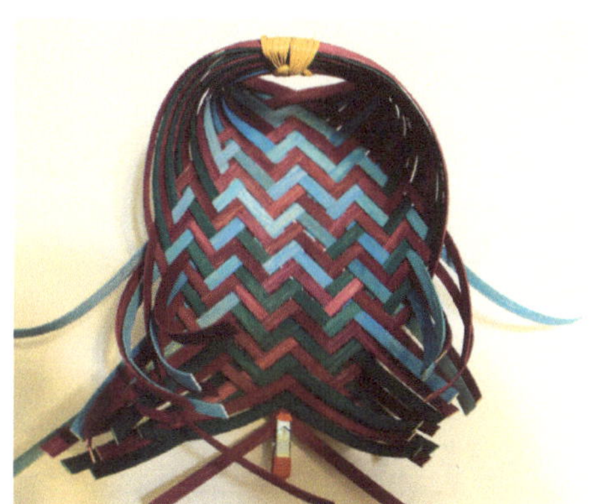
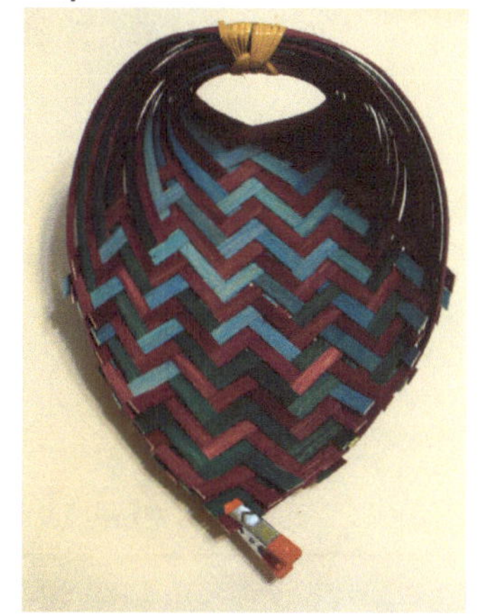

Tug and shape as you go. Trim the excess weavers. Glue tip if desired.
Finish with extra pieces and lash to tray with cane.

Butterfly Knot 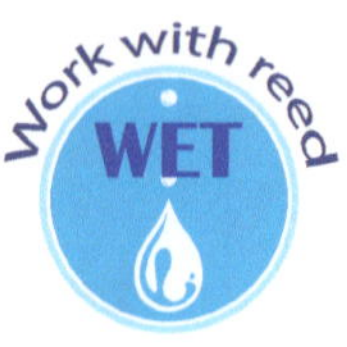

4 mm binder cane

Line up all your weavers and find the center . Clip or rubber-band them together to hold in place while you make your butterfly knot.

Using common or #4 binder cane, hold a tail behind the stack. Make a "U" on top, then feed the tail behind the stack. Make an inverted "U" being sure not to twist the cane.

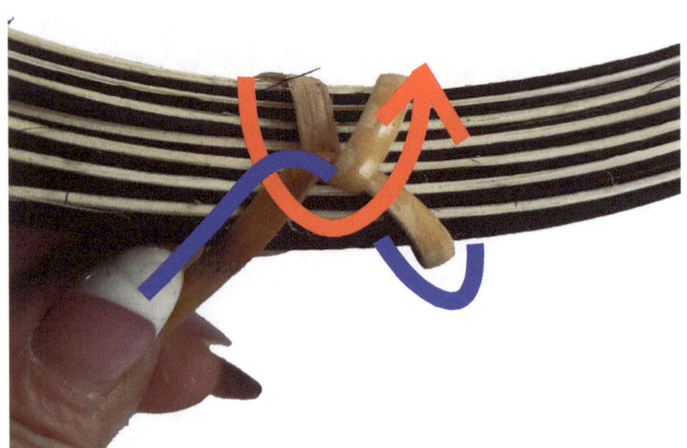

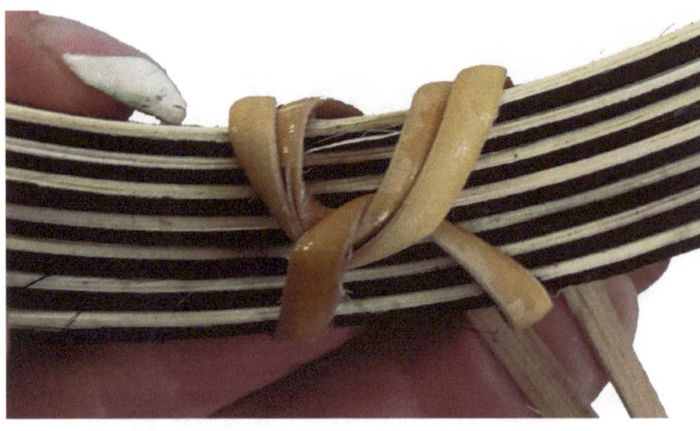

Repeat the "U" on top, keeping the shiny side on top. Keep tight.

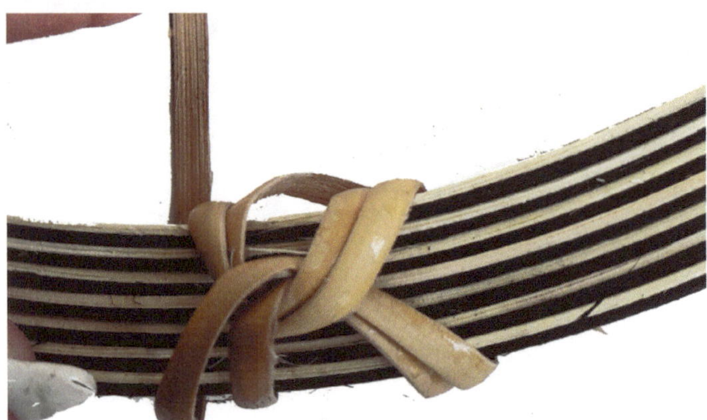

Repeat the inverted "U" on bottom.

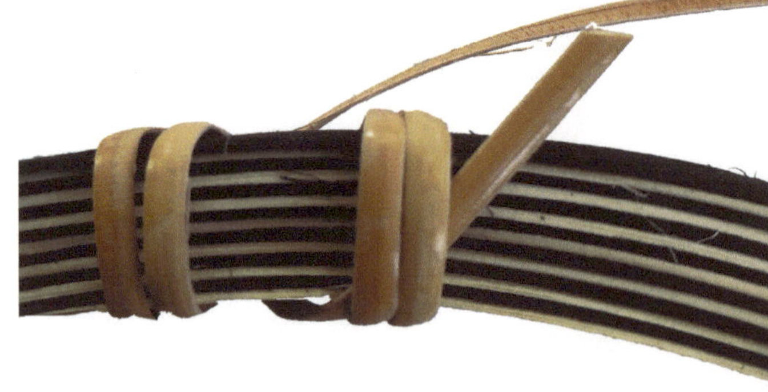

Make sure to catch / wrap the tail to secure it.

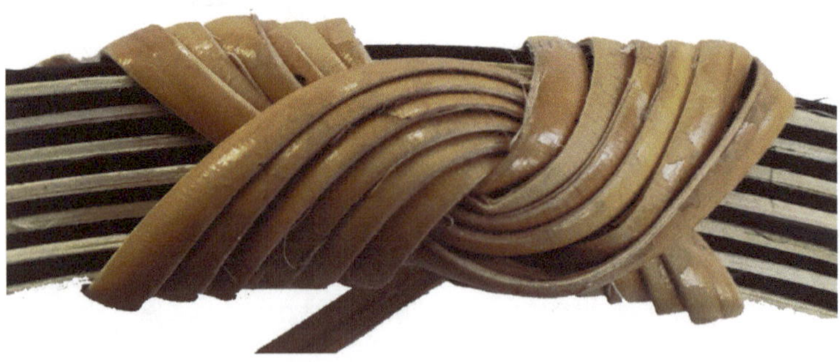

Keep repeating until you fill up your space.

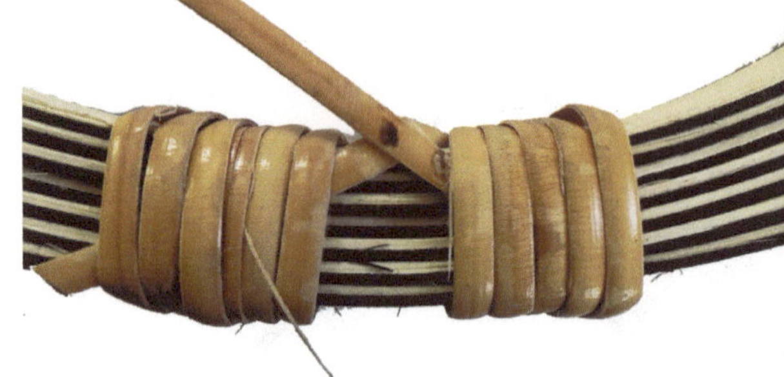

Feed the cane through loops in the back to end and trim both ends.

31

"Sew" the binders on. Insert cane in between layers, wrap to the left of end. pull tight then start weaving from the bottom every 2 staves (weavers). Clamp. If desired, add a spot of glue at point of tray. Contimue lashing around the edge. Do the same thing with end as beginning...lash to the end then tuck end in between binding layers. Pull tight and snip off.

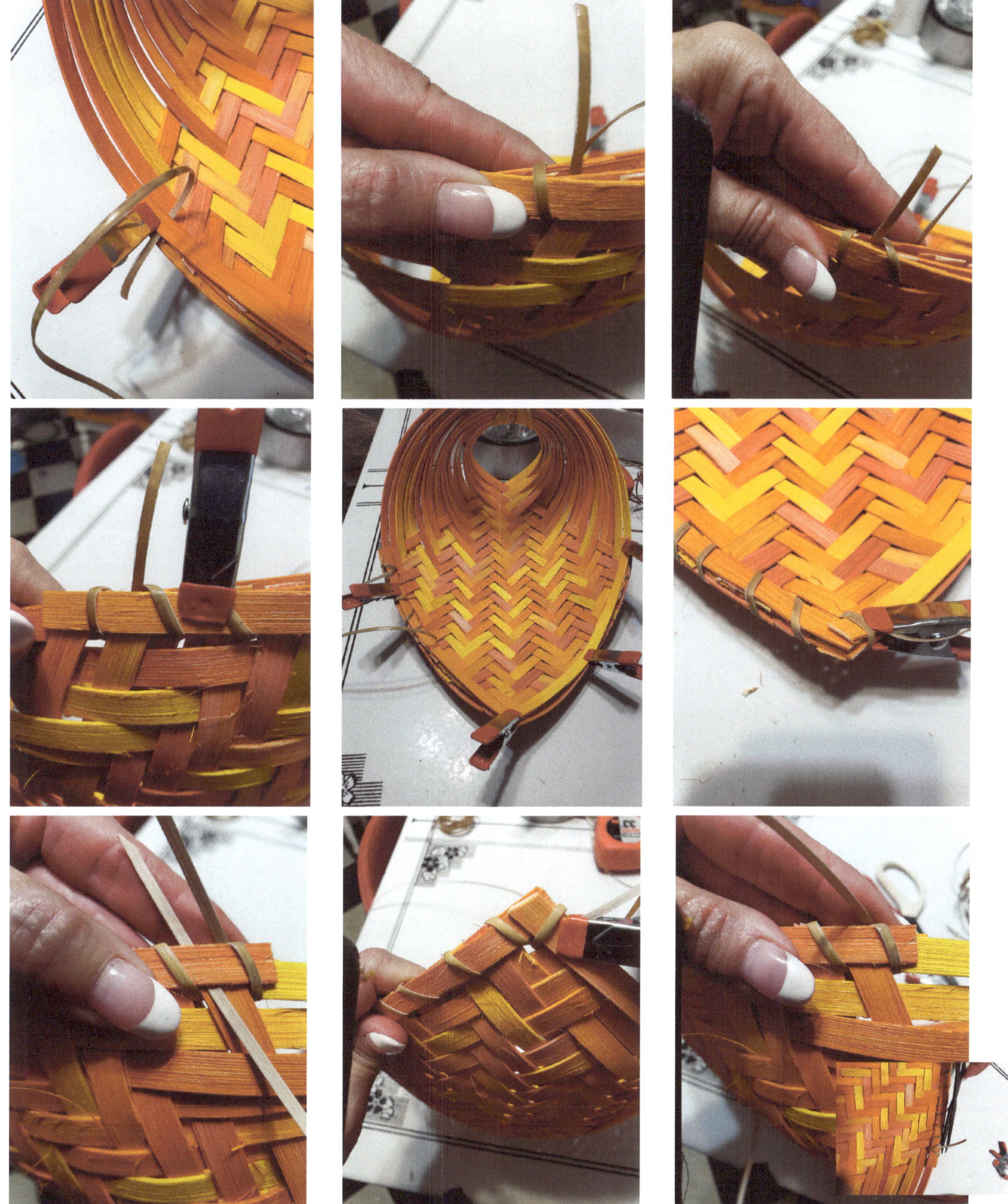

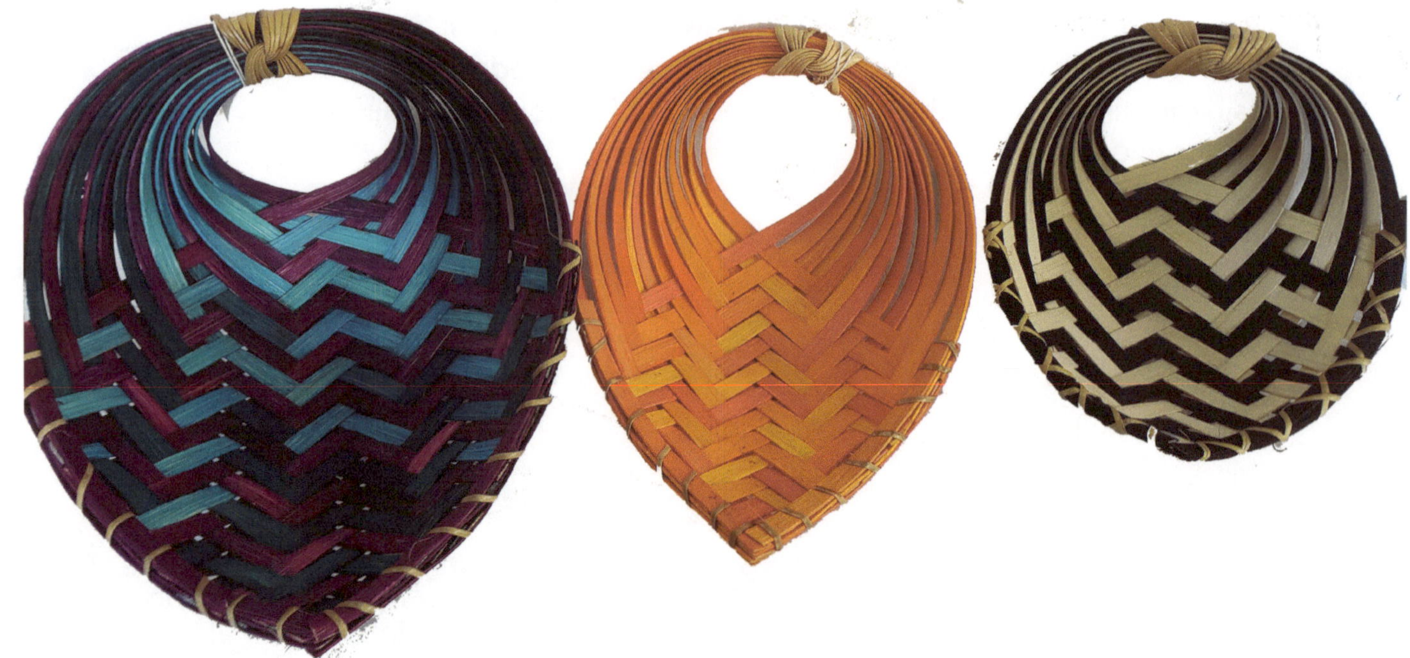

Purple and Teal
18 - 3/8" reed 37"
Tray size 10" long / 9' wide

Space-dyed reed
13 - 3/8" reed 33" long
Tray size 10" long / 8" wide

Black and natural
14 - 3/8" reed 29" long
Tray size 8" long / 8" wide

Plus: 4 shorter pieces to bind sides. Cane for knot and wrap (common or #4 binder cane)

The Japanese Leaf Tray is tradionally used as a flat tray to serve hor d'ourves. The pattern
I made calls for a bit more tension at the back. The tension creates more of a curved shape.
Use it to hold small items, as a cornucopia, or set with the point upright to hold a vase,
candle jar or salt lamp. If I am at a Renaissance Faire, it ends up on someone's head as a hat.

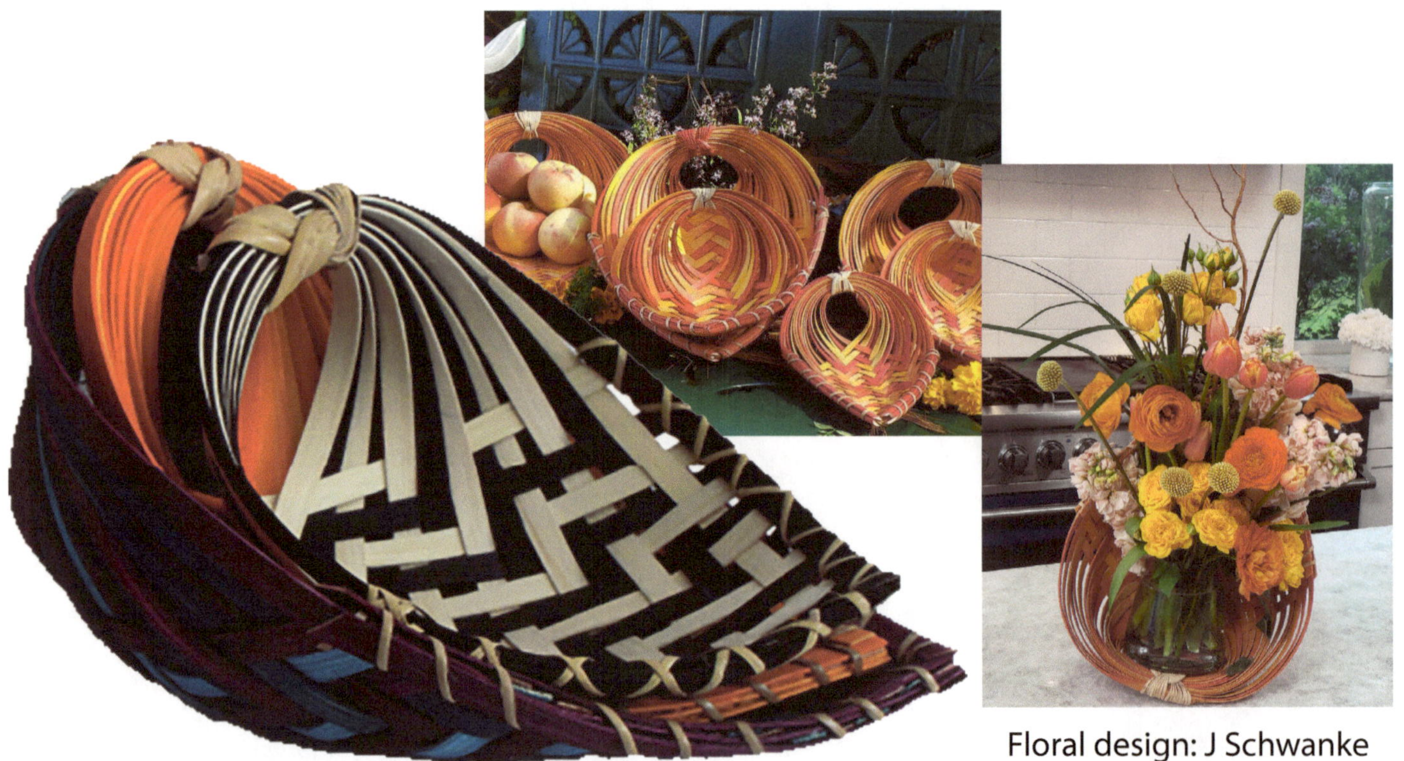

Floral design: J Schwanke

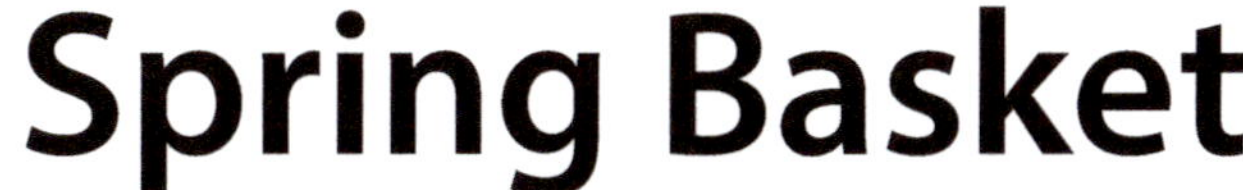

Spring Basket

Horizontal warp: 5 - 3/8" flat reed 28"
Chicken feet: 4 - 3/8" flat reed 19"
Vertical warp: 15 - 3/8" reed 21"
Handle: 2 - #6 round reed 40"
Rim - 2 - 5/8" flat oval reed 36" Rim filler 36" #6 round reed
Weavers: 5/8" flat reed, 3/8" flat reed, 1/4" flat reed (colors)
Twining: 20' #3 round reed
Lashing: 12' - 1/4" flat reed

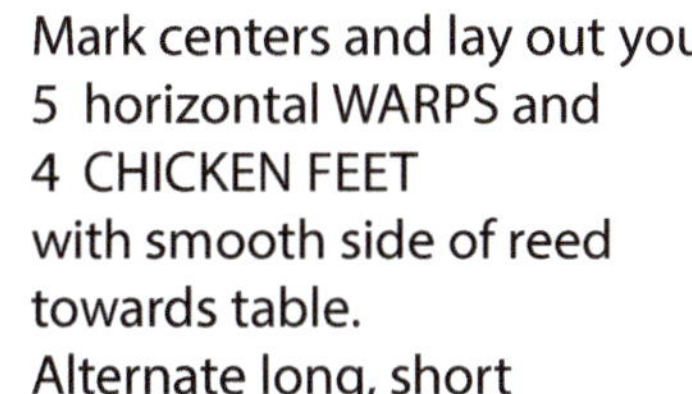

Mark centers and lay out your
5 horizontal WARPS and
4 CHICKEN FEET
with smooth side of reed
towards table.
Alternate long, short

Use a spoke weight, level or
ruler to hold flat.

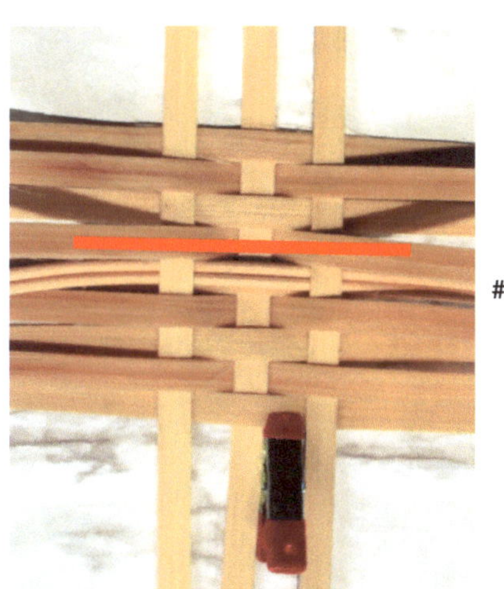

#6 round
reed

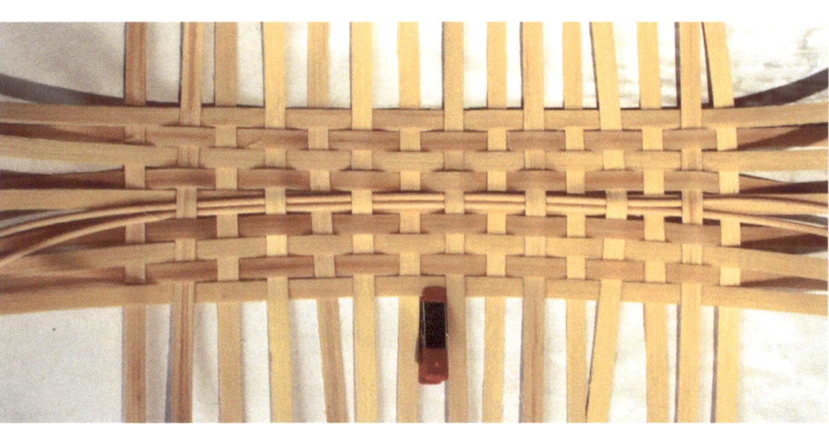

Begin weaving with the vertical WARPS
marking the center, and incorporating the
round reed HANDLES into the weave.

Finish weaving all the WARPS

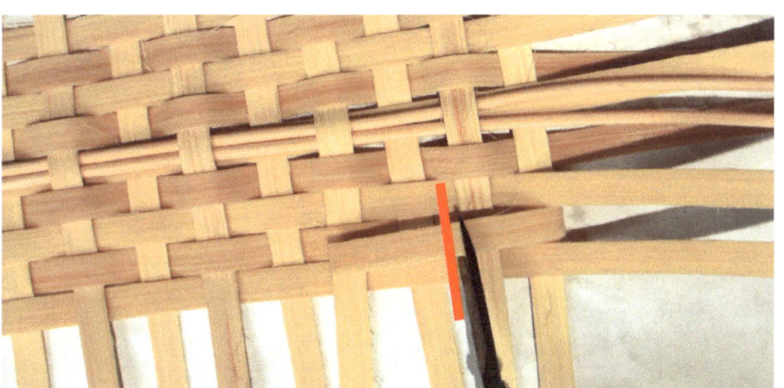

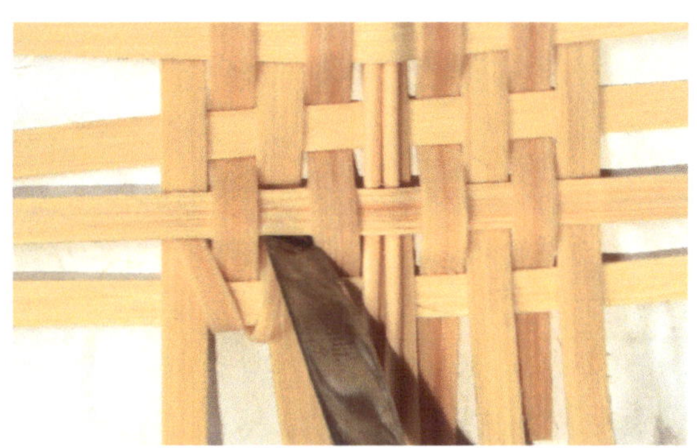

Make CHICKEN FEET by cutting them to outside of second WARP, then split and tuck as shown.
Use a weaving tool or butter knife to ease ends in.

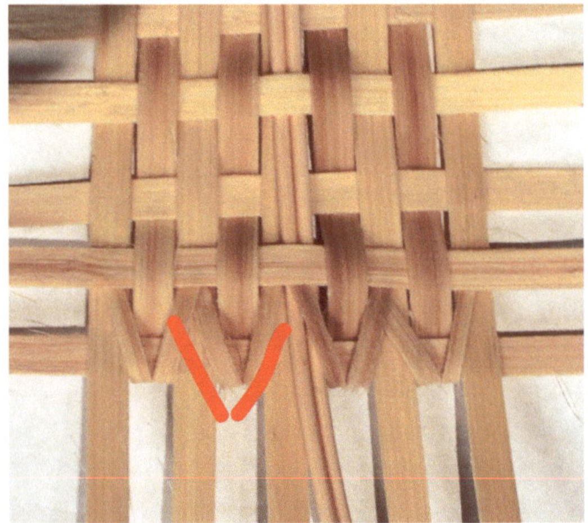

Finished CHICKEN FEET.

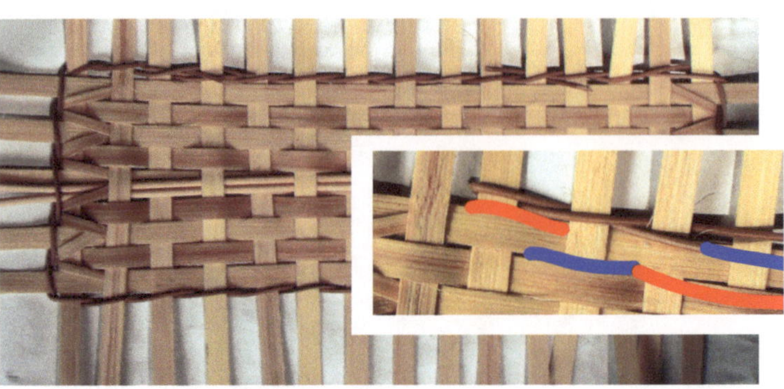

Using small ROUND REED twine around warps. Go all around the basket, overlap 1-2 warps at the end. Trim. Twining: if reed is OVER it goes UNDER, repeat .

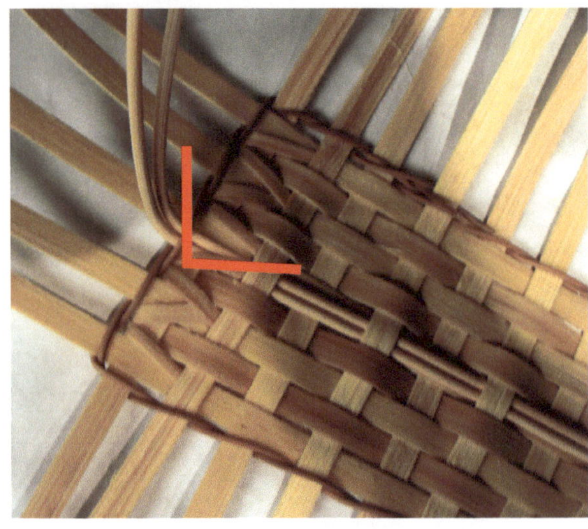

Make sure the ROUND REED handles are soaked. Upright (bend) at 90 degrees.

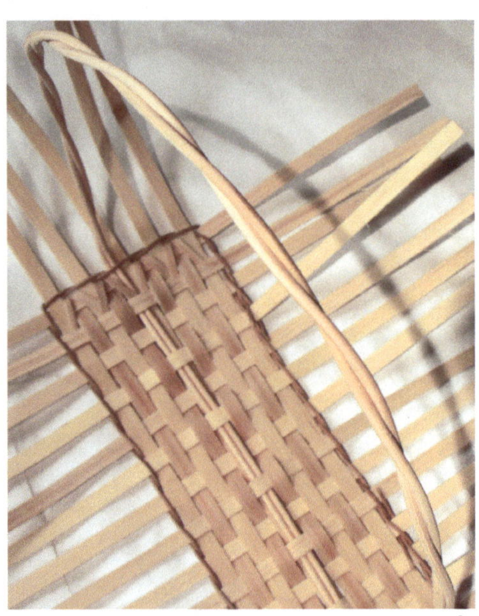

Twist two ROUND REED together and at base of basket on other side.

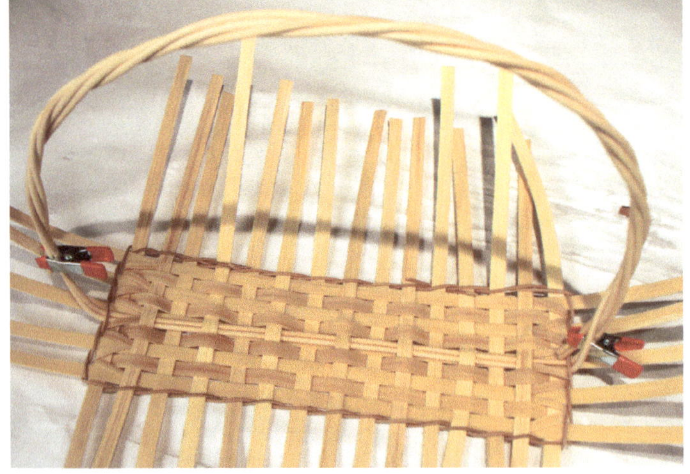

Nestle the other two ROUND REEDS around the first two and clamp. You can adjust your handle height.

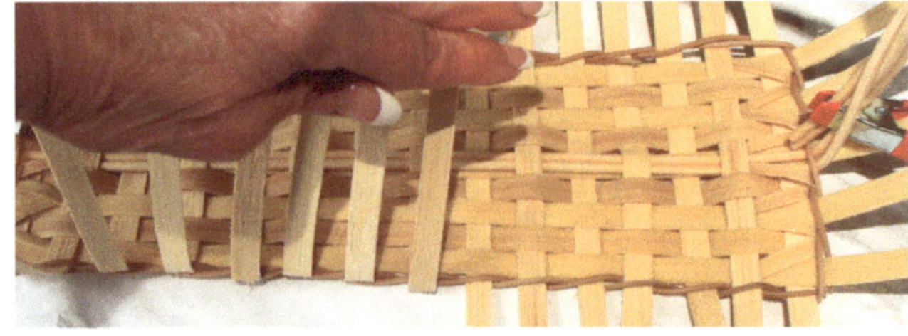

UPRIGHT your WARPS

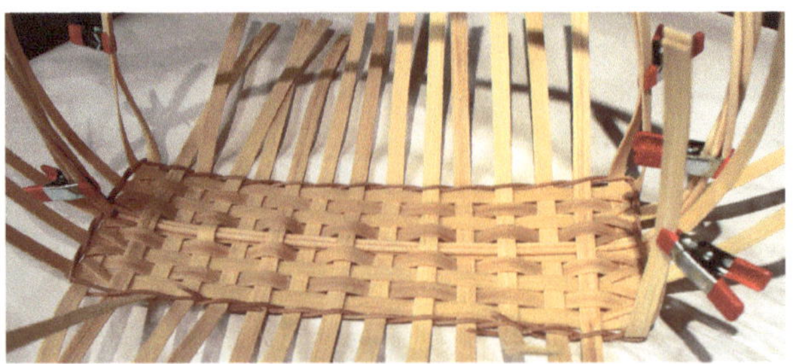

Clamp four corners to begin to weave. Be sure to incorporate handle.

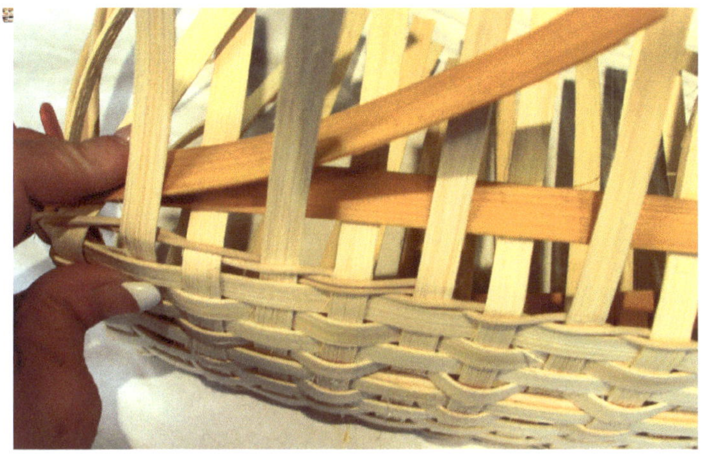

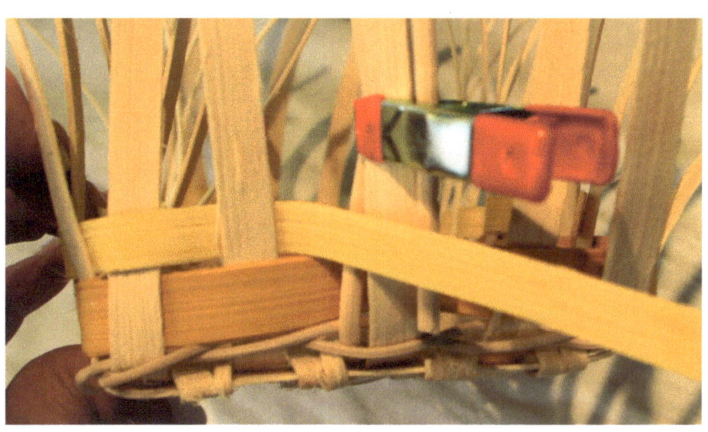

Weave the 5/8" WEAVER.

Weave the 3/8" WEAVER.

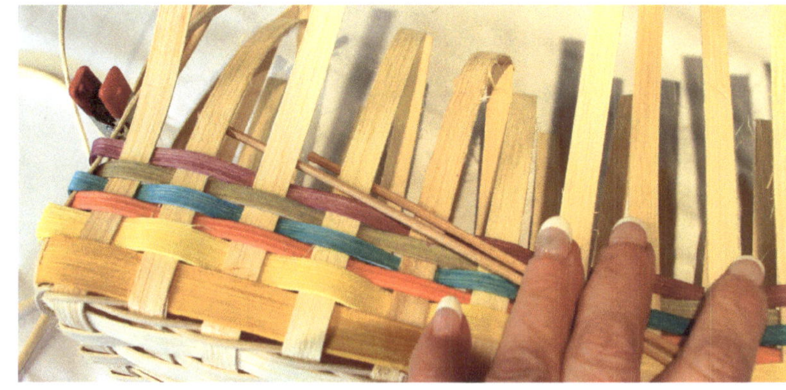

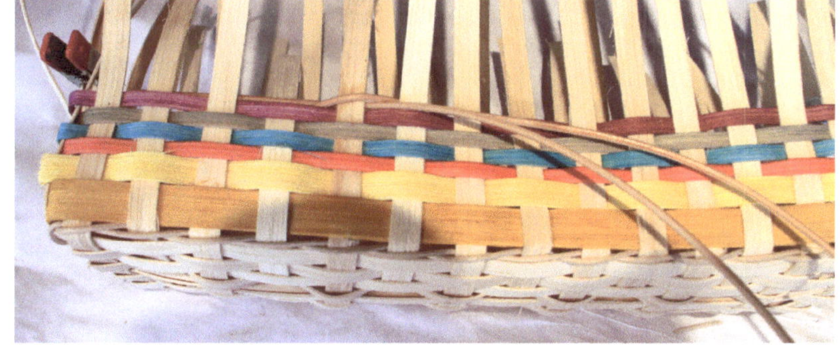

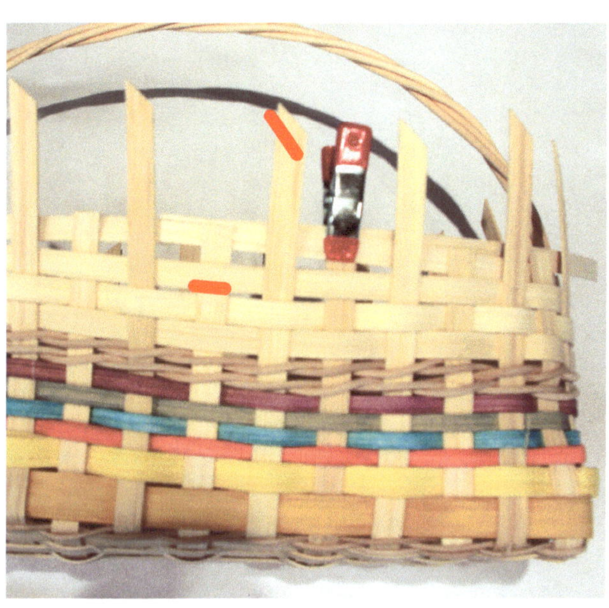

Weave your 1/4" WEAVERS, then TWINE two rows above them with round reed.

Weave 3 more 3/8" WEAVERS then add a 3/8" FALSE RIM behind the WARPS. Trim every other stave above the false rim, and trim the others about 3".

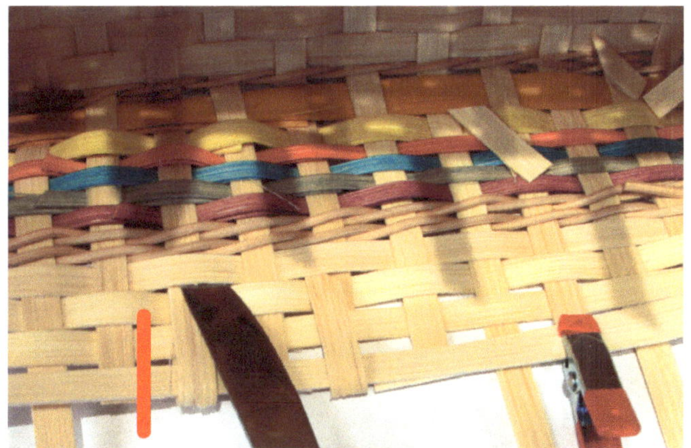

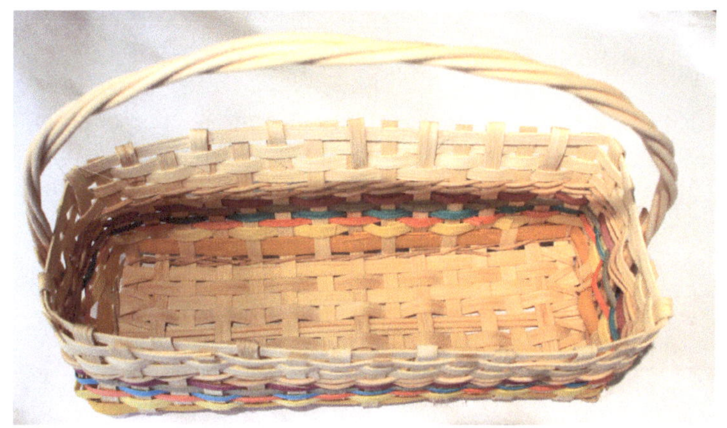

Tuck the WEAVERS over the FALSE RIM and tuck into the first or second WEAVER.

36

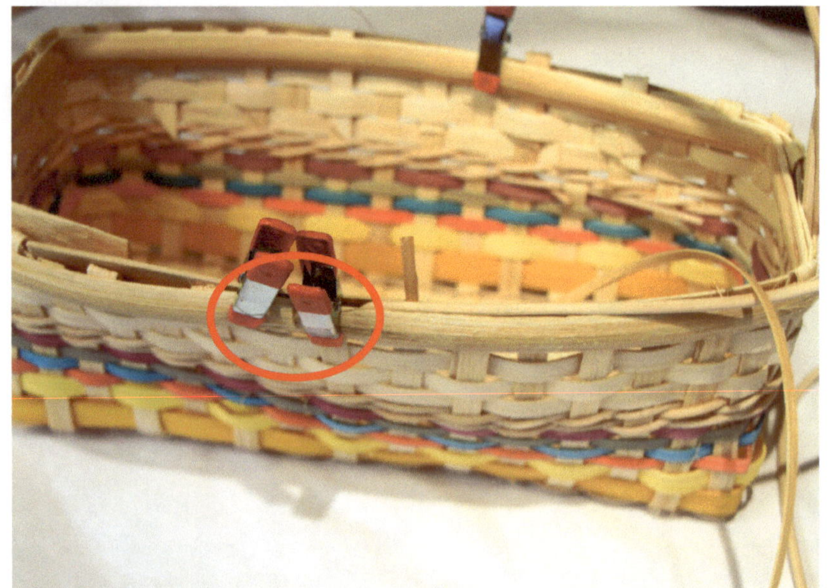

With a utility knife, SCARF (remove some material to make thinner) on the top side and bottom side of the ends of flat oval reed about 1.5 - 2".

Overlap at SCARF and clamp to rim. Put ROUND REED rim filler in between inside/outside rim.

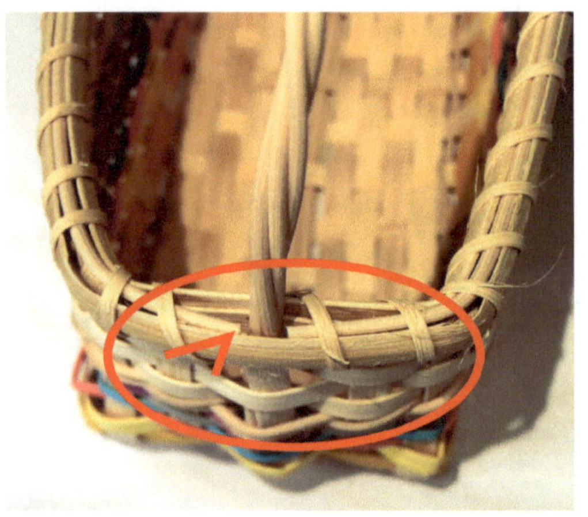

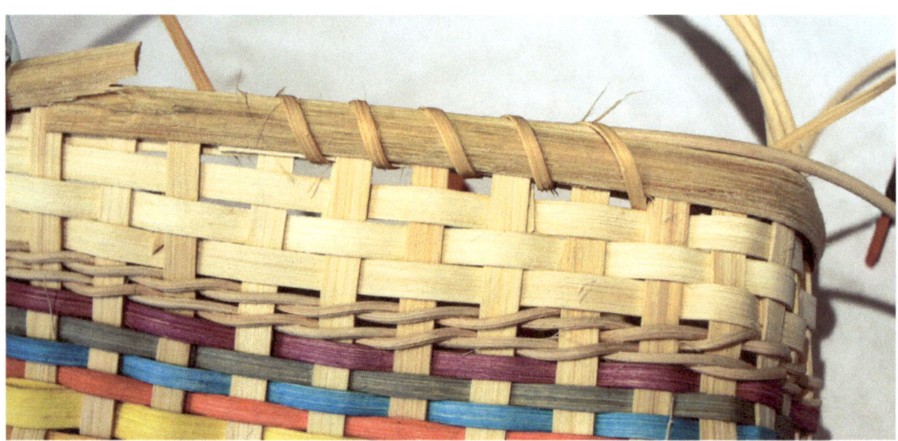

Cut your RIM FILLER on the sides of the twisted reed handle

Lash tightly together with 1/4" flat reed. Leave a tail to tuck into weavers at beginning and end.

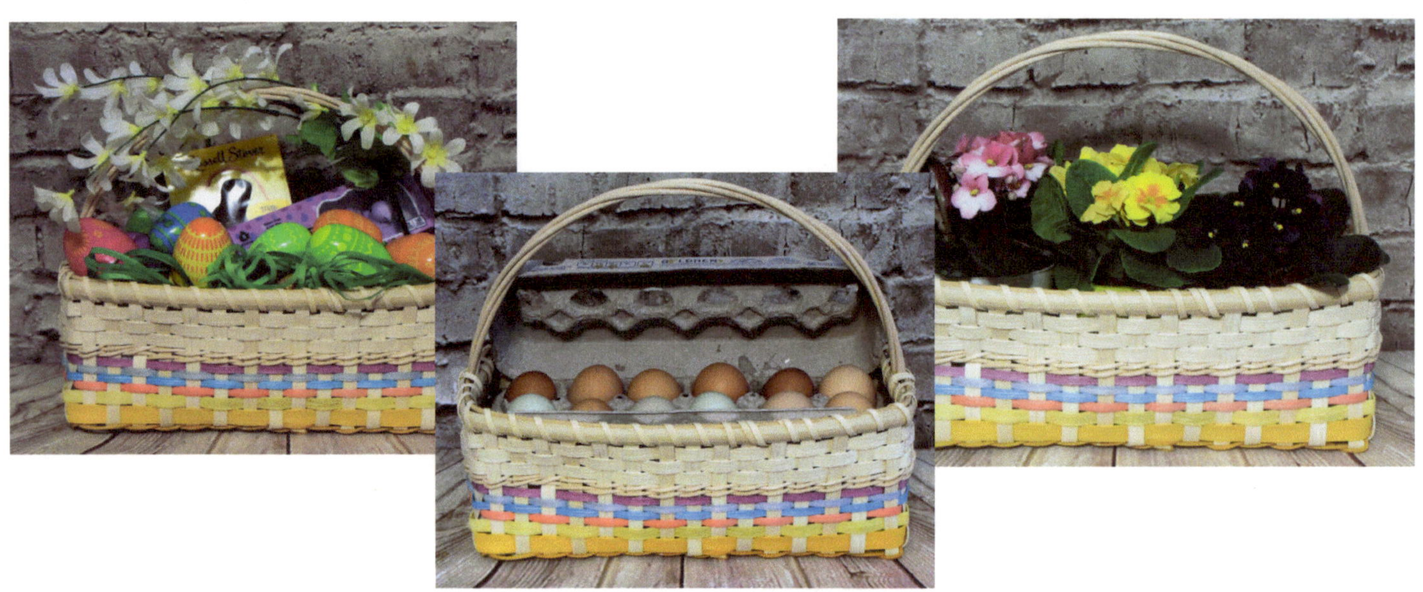

Egg Basket

2 / 8" oak hoops, # 6 round reed,
1/4" flat reed (highlight color and natural)

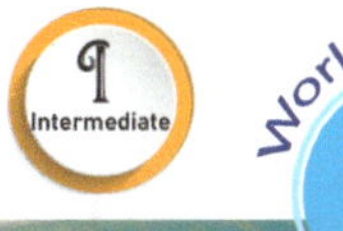

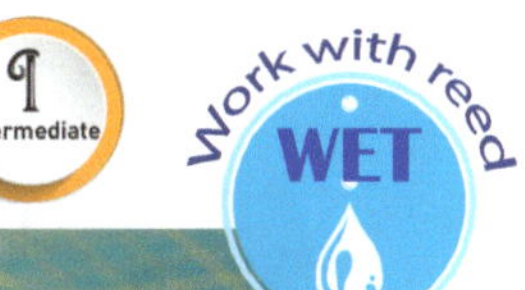

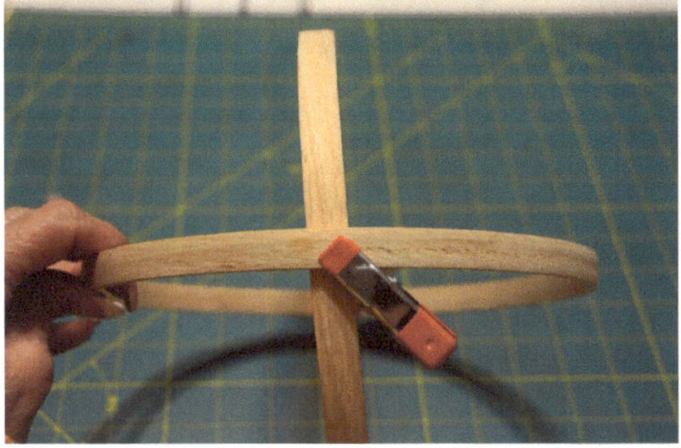

Mark centers of hoops.
Clamp hoops at midpoint.

Clamp or zip #6 round reed on rim.
Cut at angle to meet

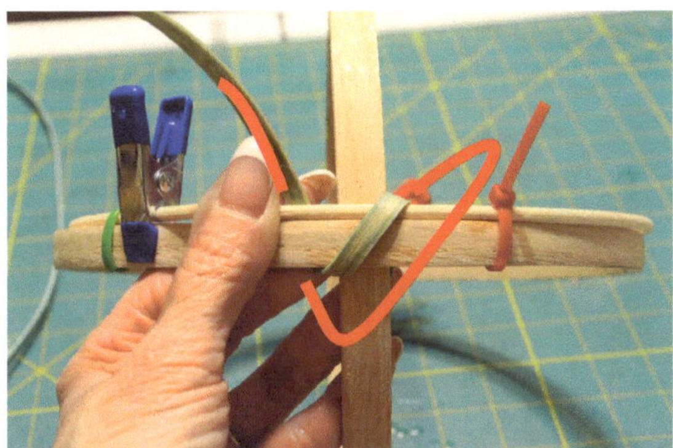

Wrap # 1: hold tail behind hoop,
go SW (southwest)

**Use
zip-ties
if easier**

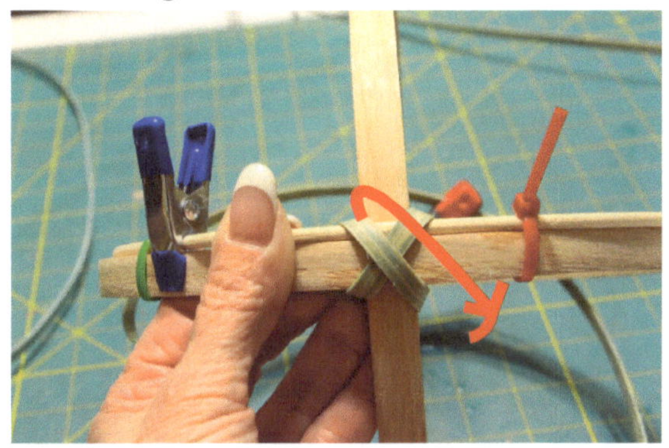

Wrap # 2: wrap behind left side of horizontal
hoop, go SE (southeast)

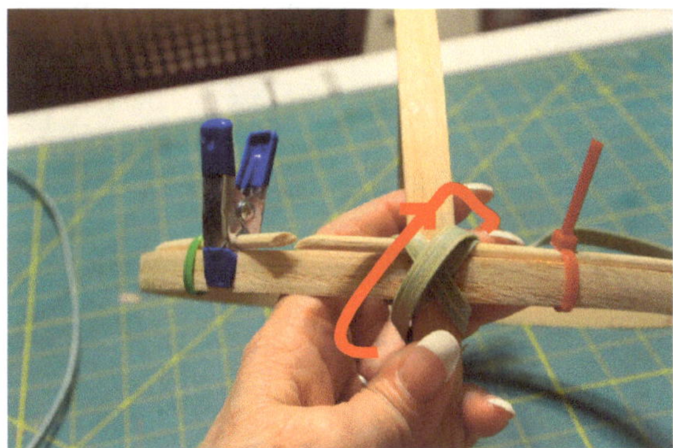

Wrap # 3: wrap behind bottom of vertical
hoop, go NE (northeast)

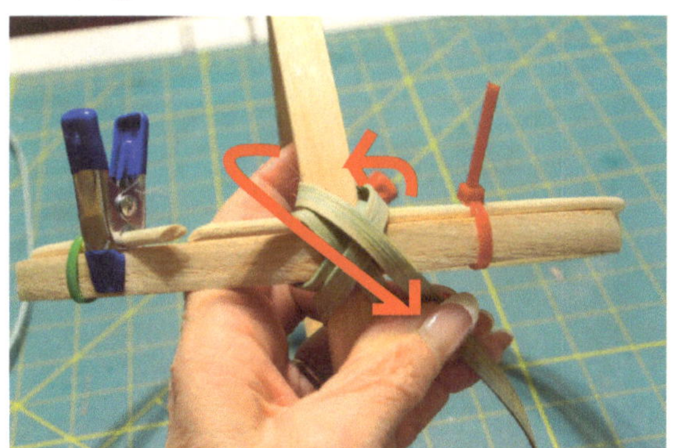

Wrap # 4: wrap behind top of vertical
hoop, go SE (southeast)

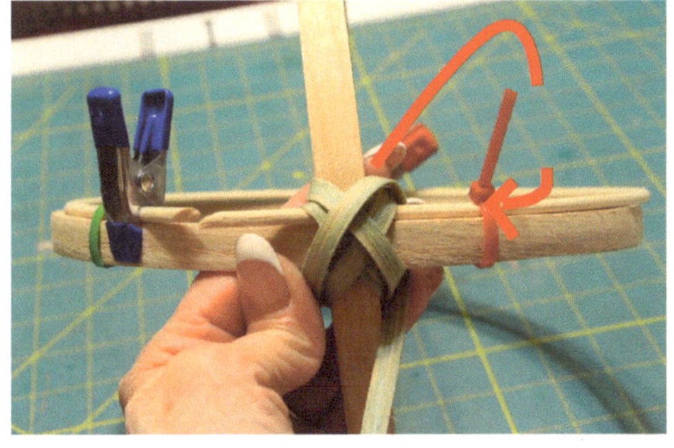

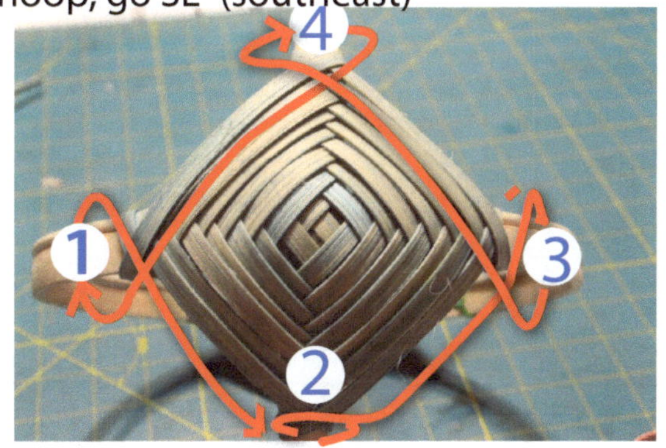

Return to wrap #1, repeat sequence 8 times or to desired size (8 rows solid color God's Eye)

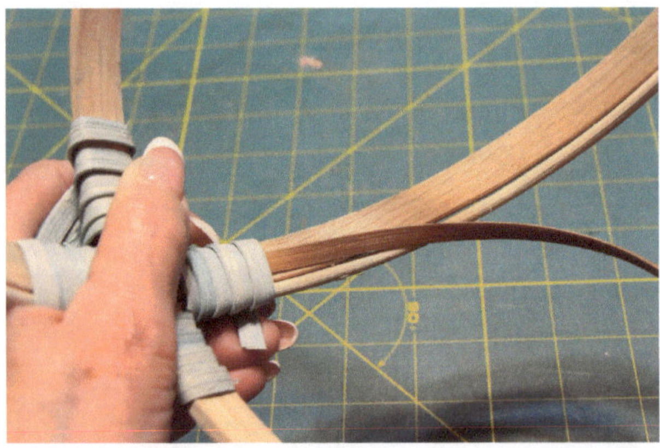

To vary the colors on God's Eye, do 4 wraps accent color then add in next color. Add wrap smooth side down.

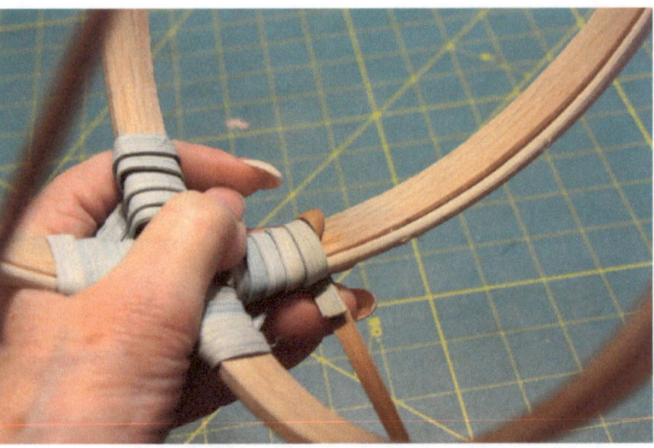

Fold 90 degrees to bring to front, smooth side on the outside.

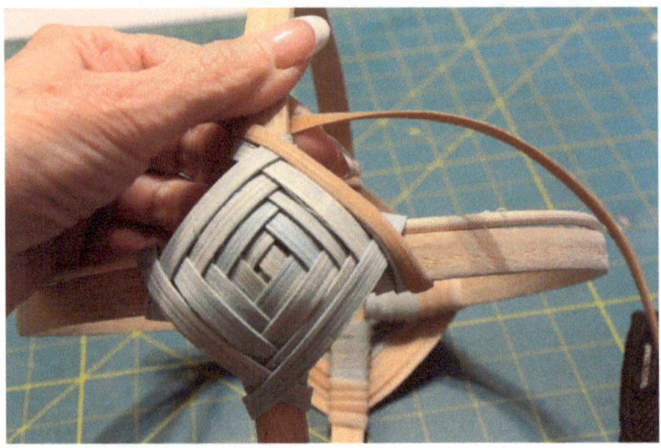

Continue pattern.

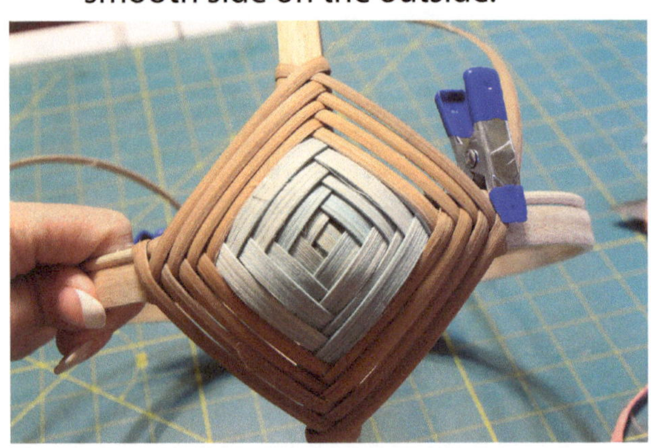

Wrap 4 more rounds.

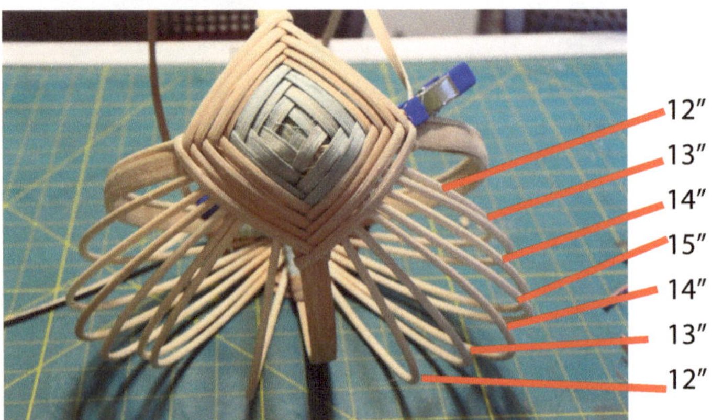

Cut 2 sets of spokes # 6 round reed. Cut ends at angle.

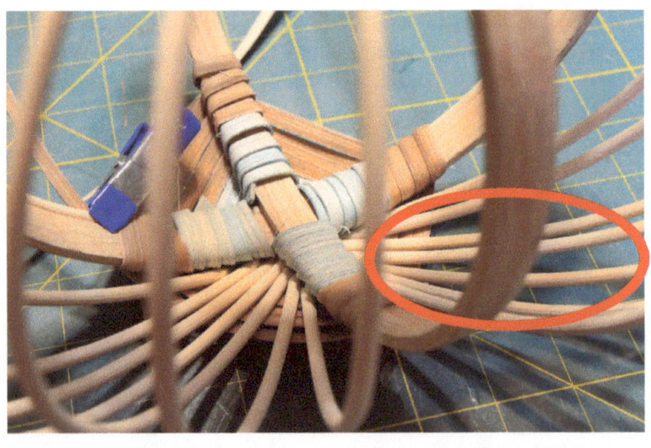

Insert spokes behind God's Eye.

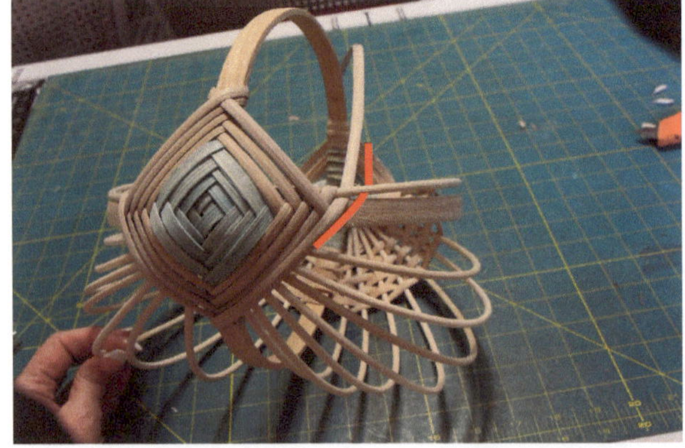

Insert tail between rim and round reed.

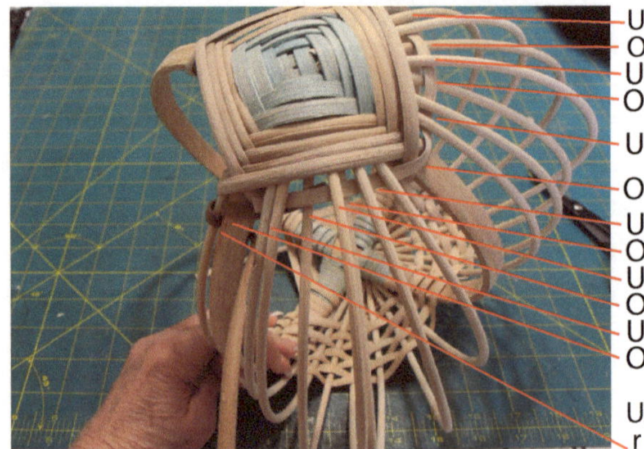

U-Under O-Over

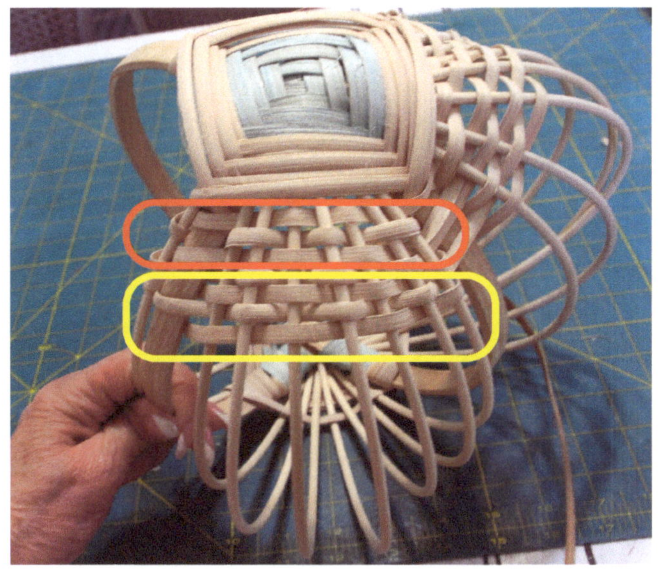

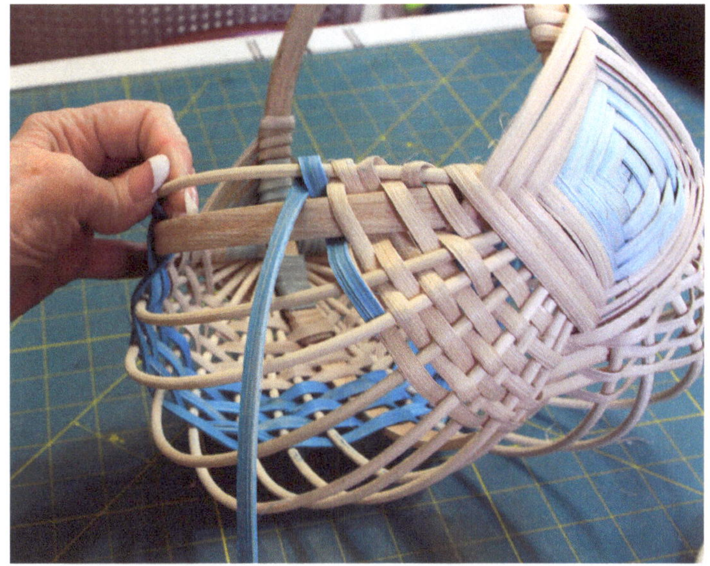

Continue pattern. When room allows weave O1, U 1. There is more space between staves as they fan out.

Add in an accent color. Overlap color for a few weaves.

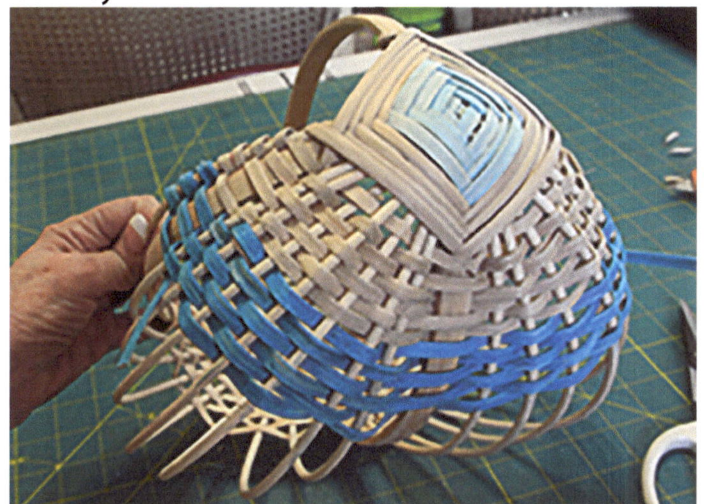

Weave 6 rows of accent color on both sides. Repeat on other side. Fill in with natural color.

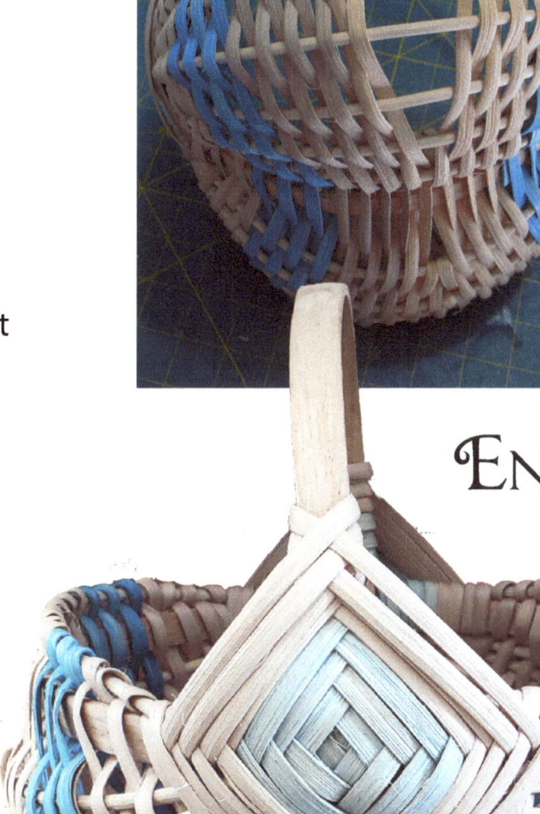

Fill in space on bottom, turning to fill space.

ᴇɴᴊᴏʏ!

Market Basket

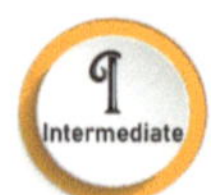

Basket size 14" wide x 9" deep by 8" high

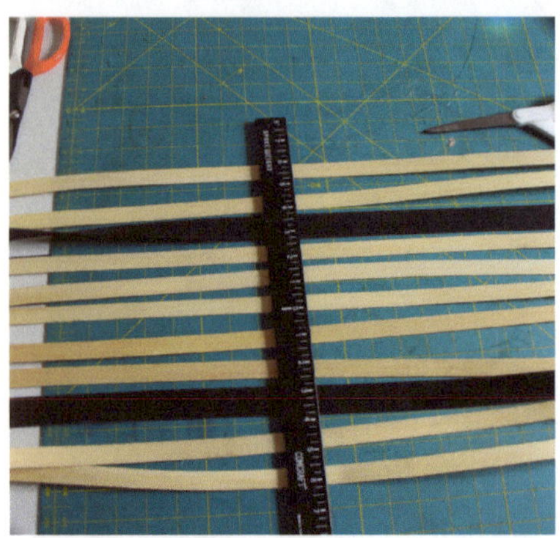

Staves : 5/8" flat reed
- 9-horizontal 30"
- 6 - vertical 28"

Weavers: 3/8" flat reed
Shaker Tape: 3 yards
Twining: #2 round reed
Rim: 5/8" flat oval reed
- 2- 45"

Rim filler: 5" seagrass or
 # 6 round reed
Lashing: 12' - 1/4" flat reed

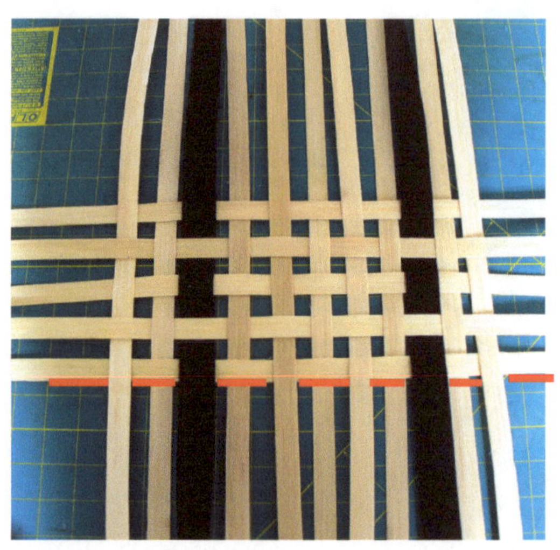

Lay out your 5/8" staves and Shaker Tape Straps
2 reed / strap/ 5 reed / strap / 2 reed. Weight down
with spoke weight, level or piece of wood.
Mark your centers and keep them even.
Be sure smooth side is toward table, rough side inside.

Begin weaving horizontal staves beginning
in center with under/over pattern. Include
straps in pattern.

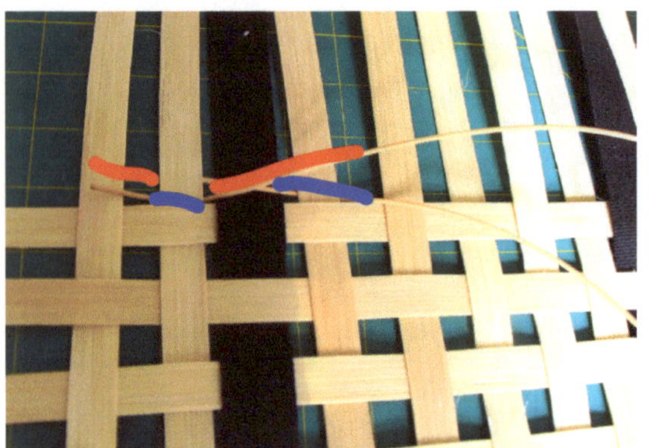

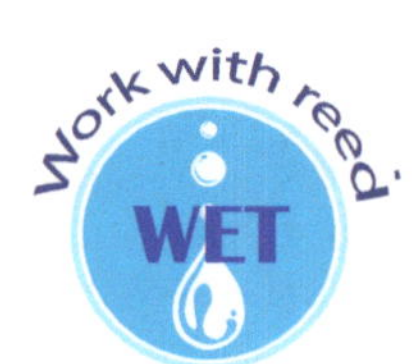

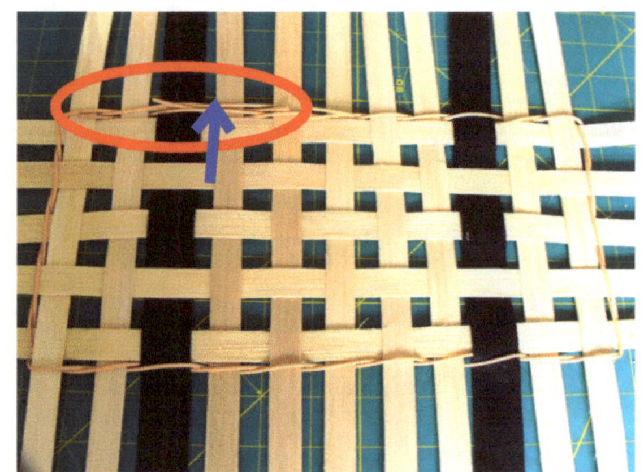

Using #2 round reed, create a lock stitch using
twining method. Lock in each stave going under/over
each stave with the round reed.
Under left, over right, repeat.

Overlap the ending a couple rows.
Cut round reed on top of the stave to end.

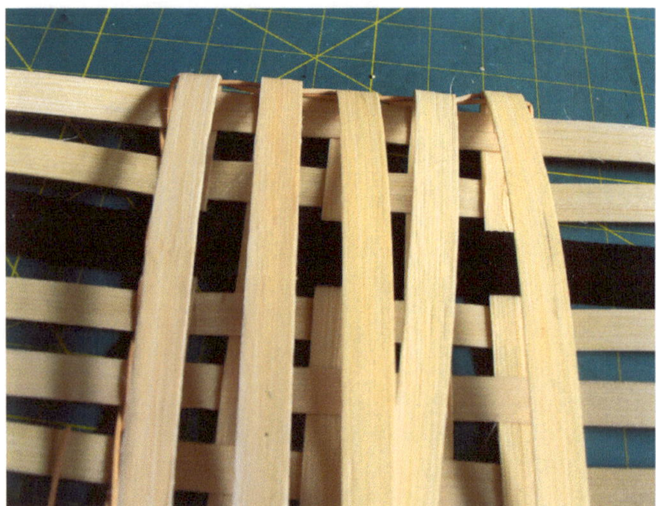

"Upright" (fold staves at 90 degrees) on all sides.

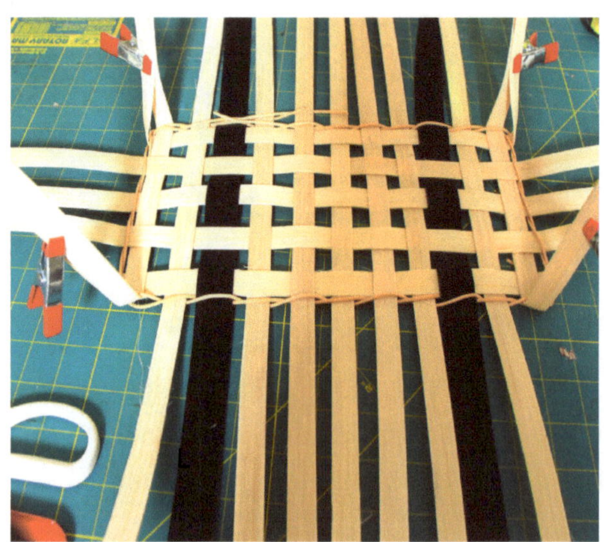

Clip all 4 corners before beginning weavers.

41

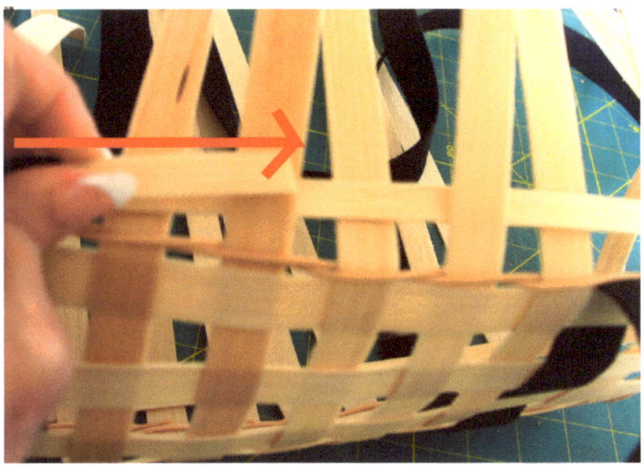
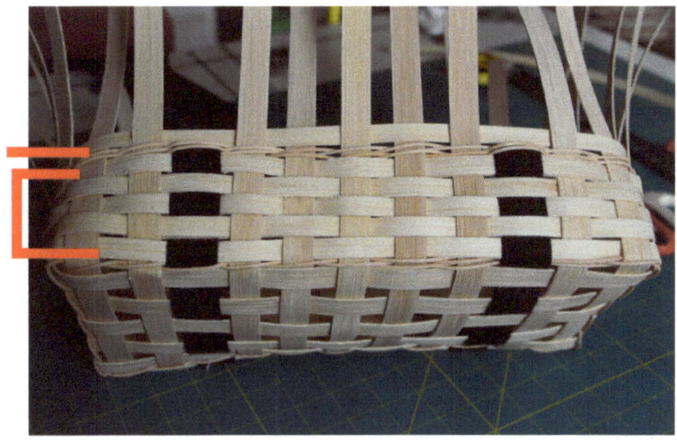

Begin weaving each row separately using over 1/ under 1 in a single row, overlapping at least 3 staves at end.

Continue weaving with 3/8" flat reed for 5 rows then do a double row of #2 round reed twining.

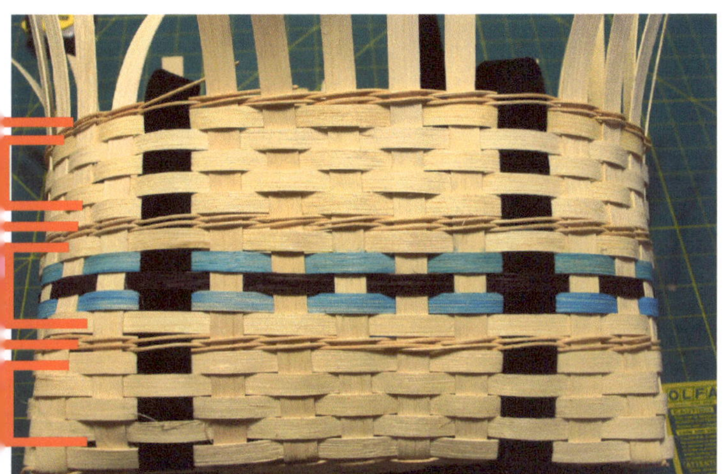
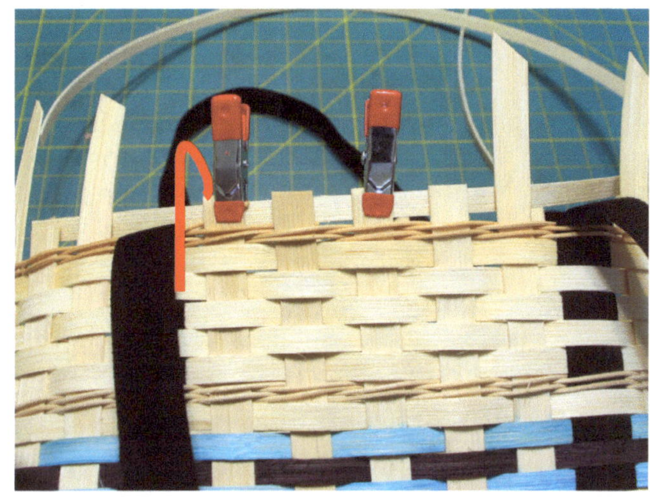

Add 1 natural reed then do 3 accent rows with 3/8" dyed reed. Then 1 more natural reed , 2 more rows round reed twining and 5 rows 3/8" flat reed.

Create a "false rim". Add a 3/8" reed inside after the last twining row. Bend over every other stave to the inside of the basket. This will hold the rim in place.

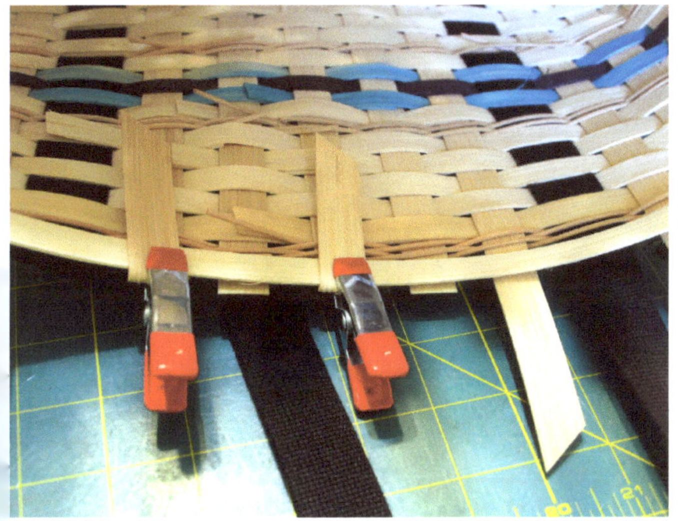
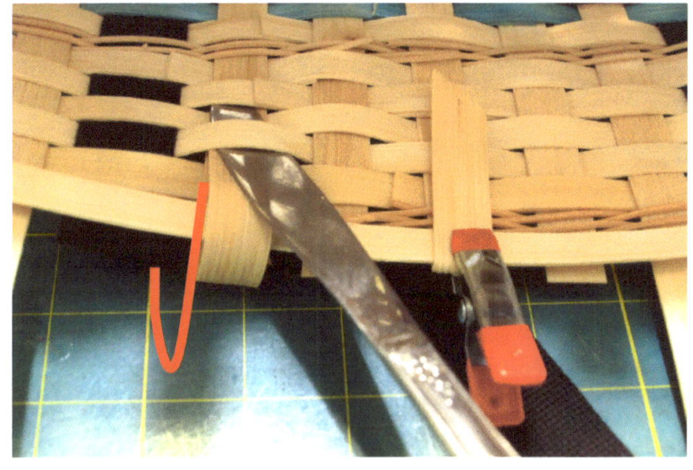

Fold over and clip every other stave.

Use a butter knife or basketry tool to tuck staves on the inside 2 rows.

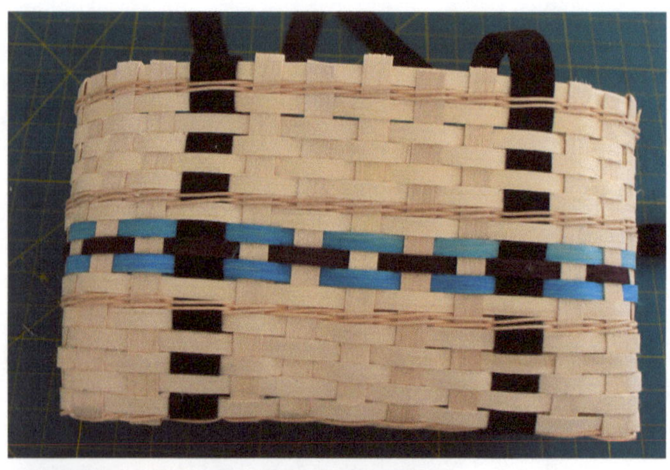

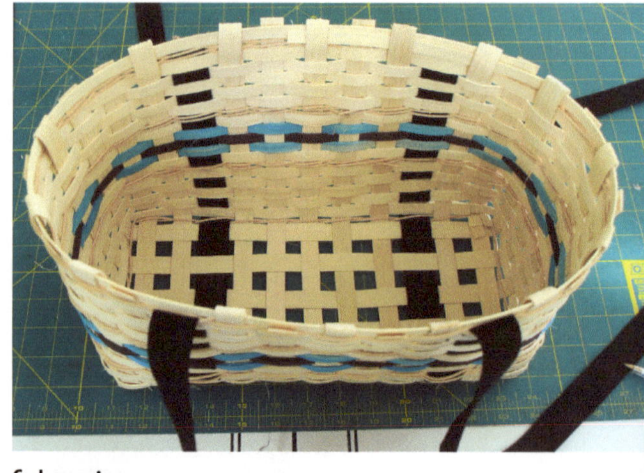

All spokes folded over false rim.

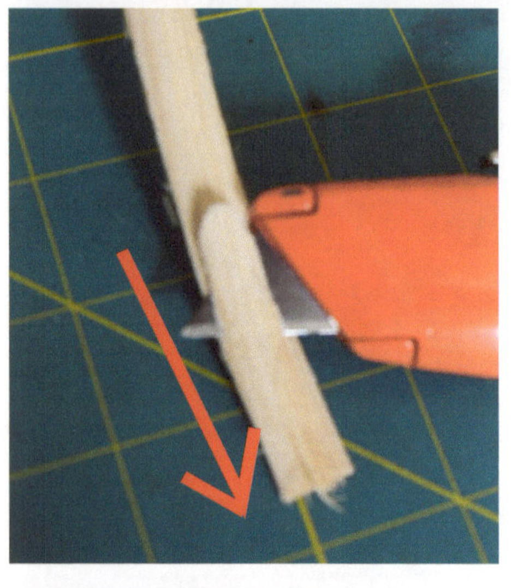

"Scarf" (trim) the ends of the flat oval reed rim. Trim flat side and oval side (opposite ends) Overlap about 1.5-2" One piece on outside one on inside.

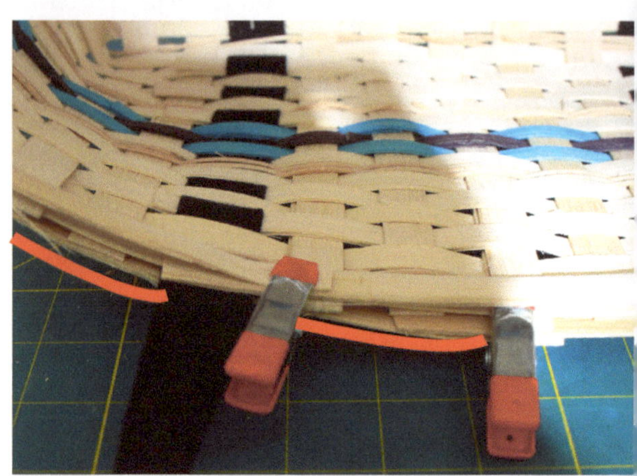

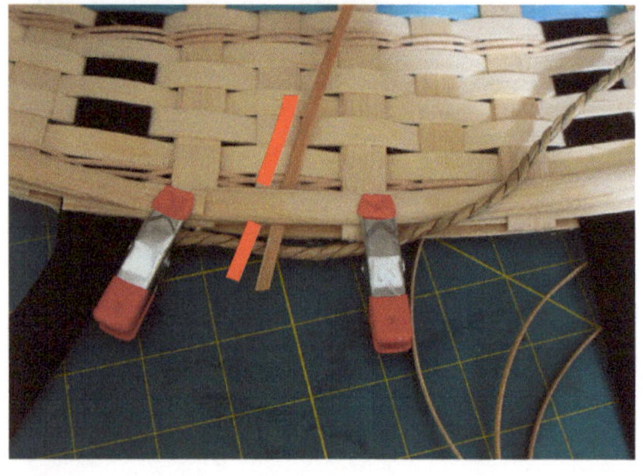

Slip 1/8" flat oval in between rims. Add piece of seagrass or 6 mm round reed in between rims as "rim filler" Sew the lashing on, looping in-between each space between staves.

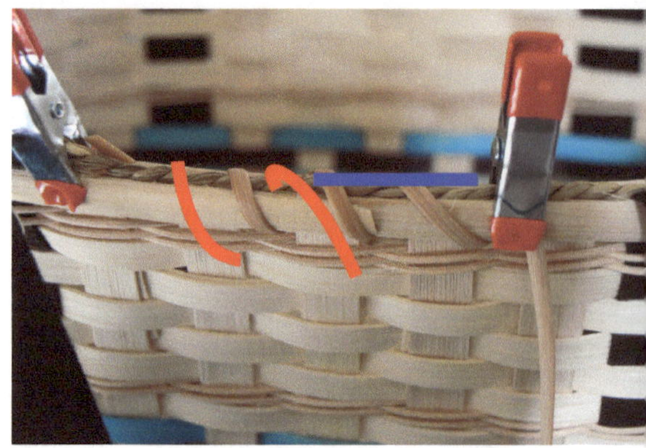

Sew straps together to fit your needs.

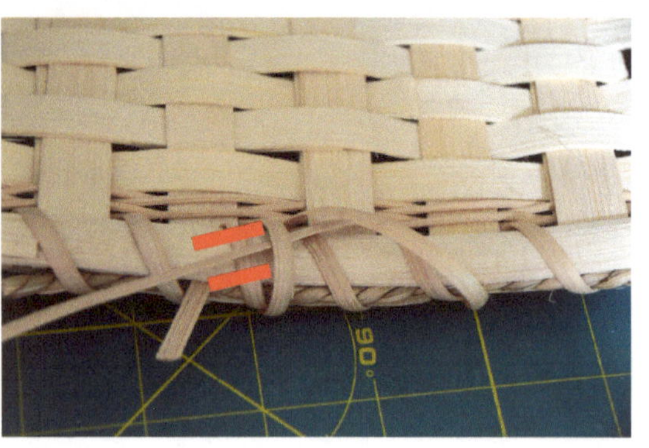

End lashing by pulling through the last 2 sewn loops . Pull tight and trim.

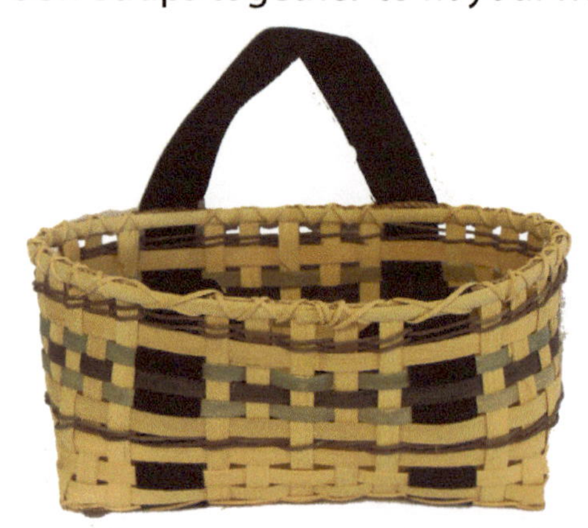

43

BACKPACKS...

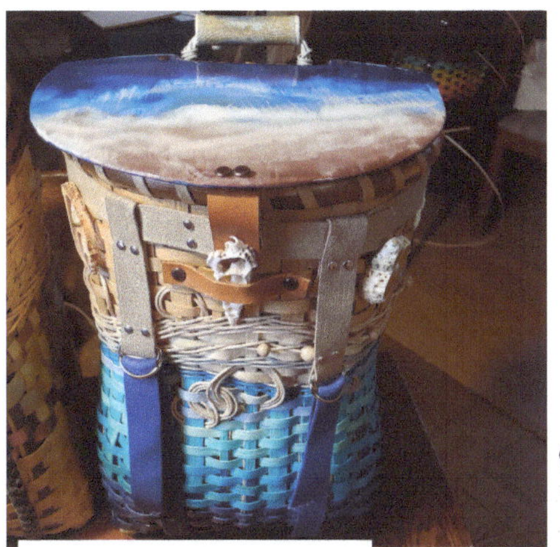 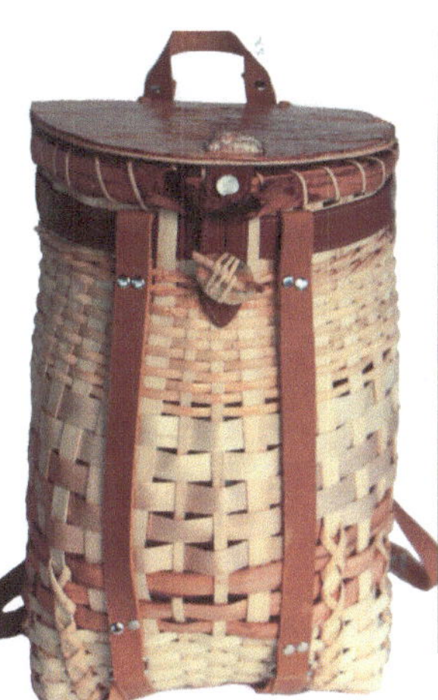 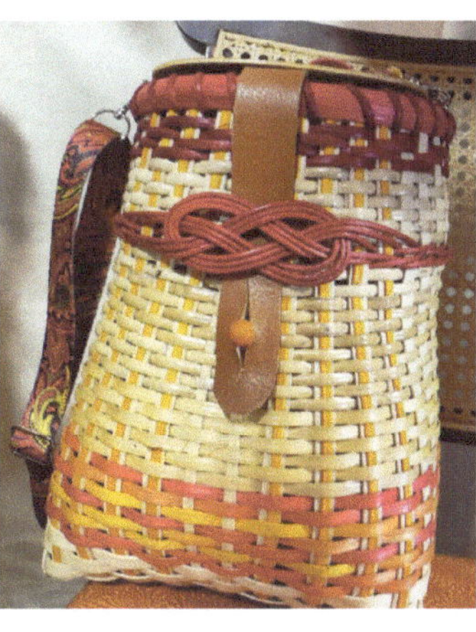 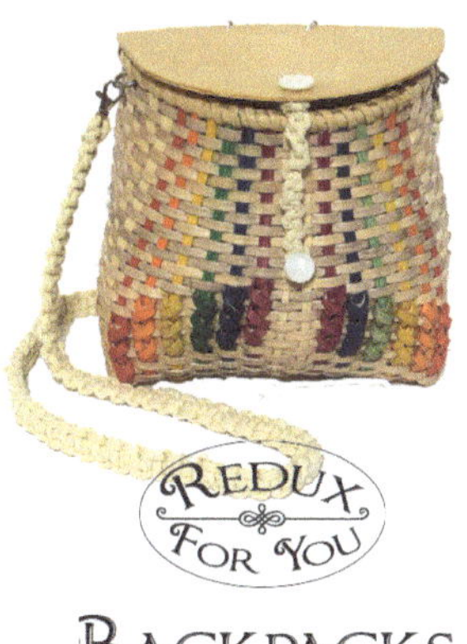

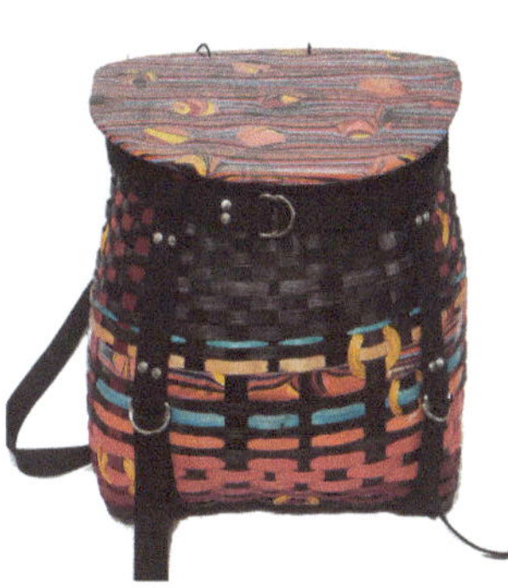 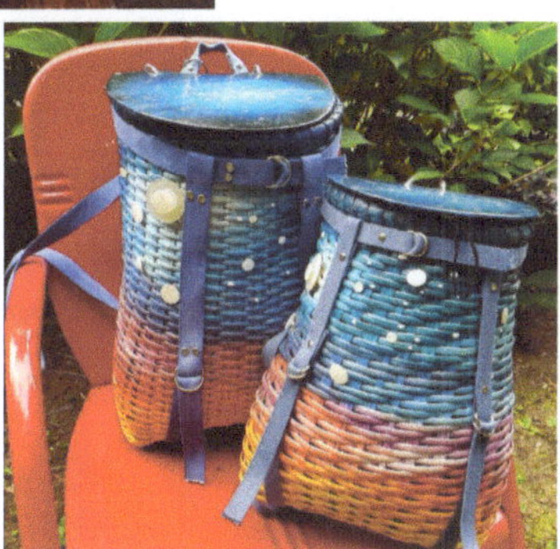 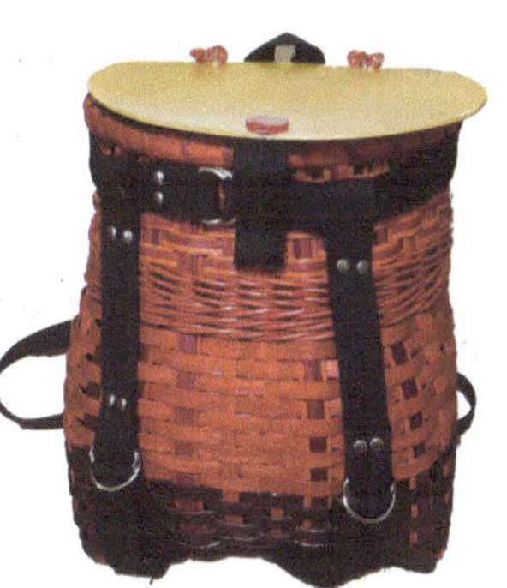 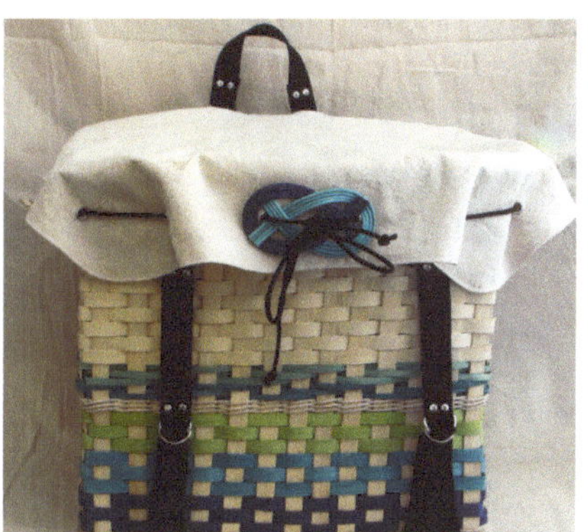

Learning the basic backpack shaping makes it possible to create more backpacks in the future. Larger or smaller, it's up to you.

The shape of the Adirondack backpack was originally designed to fit inside the curve of a canoe to ride safe and snug, and to afford optimum storage. The medium-sized backpack in the instructions is a perfect size for hiking, foraging, shopping, and farmers' markets.

Adding color or textures or other weaving styles is an adventure all to itself! Let your imagination run wild. I dye reed using Rit Dye, or add color to a backpack painting with Unicorn Spit. Unicorn Spit is a water-based glaze that can be blended as you paint. It must be sealed when dry. Instructions for dyeing reed are on pages 56 and 57.

Embellishing with belts, natural materials, cordage, and metals will give your backpack an added point of interest. Completed backpacks should be sealed to preserve the reed and the integrity of the colors.

For natural reed packs I use Tung oil, Danish oil, oil-based stains, or a natural black walnut dye. Baskets can also be stained naturally using coffee or tea.

Any weavings meant for the kitchen or children are best sealed with a food-safe mineral oil. Weavings with intense color are best sealed with Tung Oil or UV Archival Varnish. I prefer the varnish as it does not yellow with time and keeps the colors fresh.

Enjoy making your wearable art!

44

AND MESSENGER BAGS

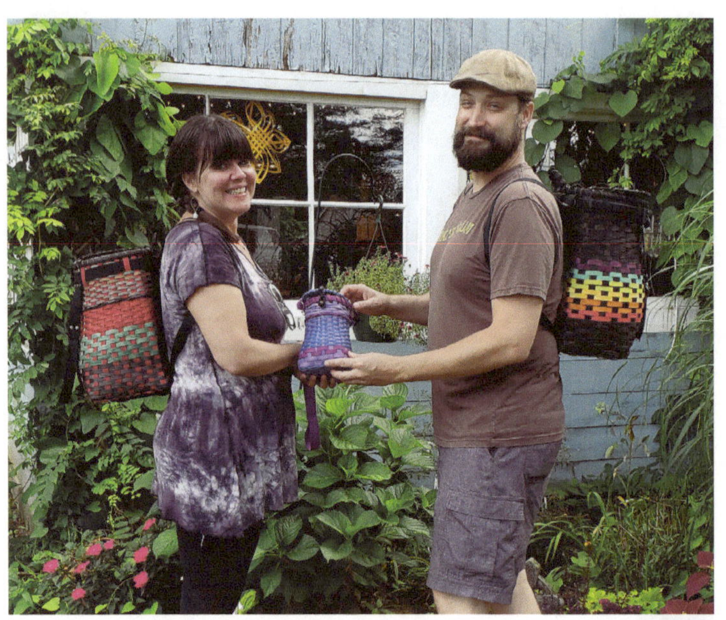

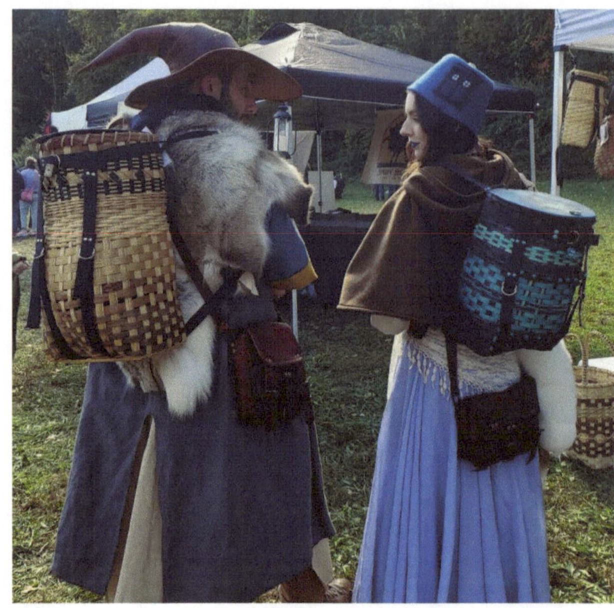

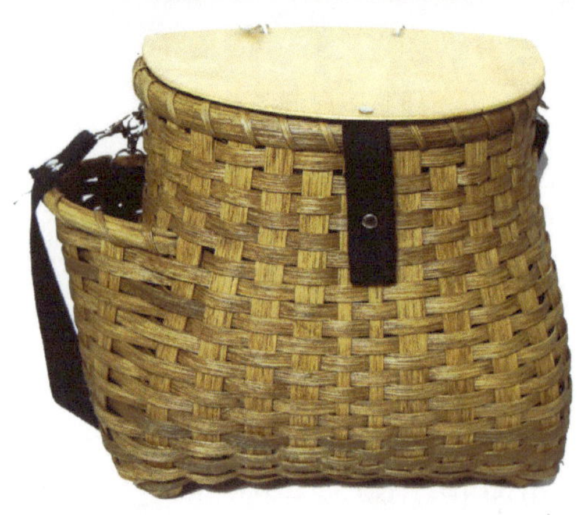

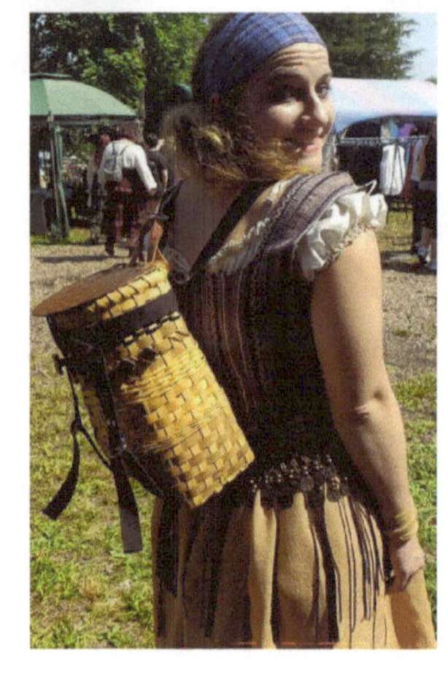

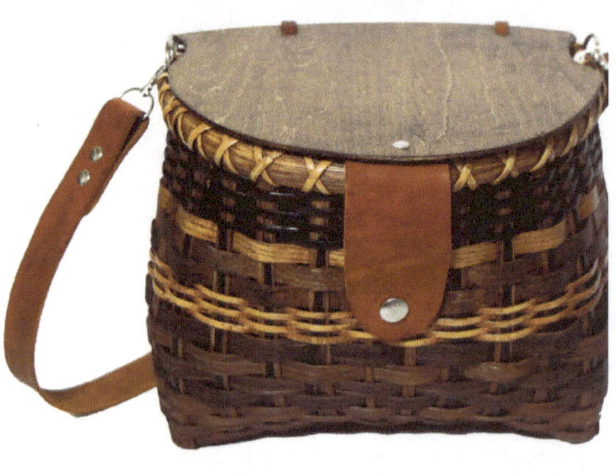

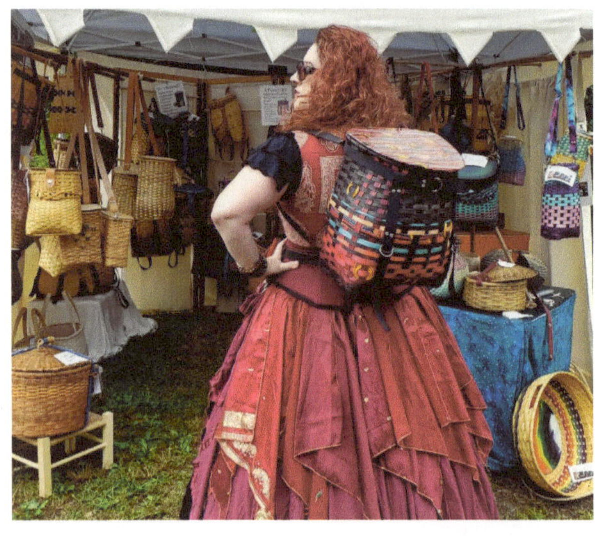

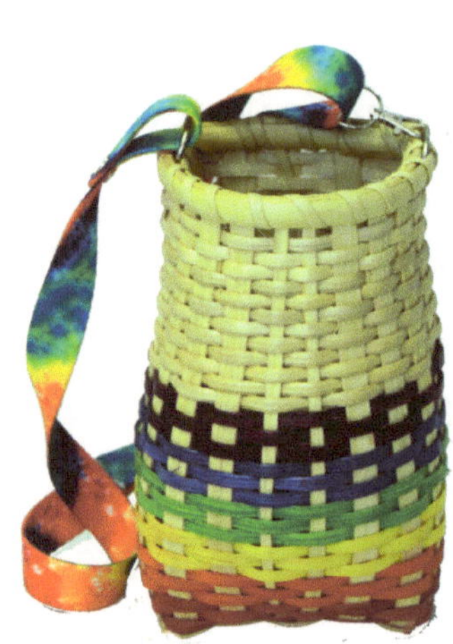

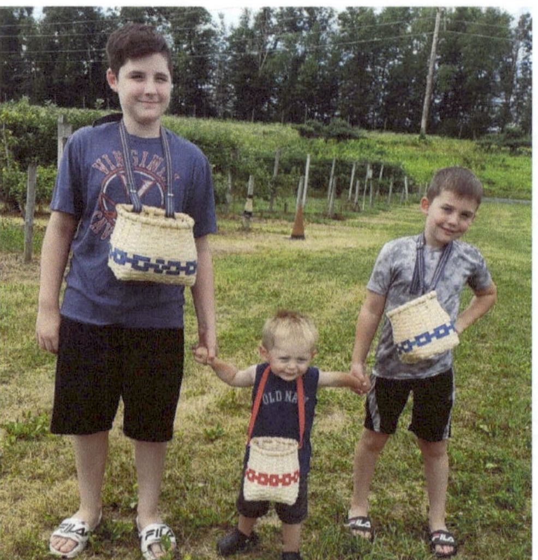

Thank you to my friends and family for allowing me to use your pictures.

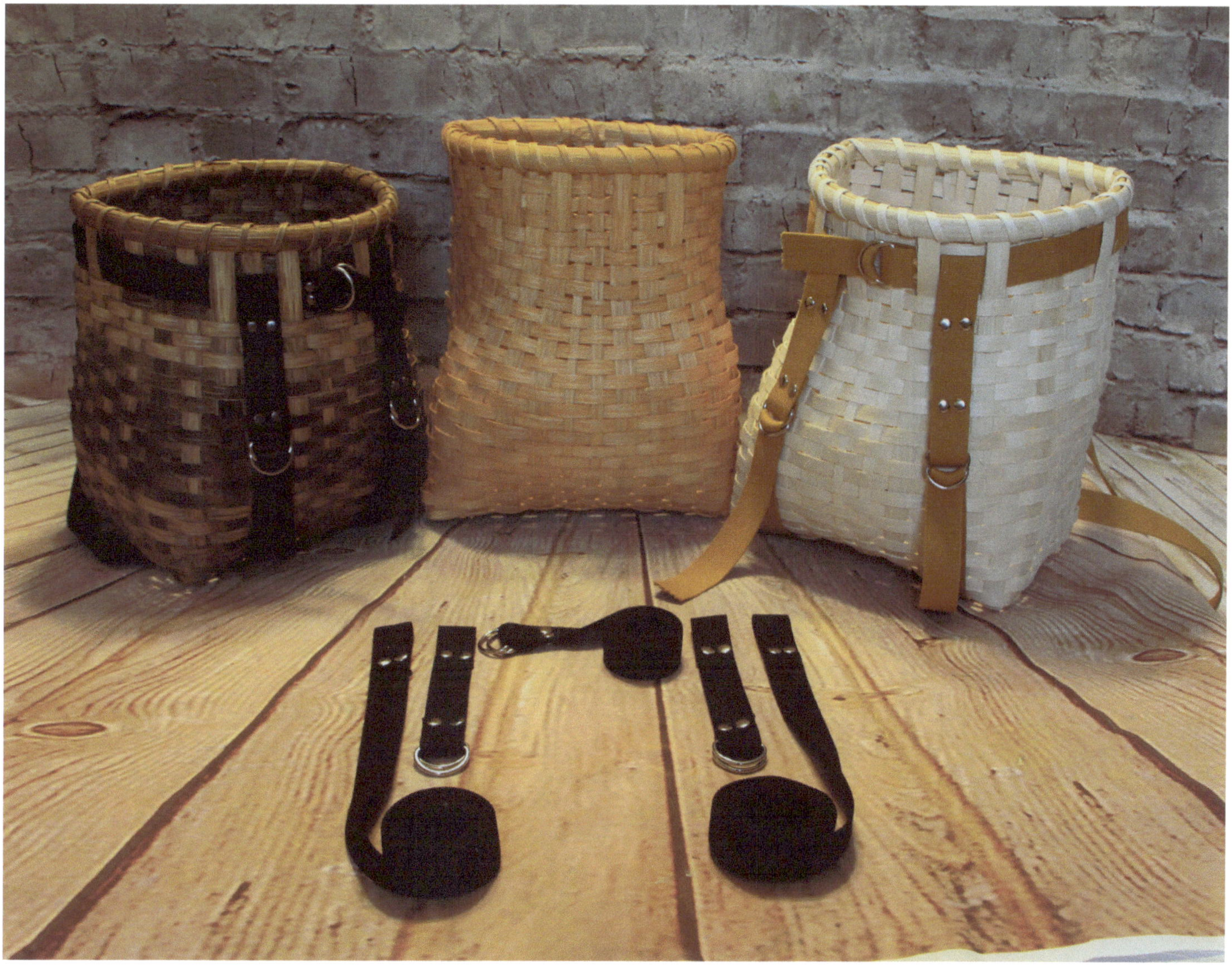

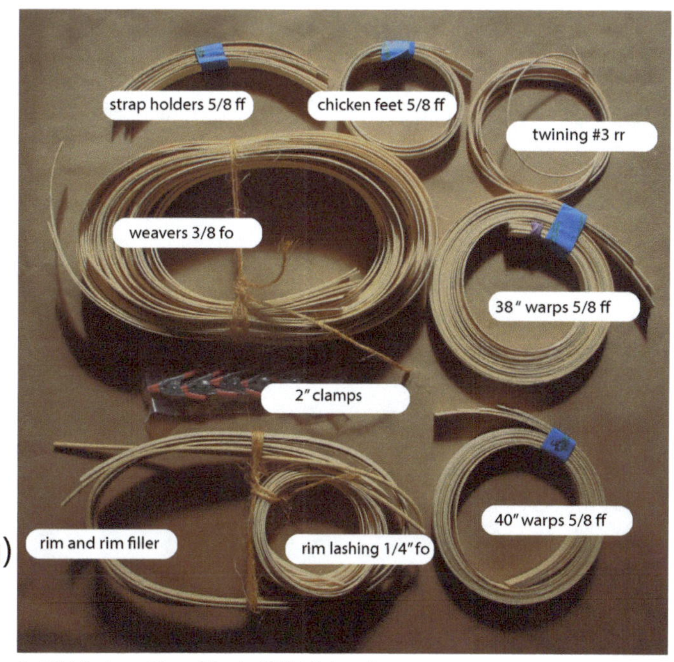

Stains: Natural black walnut, maple stain, no stain.

Medium Backpack size:

7" x 9" base / 11" tall / 9" x 9" belly
You will need: Water • clippers • utility knife

Supplies:

14: 40" 5/8" flat reed (warps)
4: 18" 5/8" chicken feet (fillers)
1/2 pound - 3/8" flat reed (weavers)
6 feet #3 round reed (twining)
Approx 80" 5/8" flat oval rim
Approx 15 feet 1/4" flat oval or flat reed (lashing)
5: 1" clamps
48" - seagrass or #6 round reed (rim filler)
8: 8" - 5/8 " flat reed (strap holders)

Medium Backpack 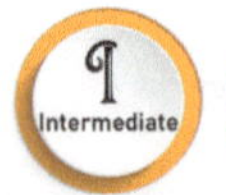 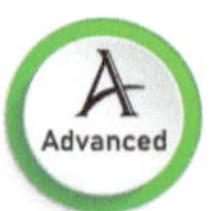

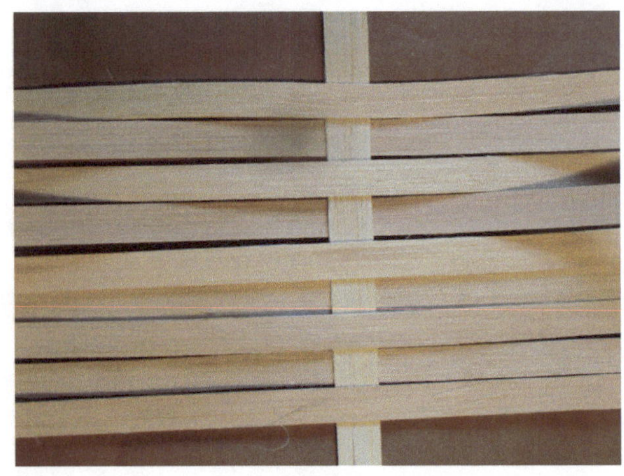

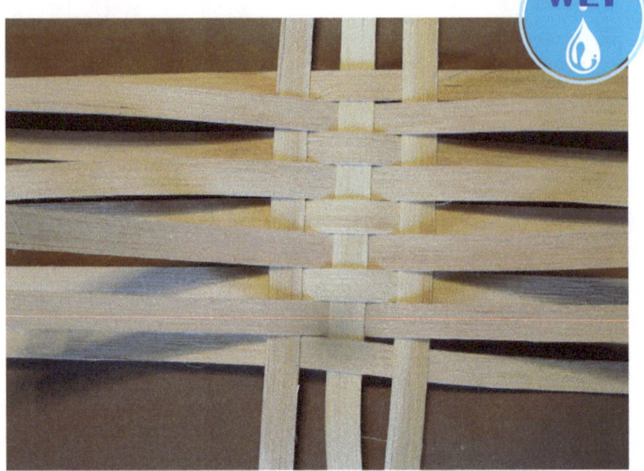

Mark center of reed with pencil. Alternate 40" warps with 18" chicken feet. Weave 40" warp in center beginning and ending with UNDER.

Weave the next warps, alternating the pattern. Begin and end with OVER. Total 9 vertical warps. *NOTE: keep smooth sides down rougher sides up.

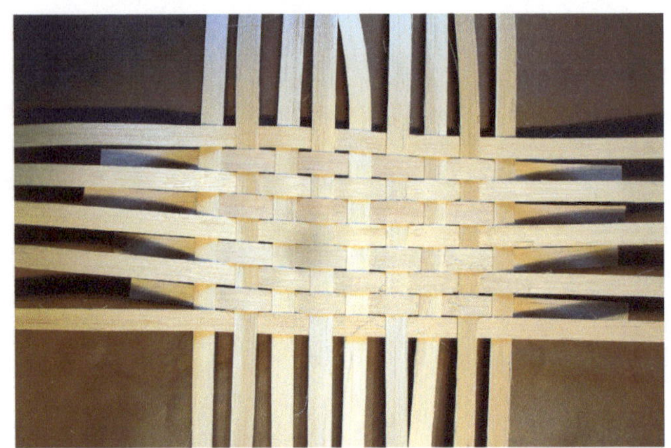

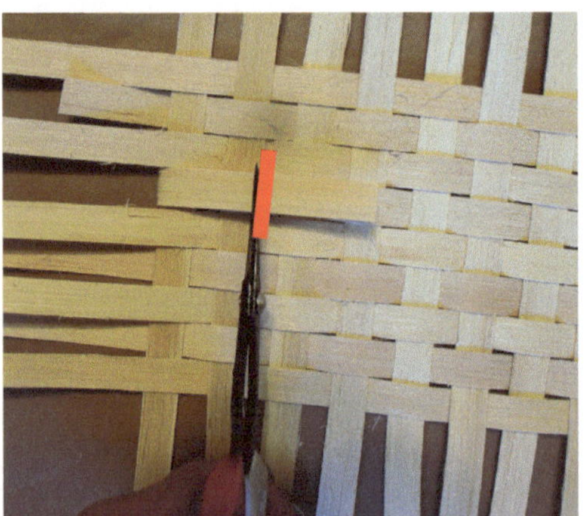

Bend over the "chicken feet" and cut past the second weave.

Finish weaving the 9- 48" pieces.

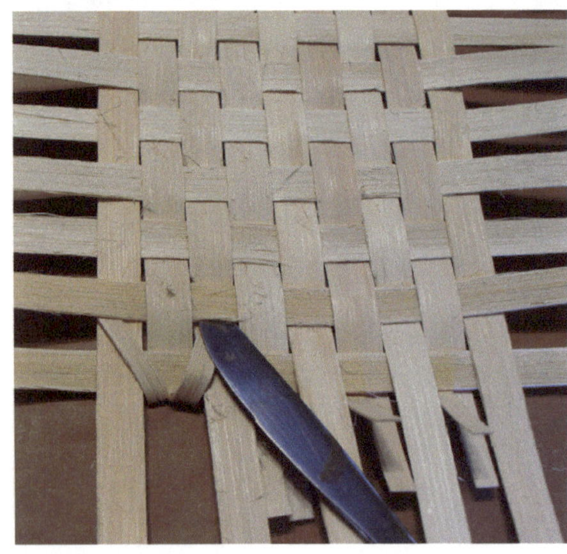

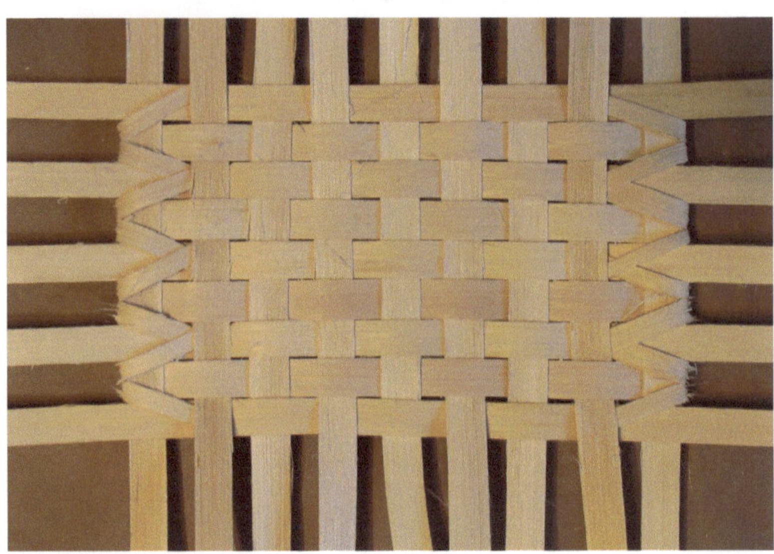

Split the "chicken feet" and tuck under the above weaver. Use a butter knife if needed.

Complete both sides. This is the inside of backpack.

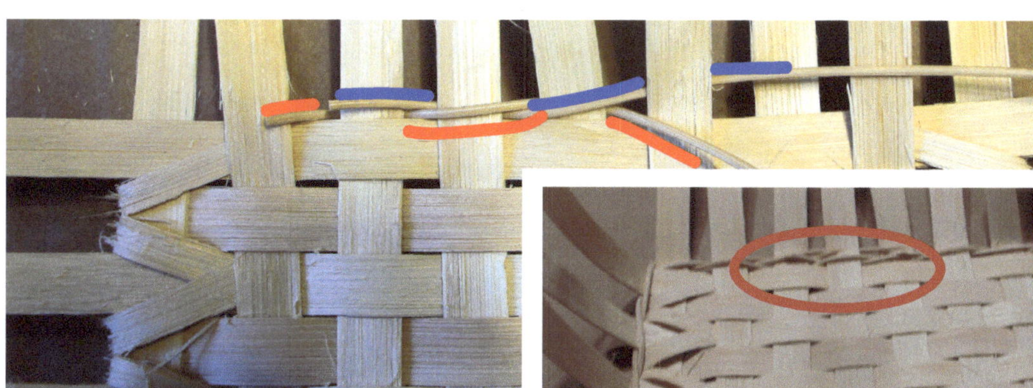

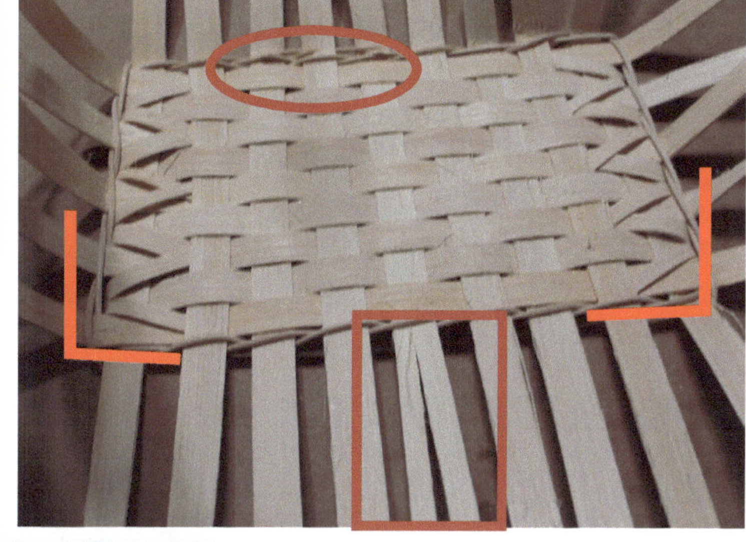

Using #3 round reed, place one end over, then under warp. Place next round reed over next warp. Cross at intersection. Continue around whole base. Overlap a couple of warps to lock.. The overlap will be the BACK of the basket.

Cut the middle warp on the front of the basket. "Upright" (fold at 90˚) back and 2 sides. Leave front flat.

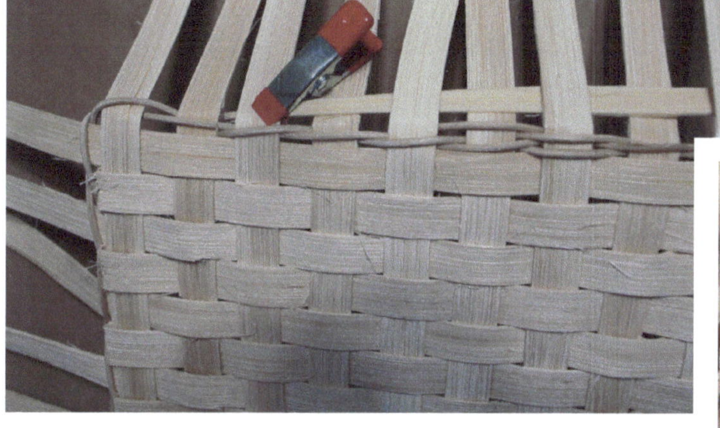

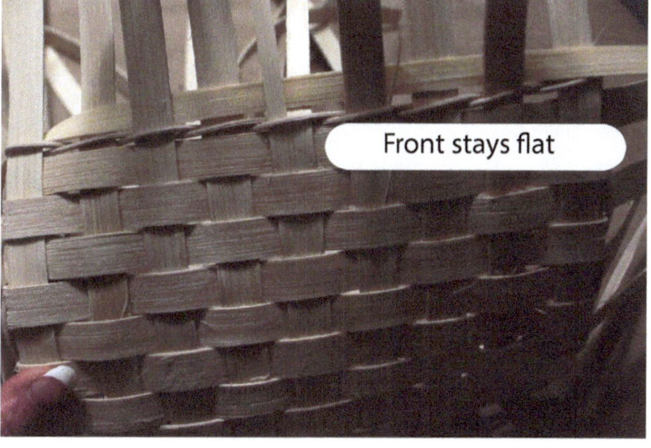

Cut a 3" angle on the first weaver. Begin weaving UNDER and OVER all around the basket. The split in front creates an uneven # of warps and a continuous weave.

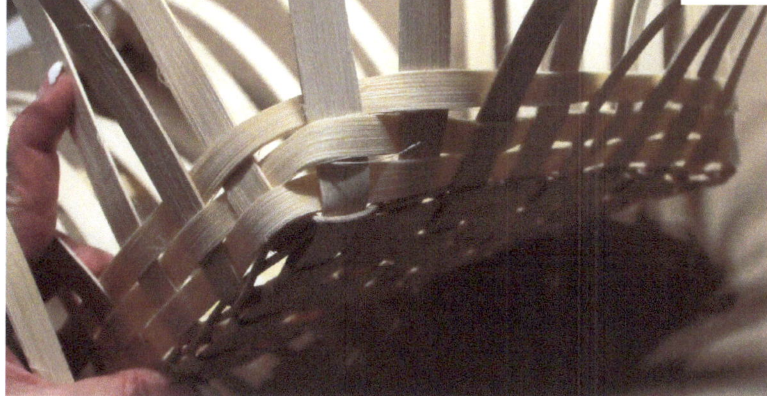

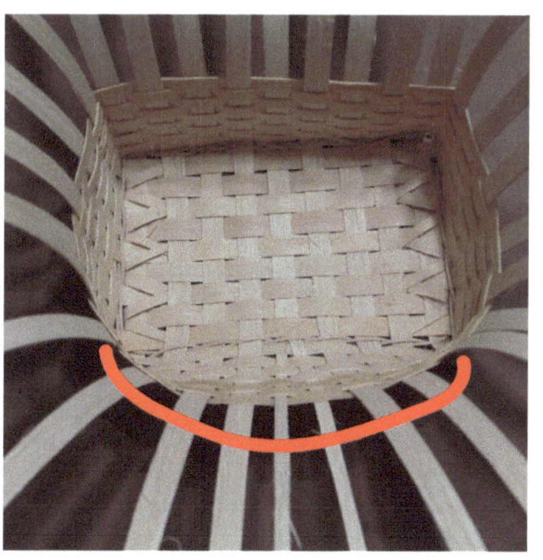

Continue weaving. When adding a new weaver, OVERLAP reed 2 warps on any side but front. Your basket will begin to take on the BELLY shape in front.

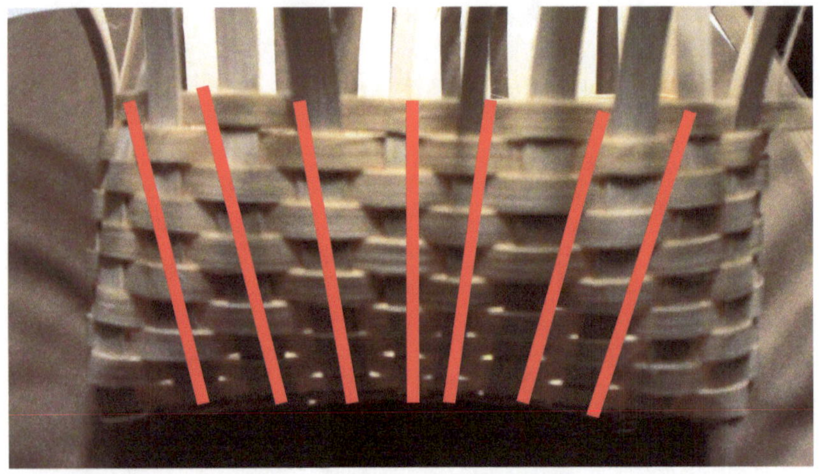

Spread weavers apart incrementally for 9 rows.

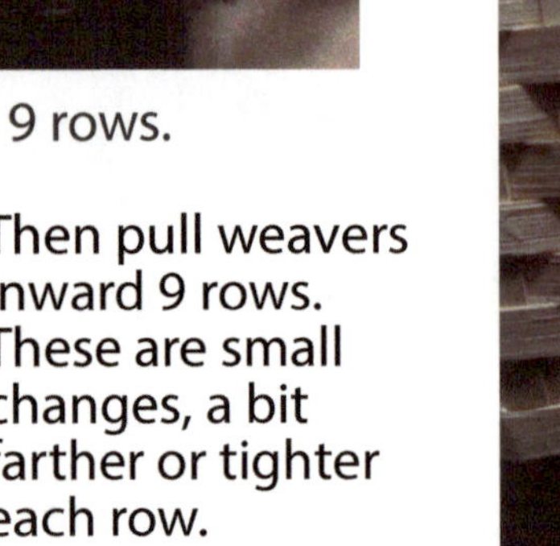

Then pull weavers inward 9 rows. These are small changes, a bit farther or tighter each row.

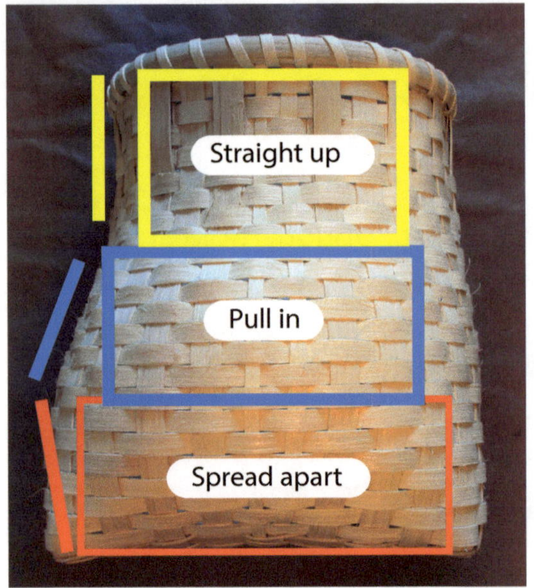

Basket structure in front.
Keep sides and back straight at 90° to base and each other, folding corners at back.

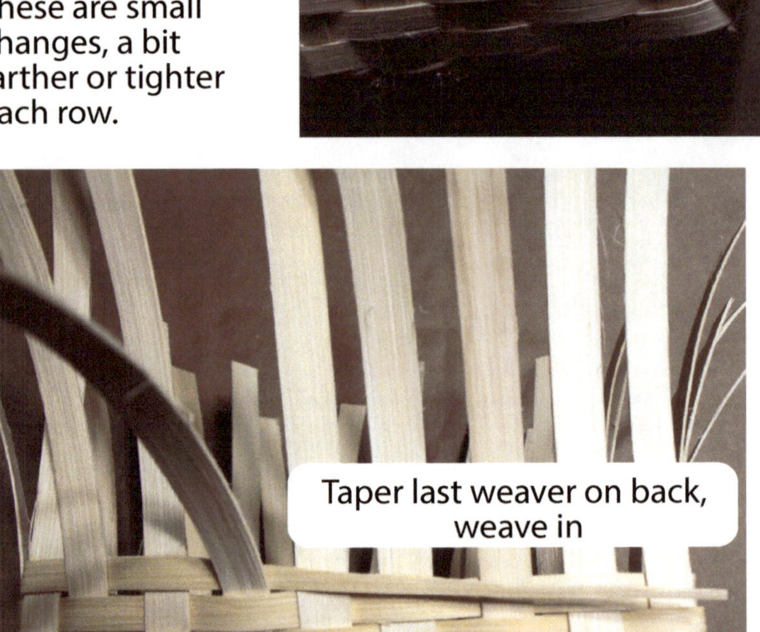

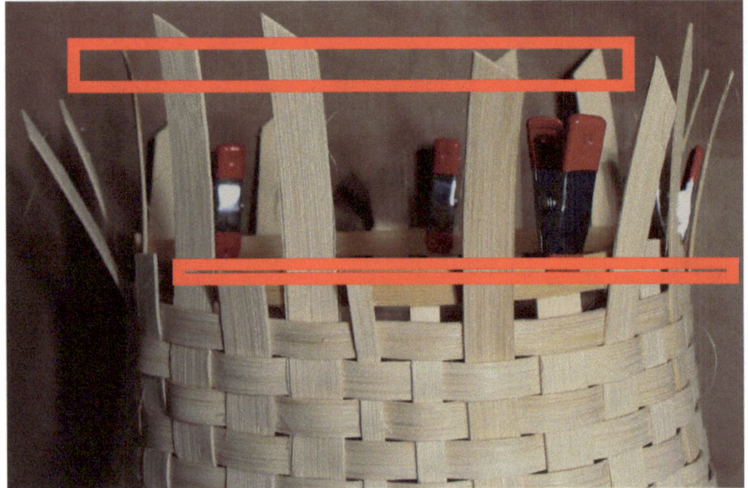

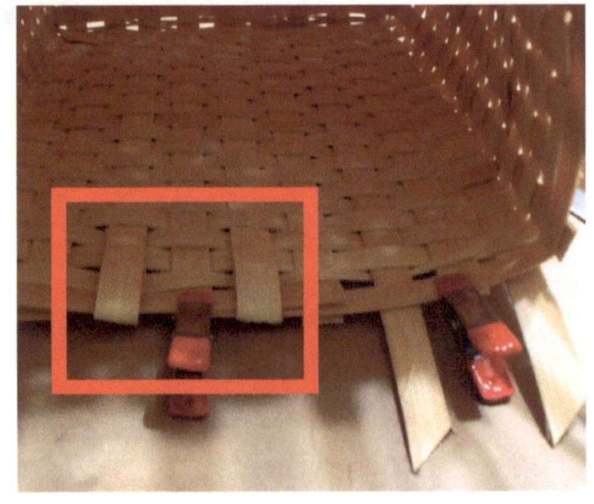

Add a FALSE RIM inside at top of basket. Cut warps at an angle 4" high, then bend over false rim and tuck into weavers.

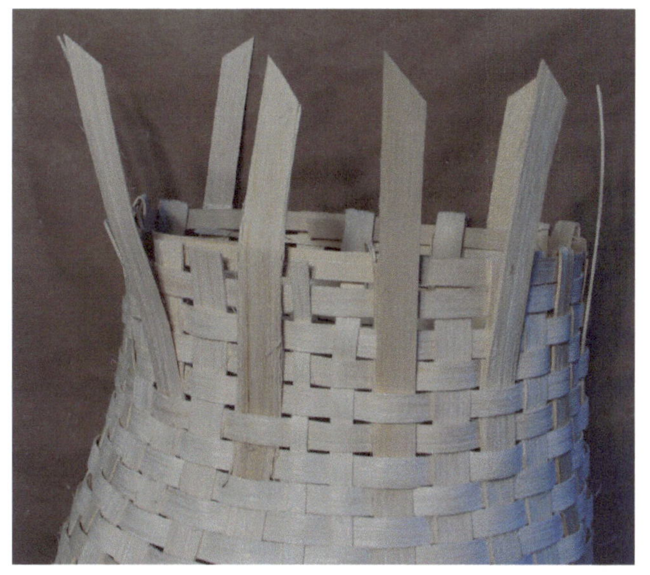
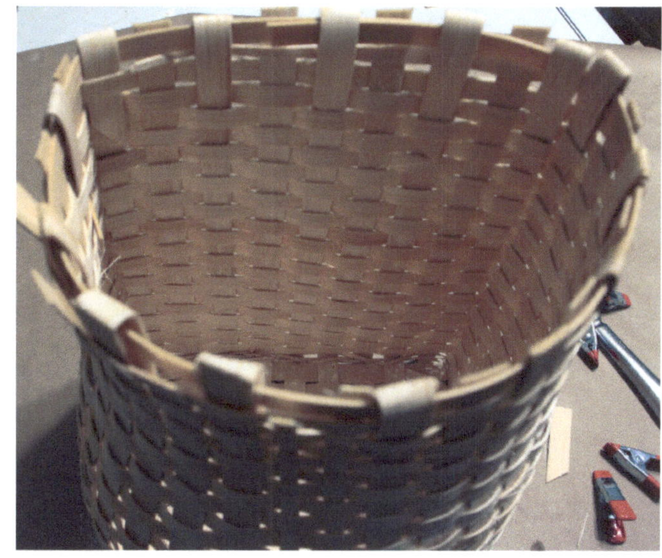

Add STRAP LOOPS (optional) if desired. Tuck into a couple weavers below loop holders. Cut flush with FALSE RIM to avoid bulk. See strap flyer for placement of loops.
 (4 front, 1 each side back corner, 2 back)

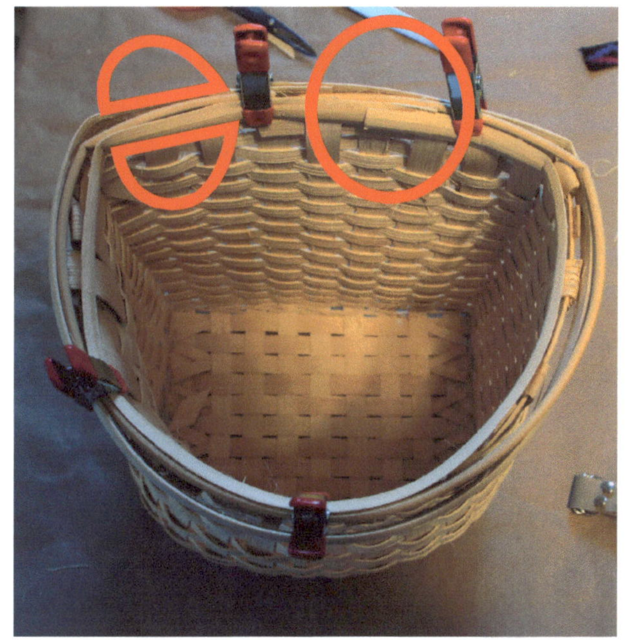
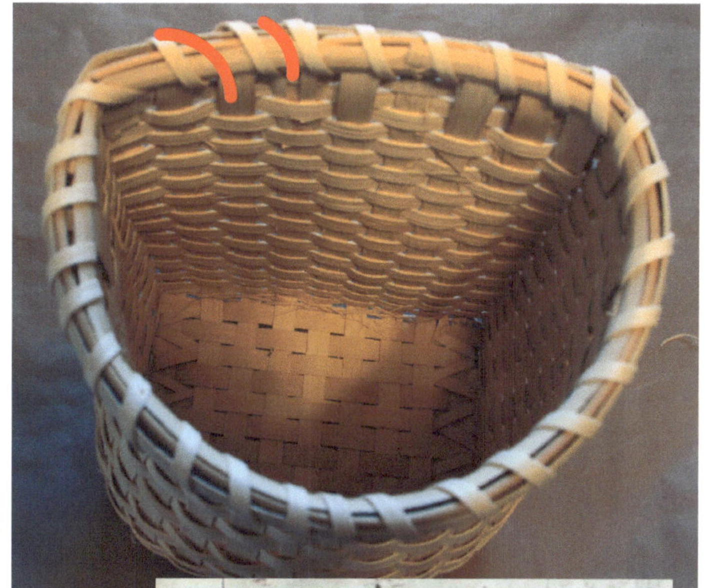

With a utility knife, SCARF (thin about 2") the top side and bottom side on opposite ends of the flat oval reed .
Overlap at SCARF with cut sides facing each other and clamp to rim. Put rim filler in between inside/outside rim. Scarf inside and outside rim.
Tuck a tail between inside rim and round reed. Lash tightly together with 1/4" flat reed.diagonally between warps, under the rim..
Leave a tail to tuck into lashing at end and pull tight. Trim both.

Stain or seal as desired. When dry, add straps on.

50

Create Your Own Design

Once you know shaping, you can make a variety of baskets.
Determine how high and wide you would like yours to be.
Extra Large backpacks can be made with 3/4" or 1" staves.
Smaller items like messenger bags and purses are woven with 3/8" flat.
Use a measuring tape or ruler, measure your height (x2) and width
of **horizontal staves** and add 8" (4" each side for tuck and fold).
Measure your **vertical staves** and add 8" (4" each side for tuck and fold).
Measure **chicken feet**: width of basket plus 6-8" (fold for chicken feet).

Here are a few variations on the backpack style weave. Be sure to split
your middle front stave for continuous weave.

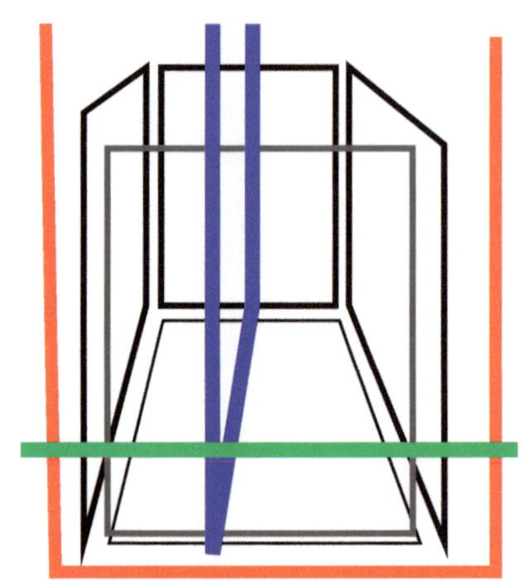

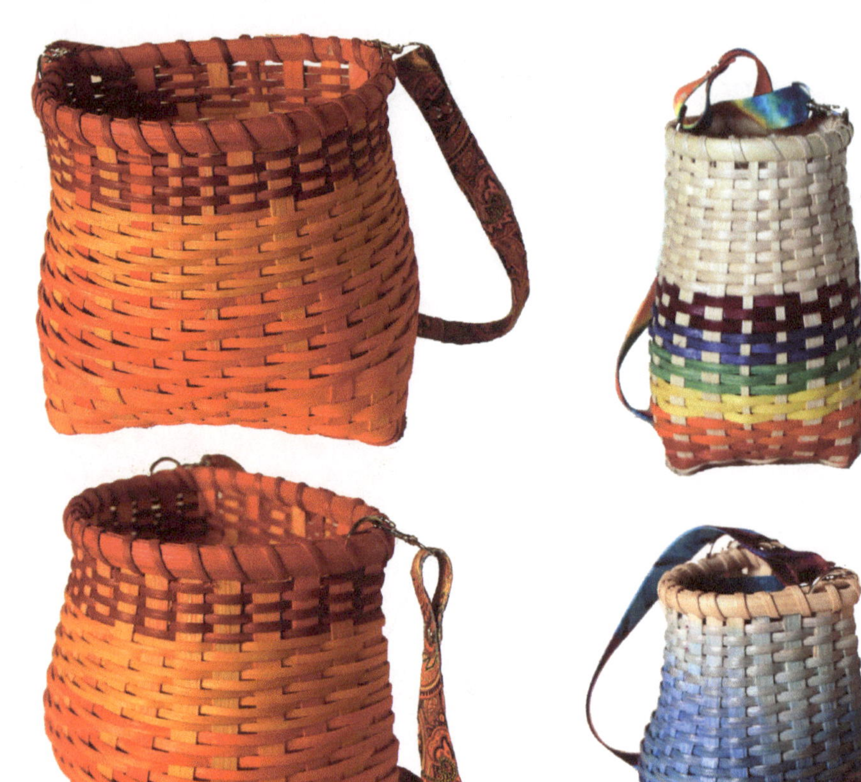

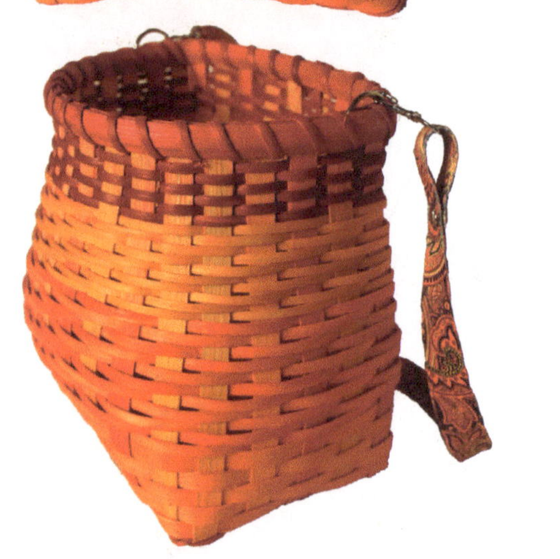

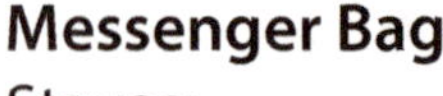

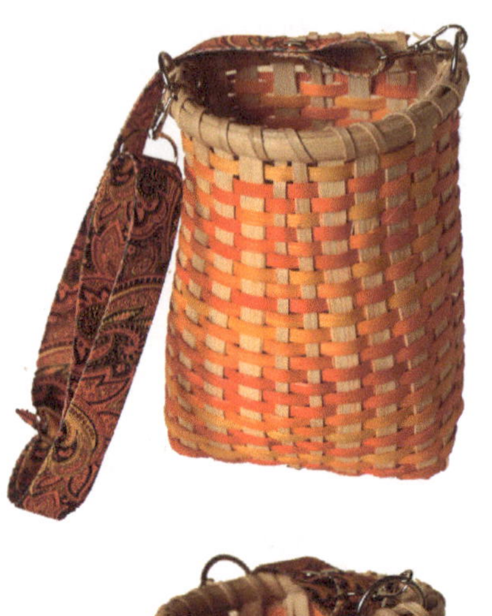

Messenger Bag	**Purse**	**Purse**
Staves:	Staves:	Staves:
9 vertical staves 3/8" flat reed	5 vertical staves 3/8" flat reed	7 vertical staves 3/8" flat reed
5 horizontal staves 3/8" flat reed	4 horizontal staves 3/8" flat reed	4 horizontal staves 3/8" flat reed
Space-dyed staves	Weavers:	Natural staves
Weavers:	Top: 1/4" flat natural and dyed	Weavers:
3/8" flat, 7mm flat oval , 1/4" flat	Bottom: 7mm flat oval	3/8" flat, 7mm flat oval , 1/4" flat
Sealed: Tung Oil	Painted with Unicorn Spit	Space-dyed reed

Backpack Straps

Straps are made with 1: Shaker Tape, D-rings and 8 mm rivets. D-rings and rivets are available through craft stores and online. Shaker tape is available through seatweaving websites.

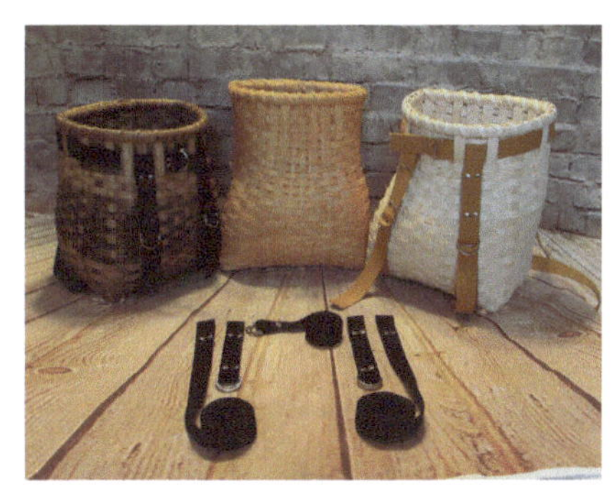

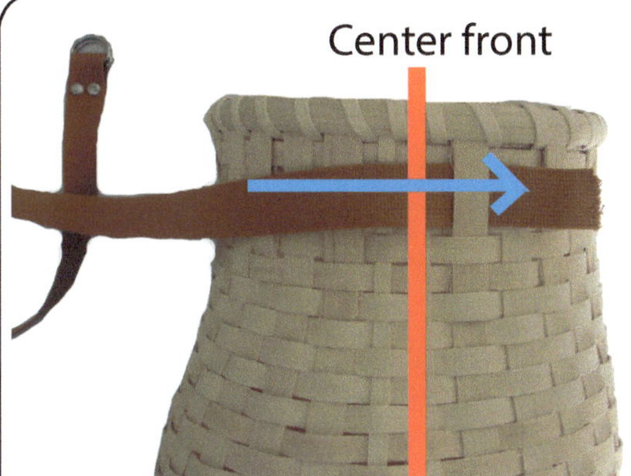

Feed the end of the backpack belt A through the first loop (d rings and 38" long)

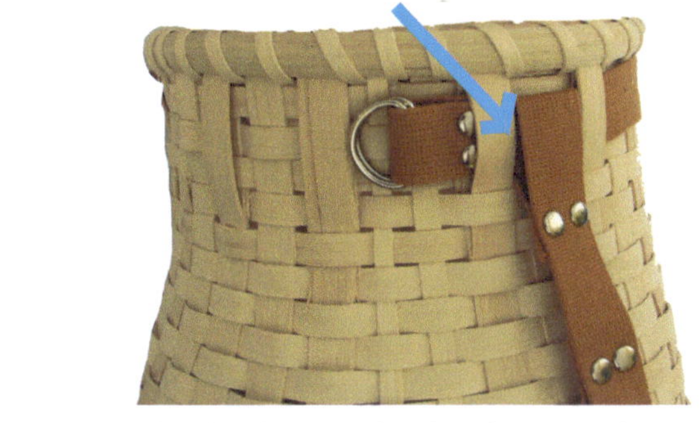

Feed the belt through the looped d rings (rivet one end, d ring other / 6" long)

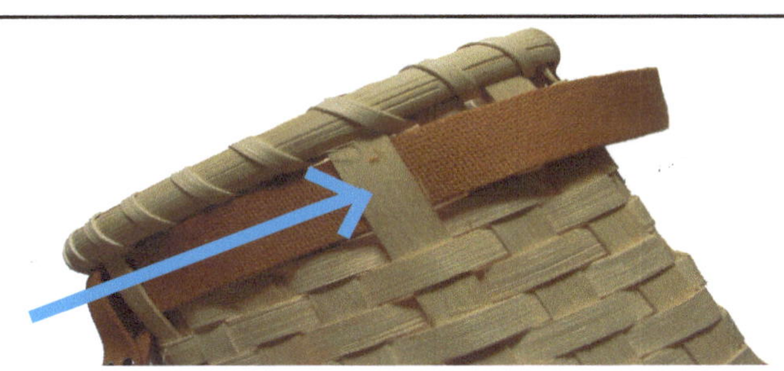

Feed belt A through right side

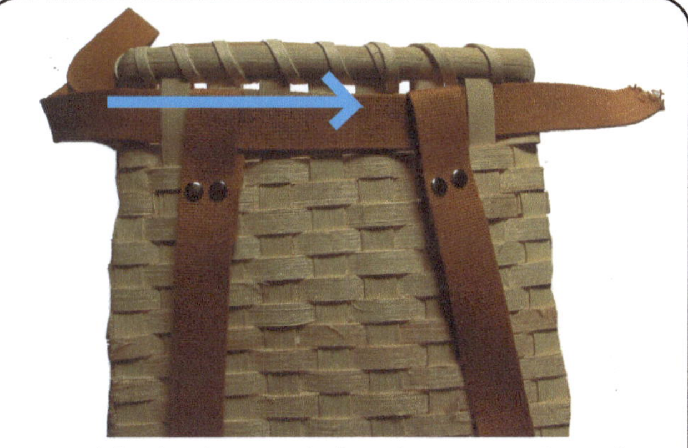

Feed belt through backstraps C and D

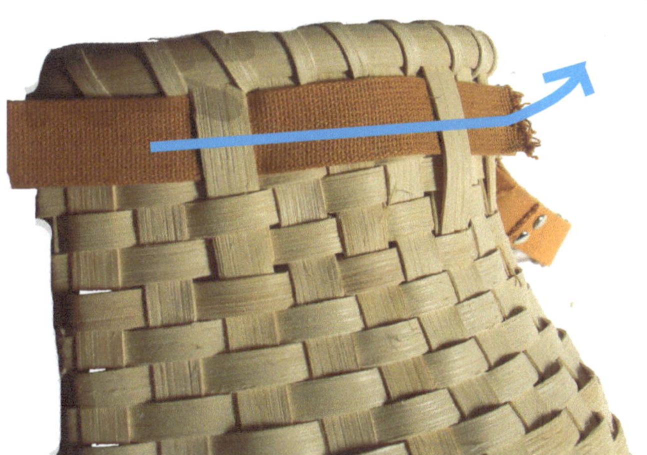

Feed belt A through to front

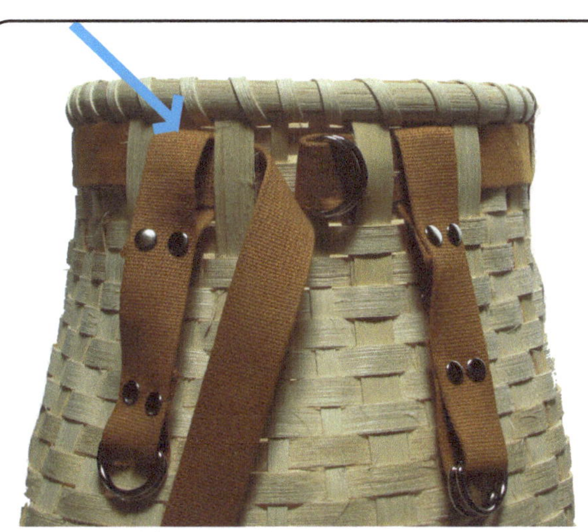

Feed belt A through loop E

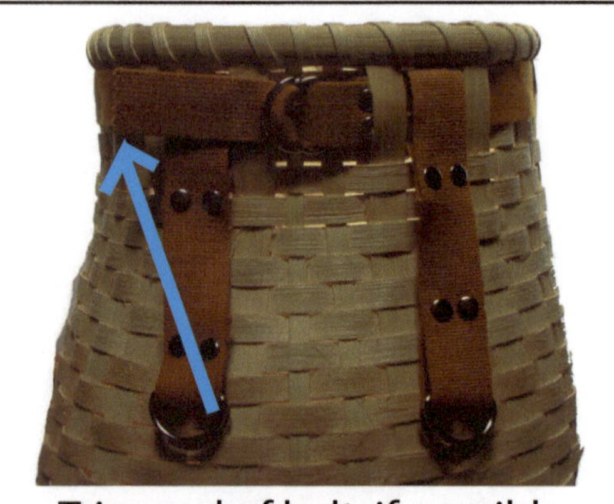

Trim end of belt, if possible, use pinking shears

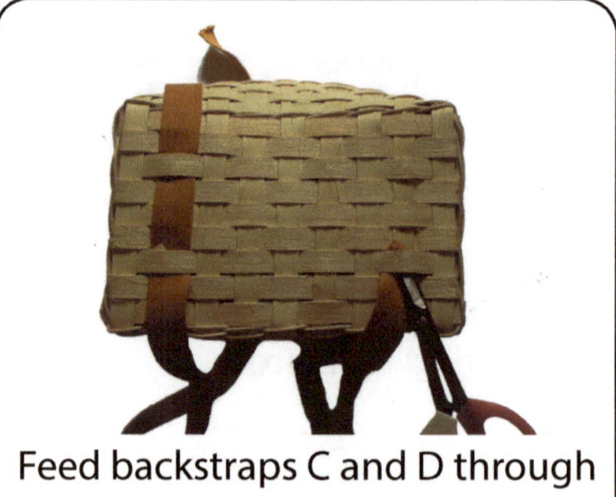

Feed backstraps C and D through bottom of backpack

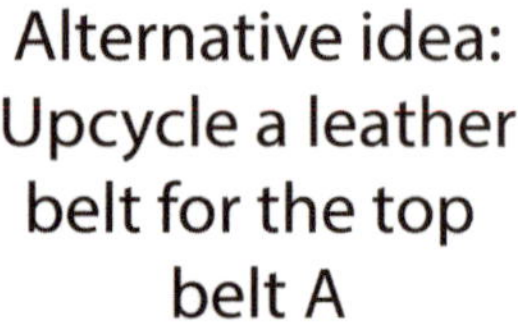

Alternative idea: Upcycle a leather belt for the top belt A

Material used is 1" shaker tape.

Adjust sizes if you make a larger or smaller backpack.

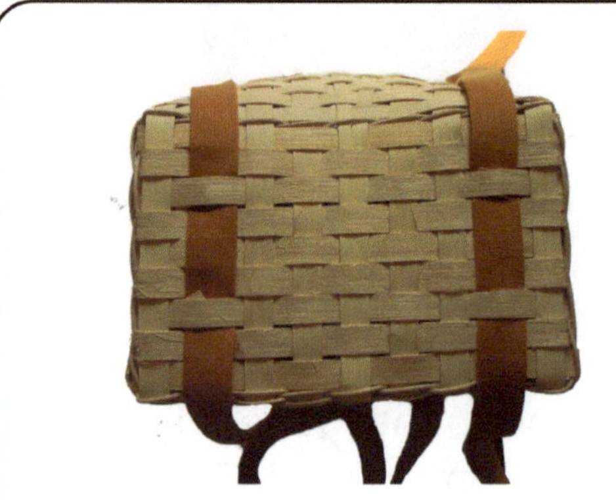

Adjust straps to length on back after feeding through

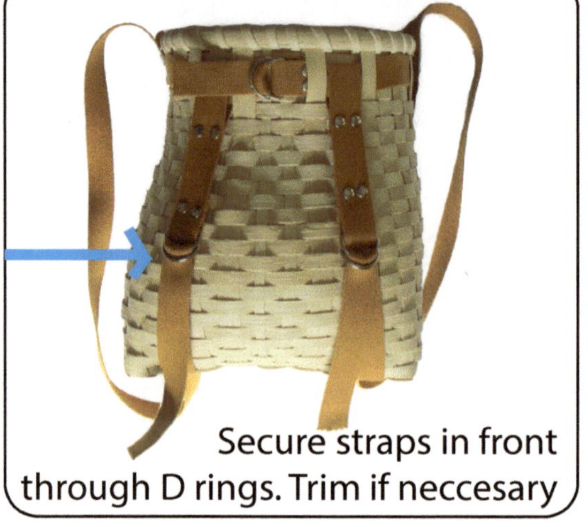

Secure straps in front through D rings. Trim if neccesary

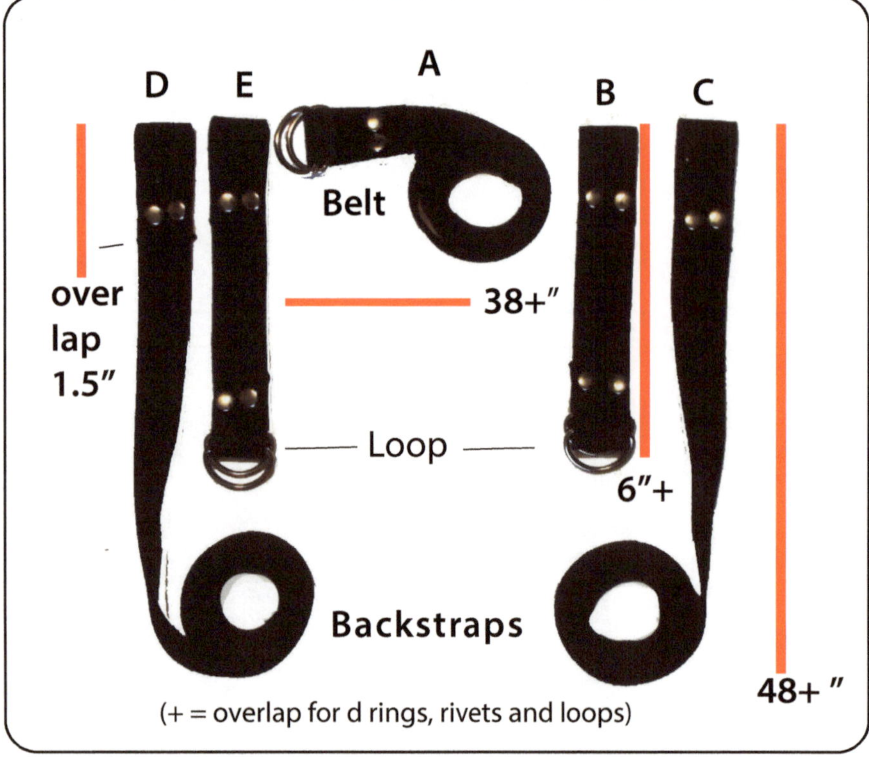

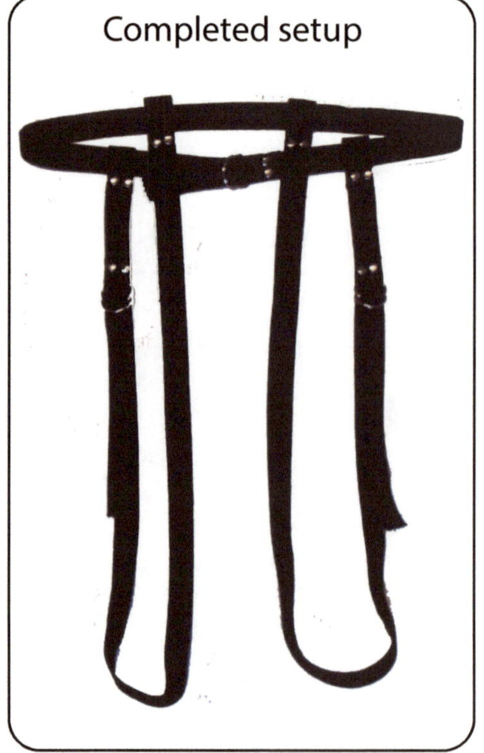

ZEN STONES

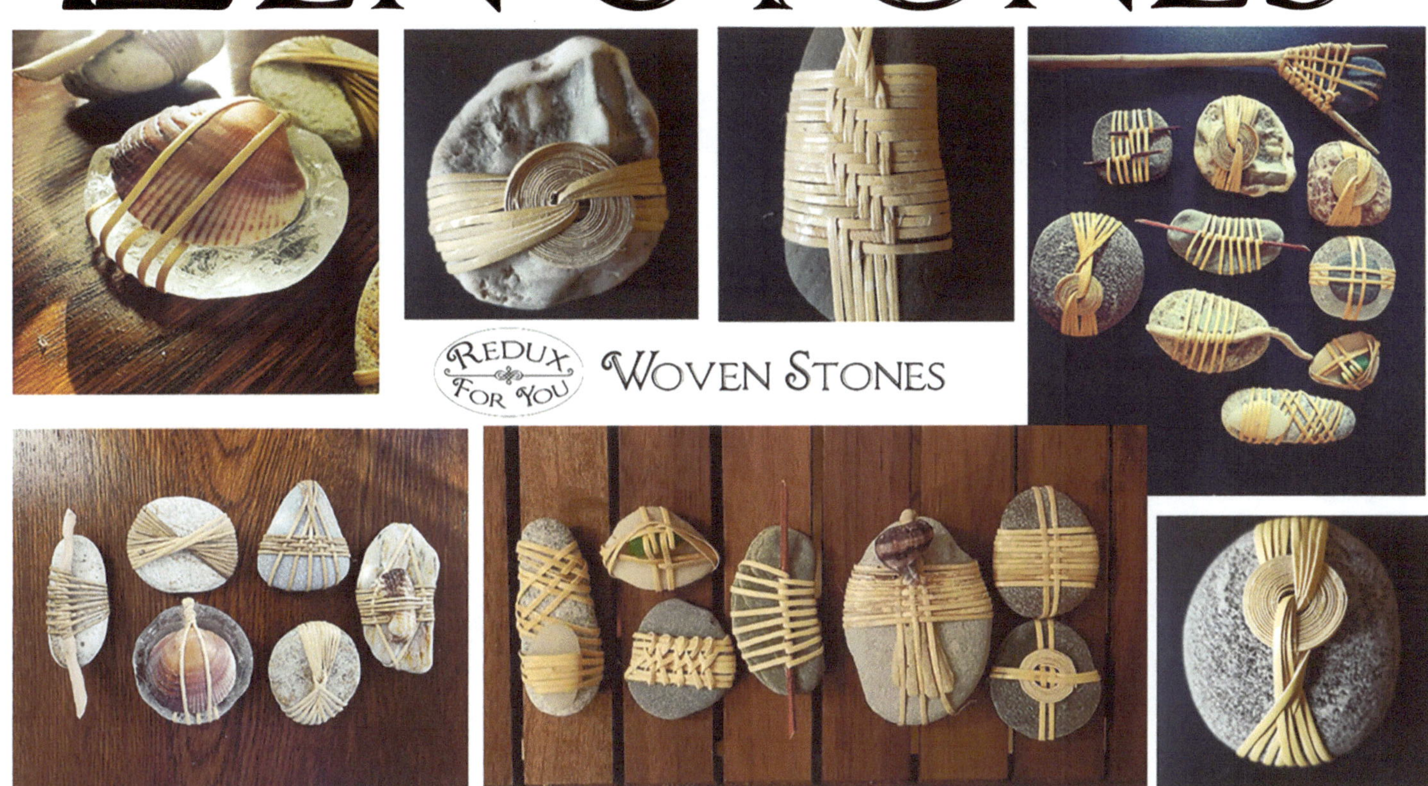

Wrapping stones can be soothing. It utilizes small pieces of cane, leather, or cord. Incorporating seaglass, driftwood, or small personal objects creates a personalized piece. It is a very portable small craft that lends itself to being done while traveling or relaxing. What a great project for a beach day or get-together with friends.

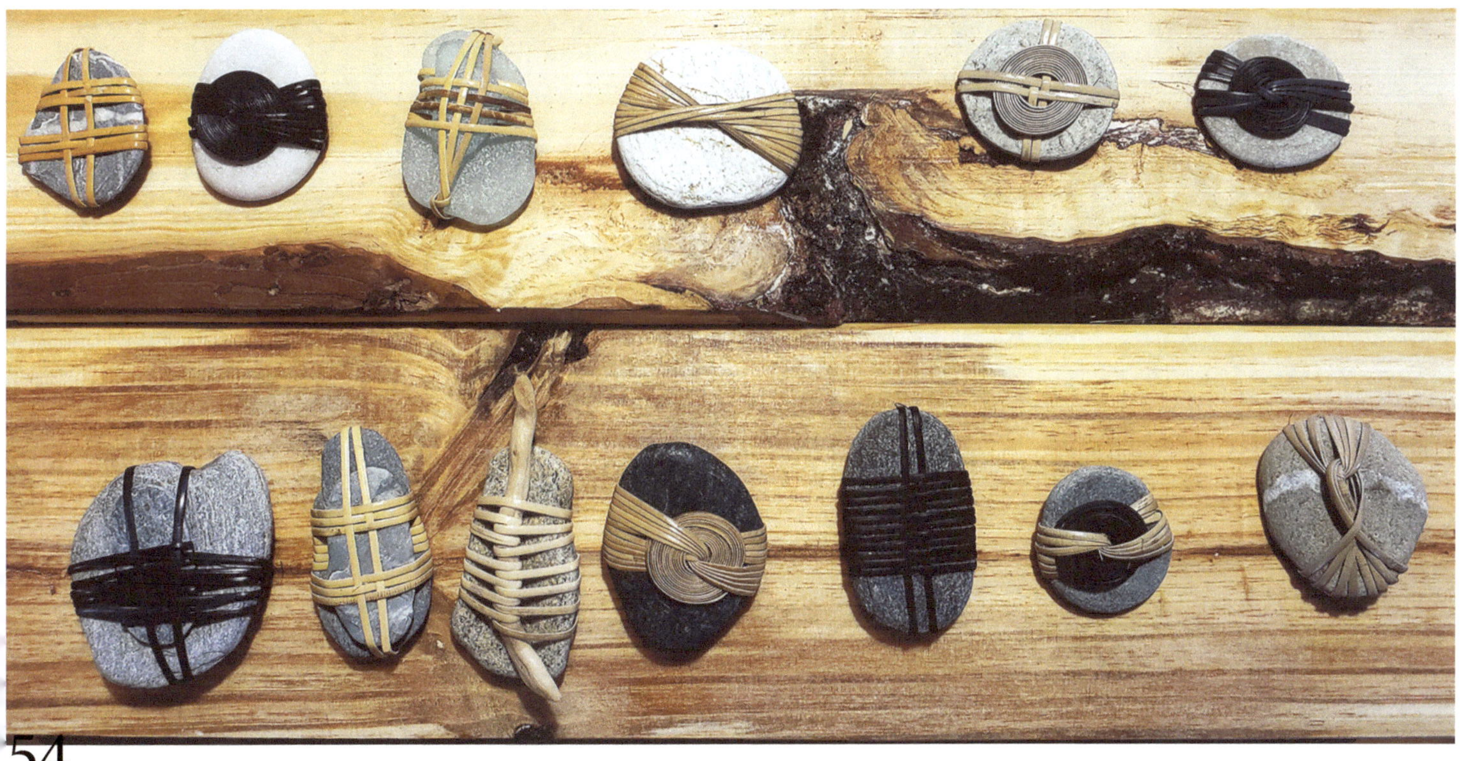

Butterfly and Moon

You can do as many or as few wraps on butterfly knot as stone allows.

For more info on butterfly see page 29 in leaf tray

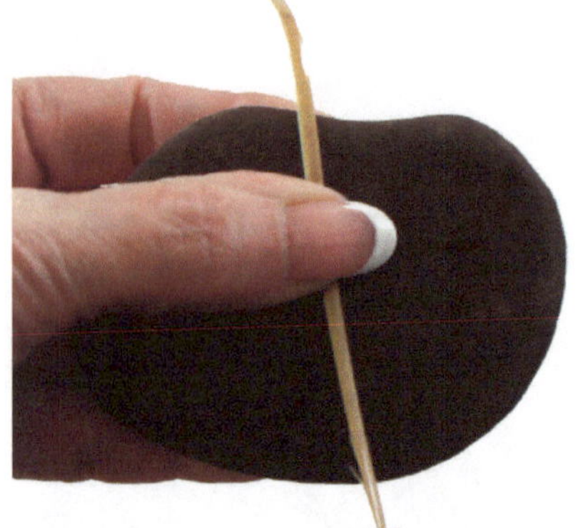

Begin cane behind stone. Leave a tail.

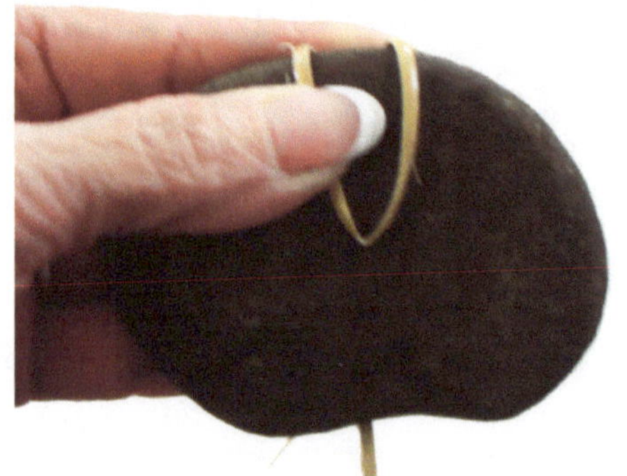

Make a U in front. Make sure cane stays flat.

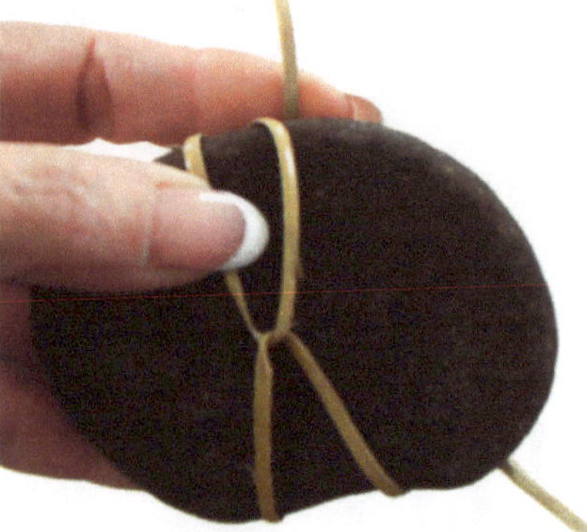

Bring cane around to front. Make a second U.

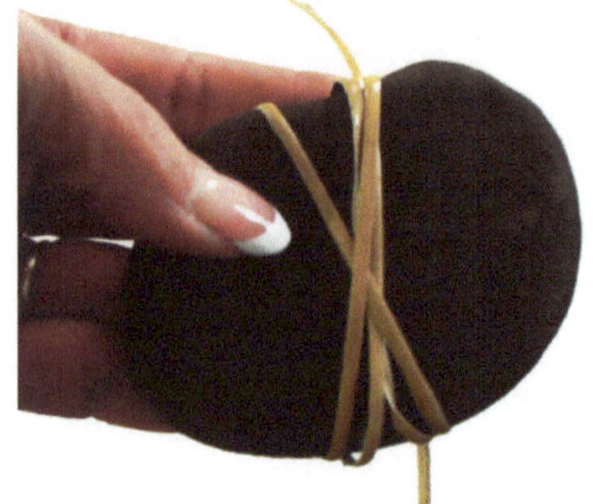

Crisscross in back. Catch the tail in wrap.

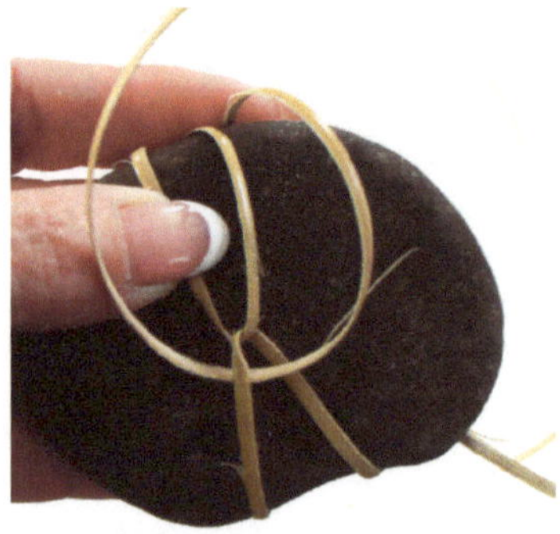

Keep making sequential wraps. Lay cane to outside of last wrap.

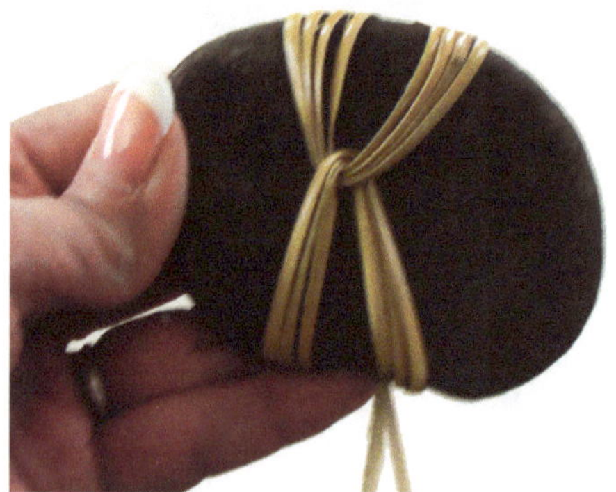

Tuck tail in back of stone: cut

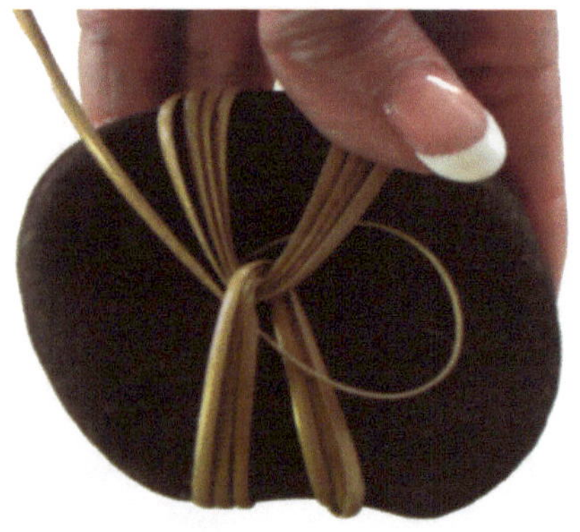

Start with a new piece on it's side. Weave under, over, under in a circle.

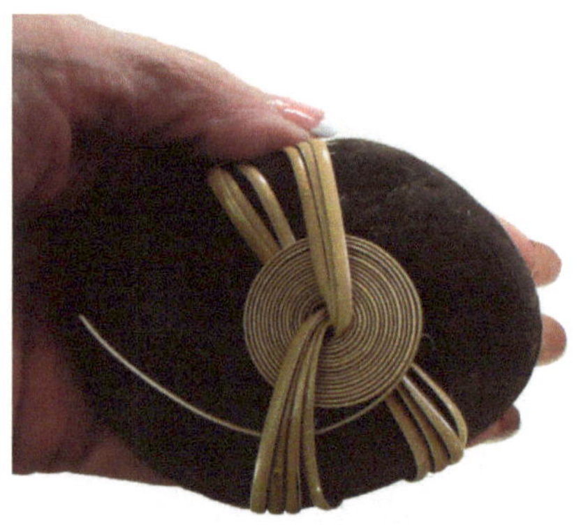

Keep wrapping snugly until desired size.

Cut end of cane, tuck in.

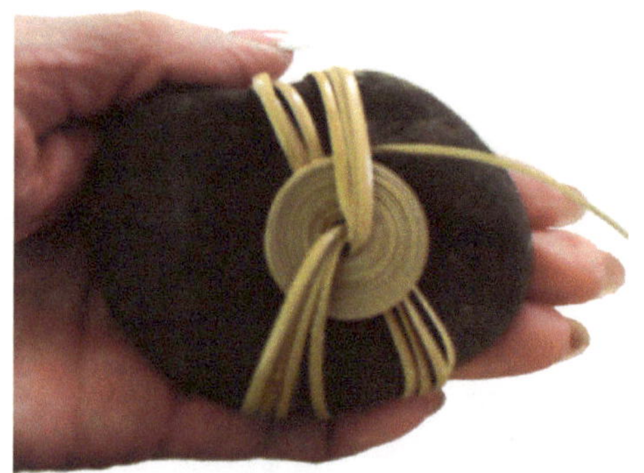

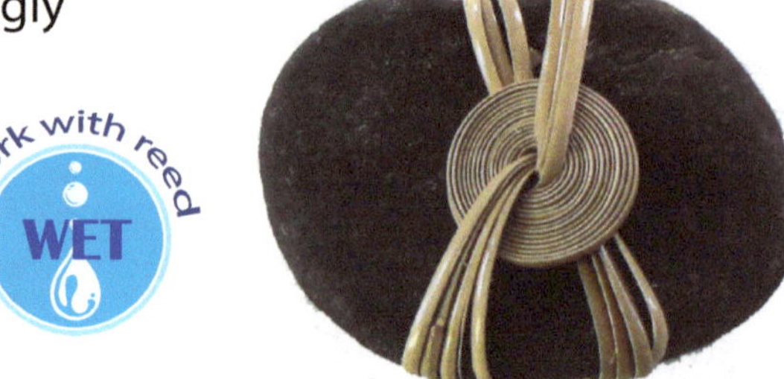

All Wrapped Up 

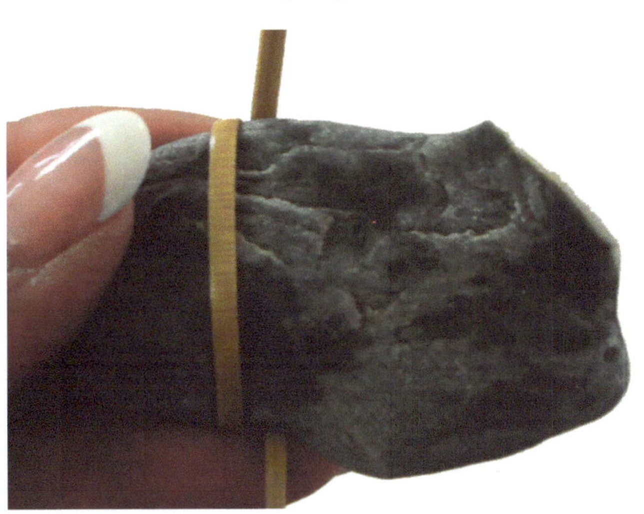

Wrap cane around back, leaving a tail.

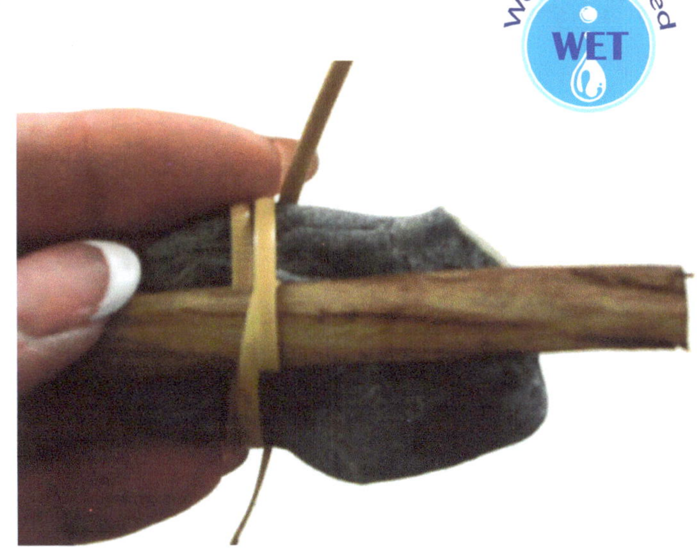

Add your stick or object.

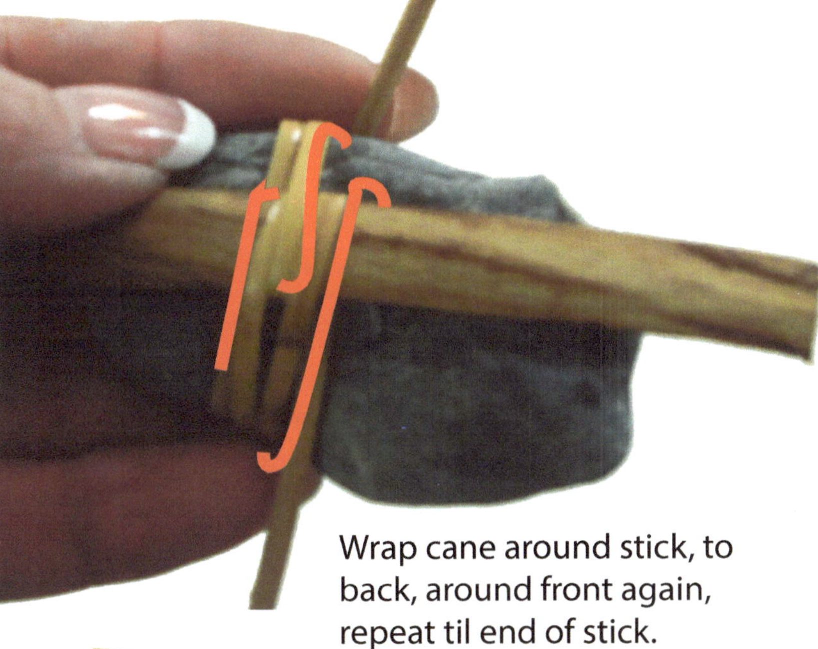

Wrap cane around stick, to back, around front again, repeat til end of stick.

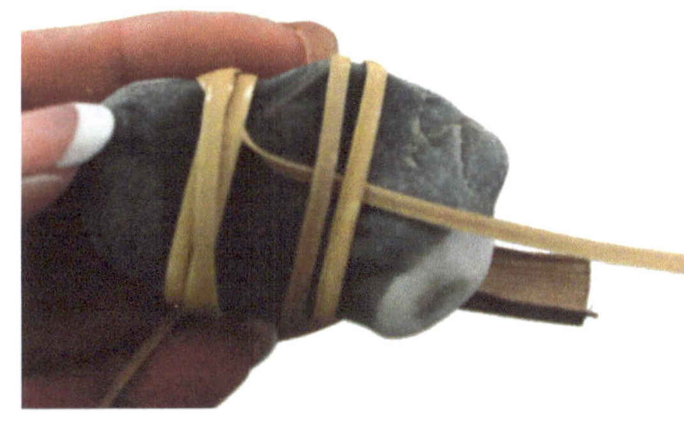

Catch tail with wrap in back.

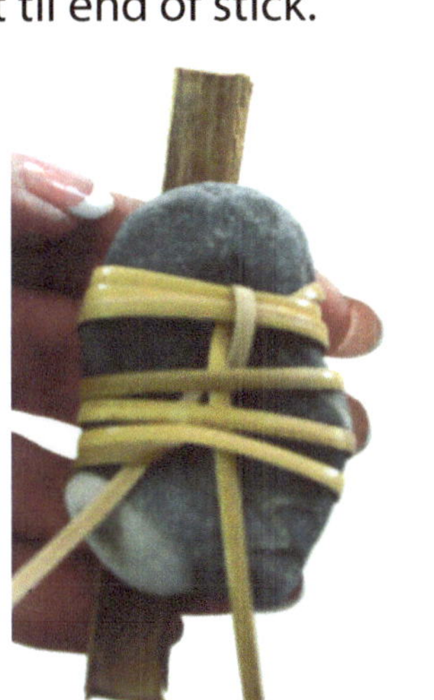

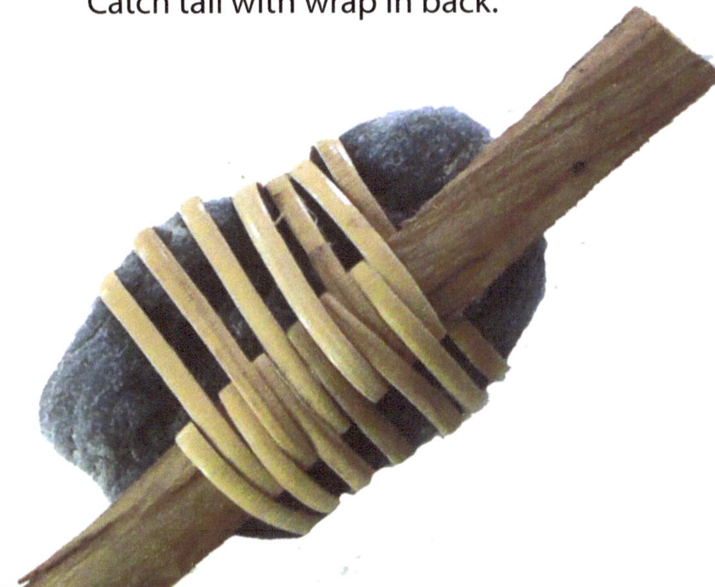

Little Weave

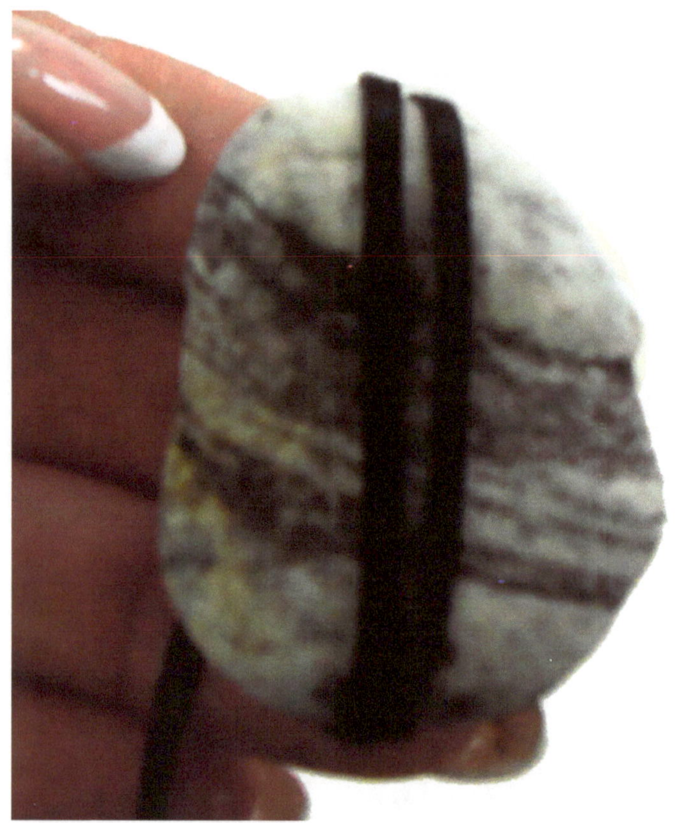

Wrap black cane around stone 2 times

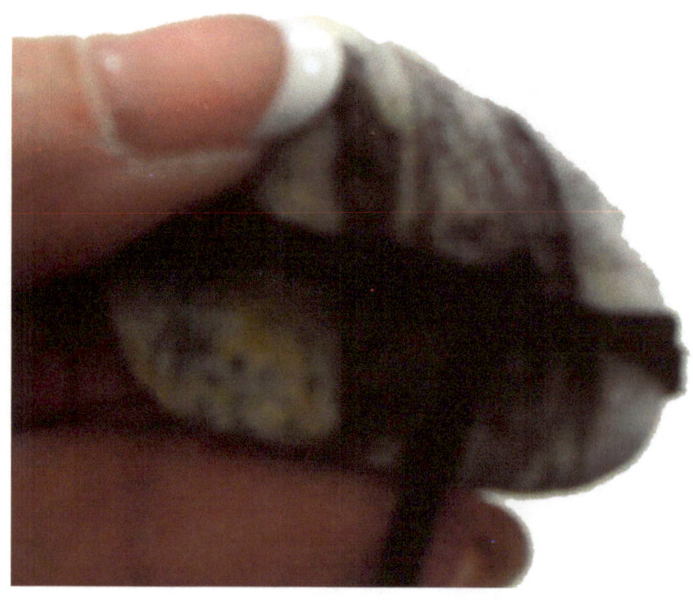

Make a right angle in back bring to front.

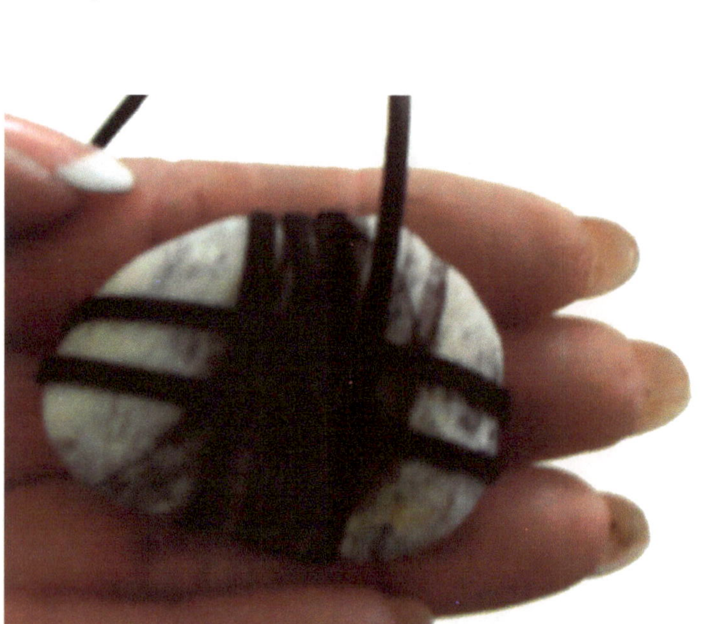

Weave over and under the 2 pieces,
bring to front and alternate for rest of stone.

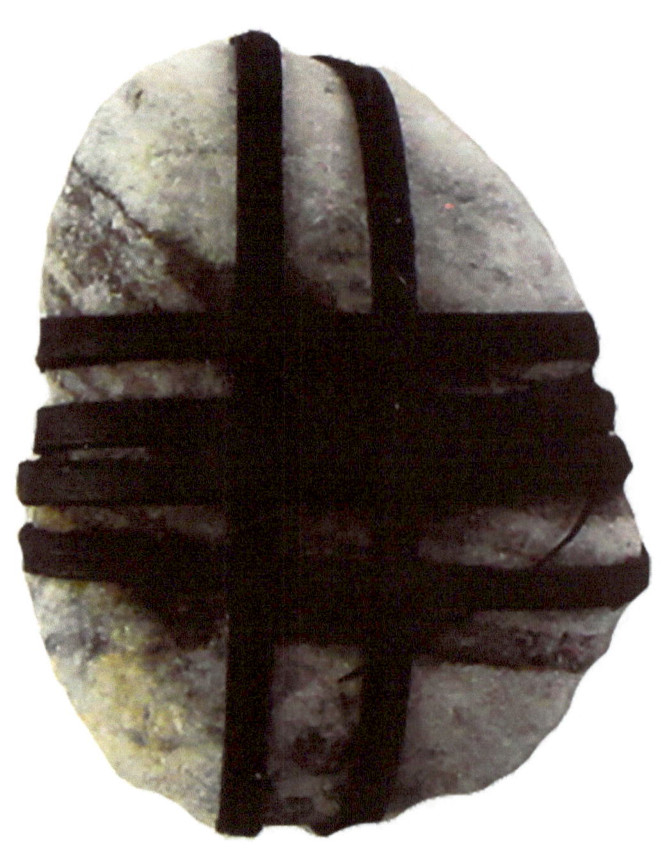

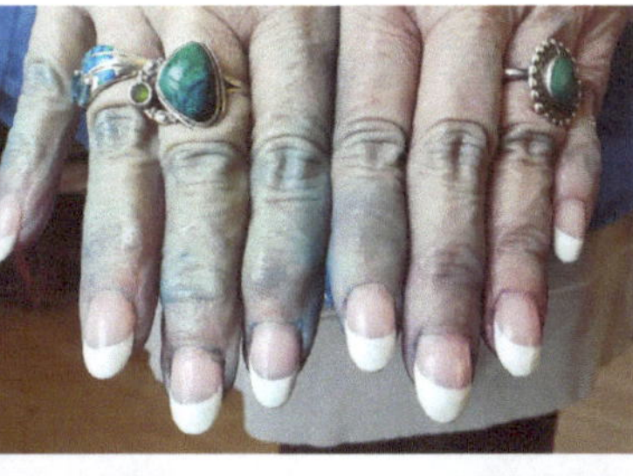

COLOR

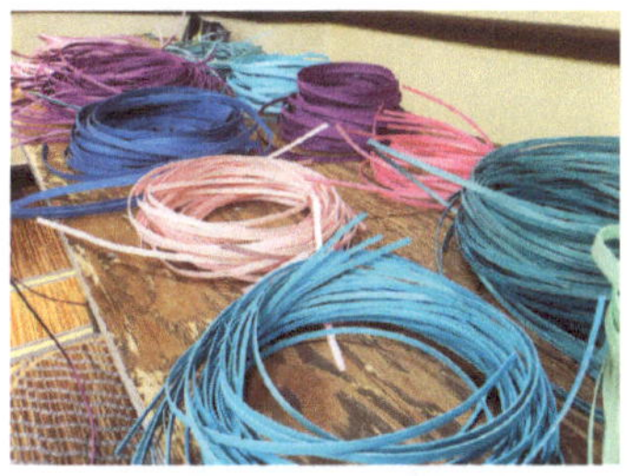

How to dye reed

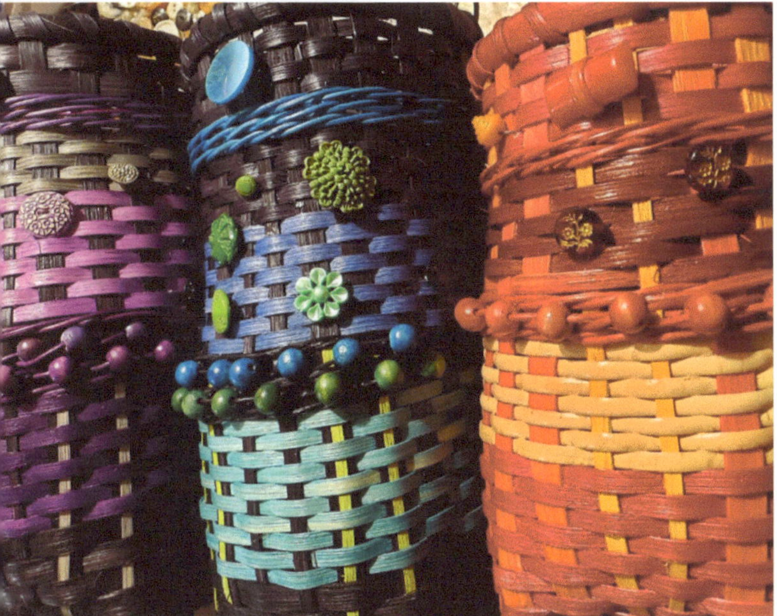

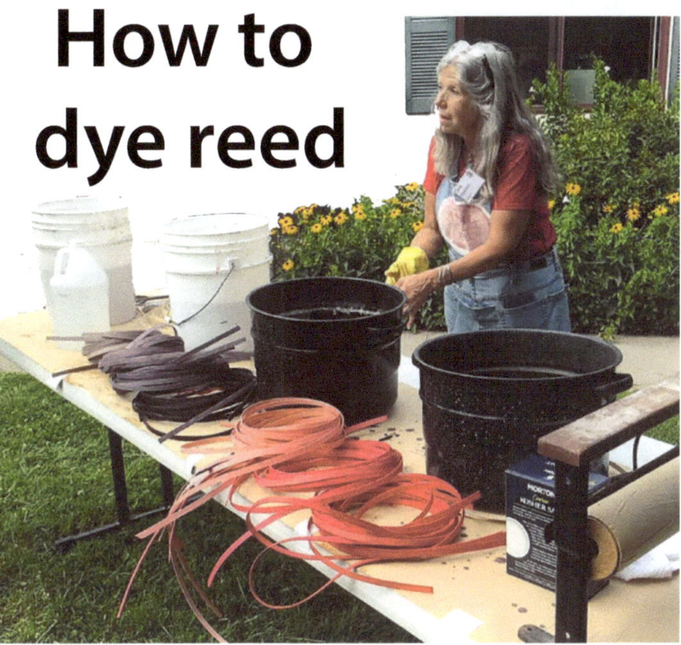

There are many different dyes to choose from. I prefer Rit Dye for a couple reasons. It is readily available with a lot of color choices. Reed suppliers also carry dyes.

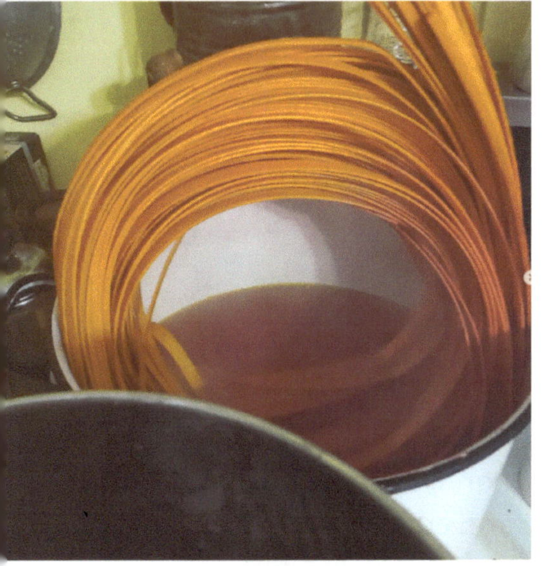

- Always use pots that are for dye only.
- Fill a large pot about half-way with water and add generous amount of plain salt.
- Choose liquid or powdered dye.
- Bring the pot to a simmer and add dye.
- Turn heat off. Do not boil reed.
- Wear gloves.
- Immerse reed in pot.
- Check on color saturation and use tongs to flip.
- Remove reed and rinse with cold water until the water runs clear.
- Give the reed a final rinse with a few gallons of cold water and about a quart of white vinegar. This helps set the dye and keep it from bleeding.
- Dye batches in tones of color by leaving in different lengths of time: Dark, medium, light.
- Dye accessories like wooden beads or webbing if desired.
- To create "space-dyed" reed, use 3 pots of color at the same session. Dip 1/3 of each bundle in each of the colors.

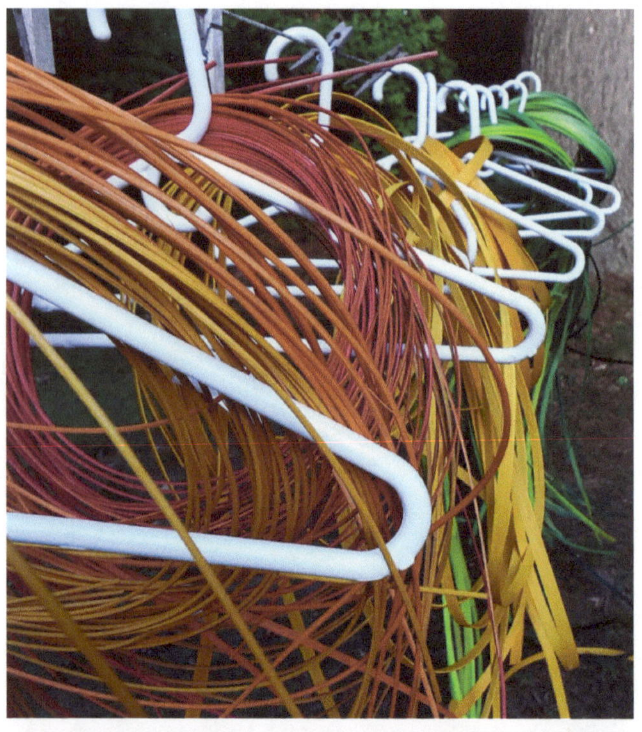

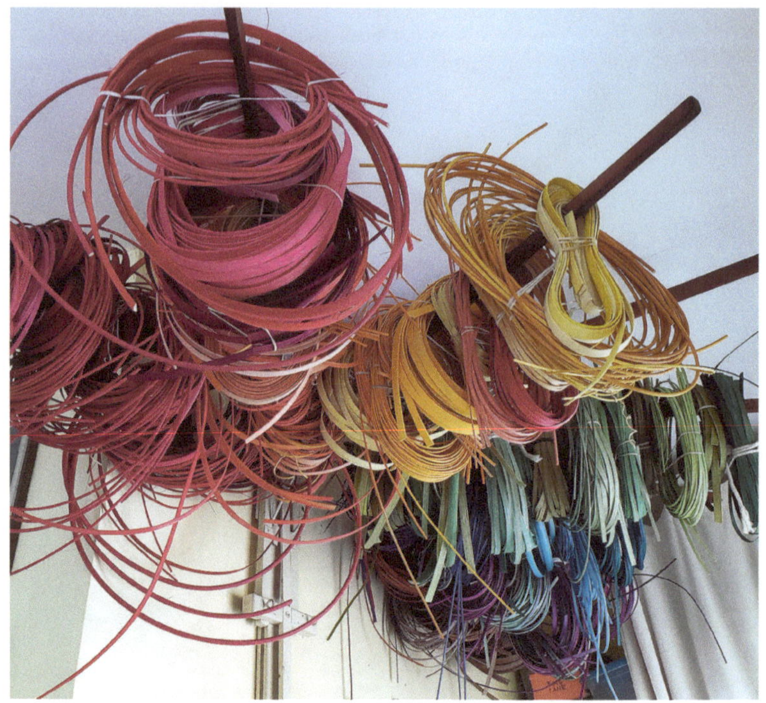

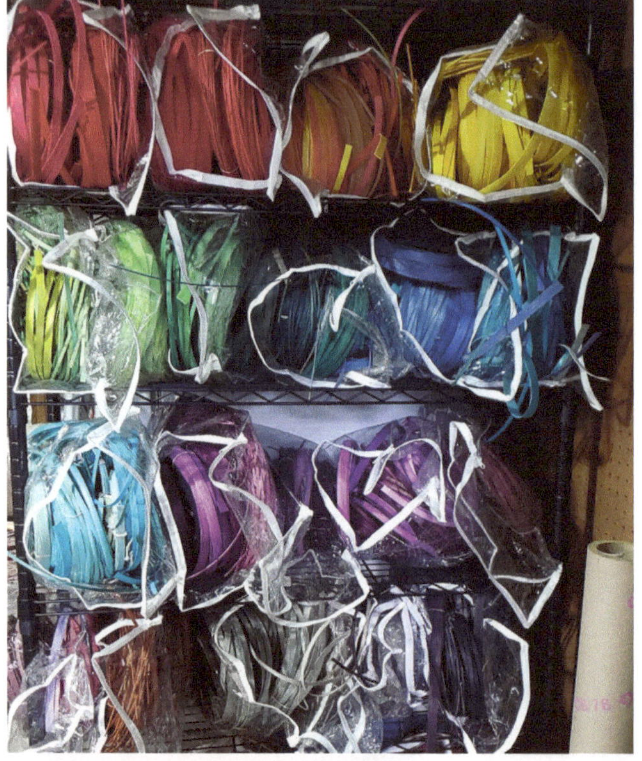

Dry Reed

- Let reed dry completely.
- Dry outside if possible.
- Never store reed damp as it will mold.
- Store hanging or in open bags.
- Add dessicant to bags to remove moisture.
- Bags in photo are zippered linen bags.

Seal Reed

- Seal reed on finished projects to prevent bleeding and maintain colors.
- Apply Tung oil finish, Danish oil or UV Archival Varnish using brush. Wipe off excess.
- Scott's Liquid Gold or Howard's Feed n' Wax are also options. Reapply depending on use.
- Do not use urethane, polyurethane. They may flake and crack after time.

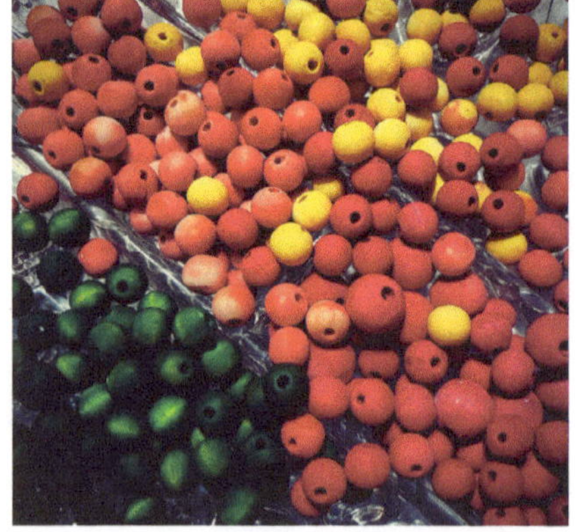

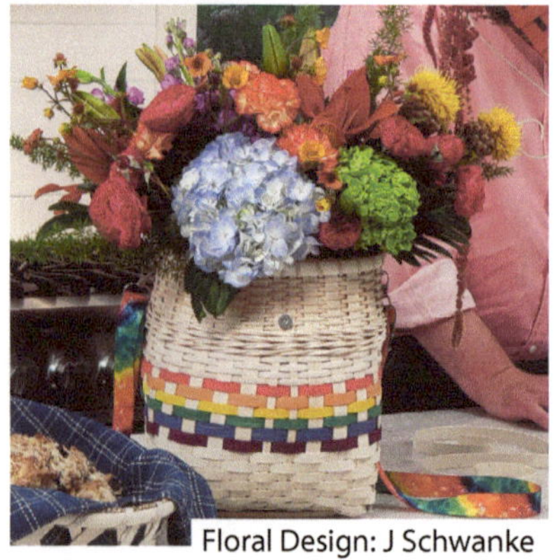

Floral Design: J Schwanke

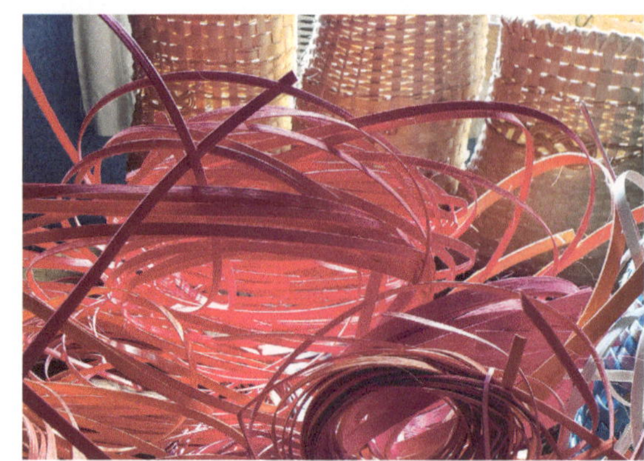

59

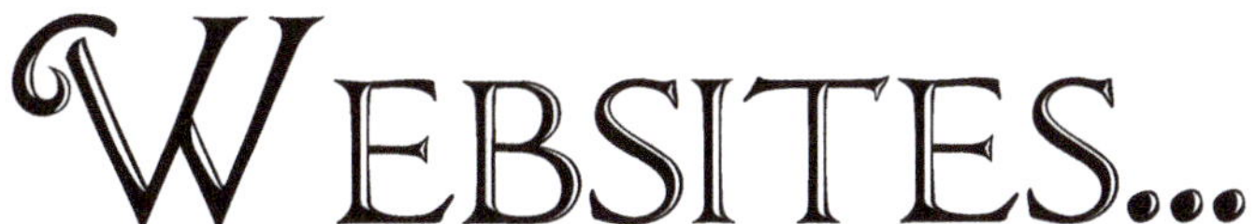
WEBSITES...

Websites:

reduxforyou.com

suemuldoonimages.com

ubloom.com/life-in-bloom

Silverriverchairs.com

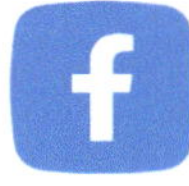  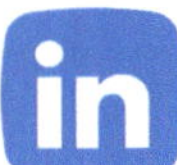

Supplies:

hhperkins.com

All materials in this book are sourced from hhperkins.com with the exception of wool and add-ons.

Wickerwoman.com

alchemyfibermill.com

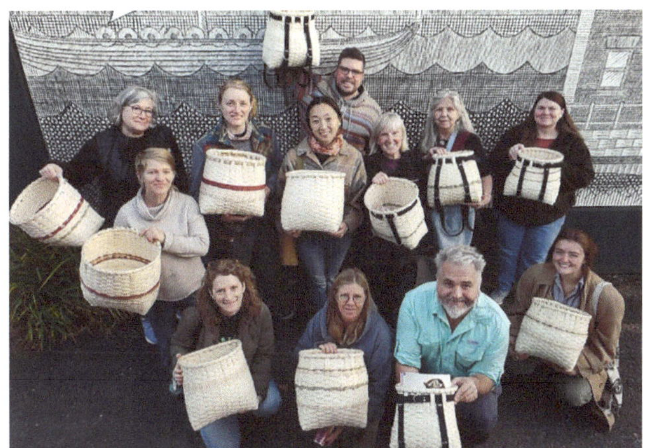

Photo: Hudson River Maritime Museum

AND RESOURCES

Guilds:

The Seatweavers' Guild

Northeast Basketmakers Guild

National Basketry Organization

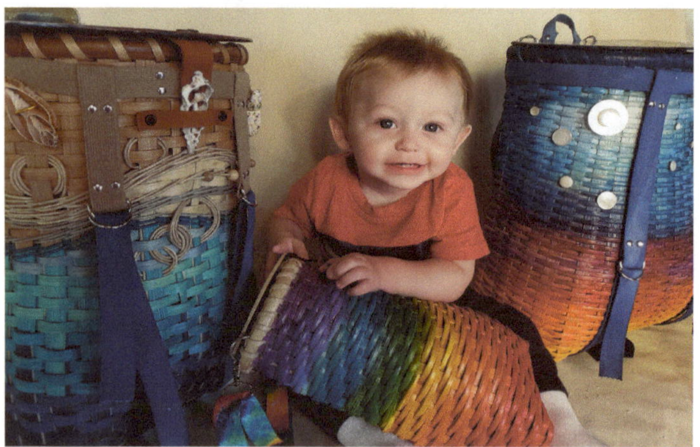

Teaching and shows at:

HH Perkins
Northeast Basketmakers Guild
The Seatweaver's Guild
John C Campbell Folk School
The CT Renaissance Faire
Robin Hood's Faire
Coventry Farmers Market
CT Valley School of Woodworking
Snow Farm
Searsport Shores Campground
Lessonface
North Bennet Street School
Arts Center East
Ashford Area Arts Council
New York State Sheep and Wool
The Fiber Festival of New England
Maryland Sheep and Wool
Mid Atlantic Fiber Association
Alchemy Fiber Mill
Gifts on the Green
Hudson Valley Maritime Museum
Waterford Craft School
Nutmeg Spinners
Jockey Hollow Spinners
Coventry Arts Guild

Find a class, festival or faire...

Calendar

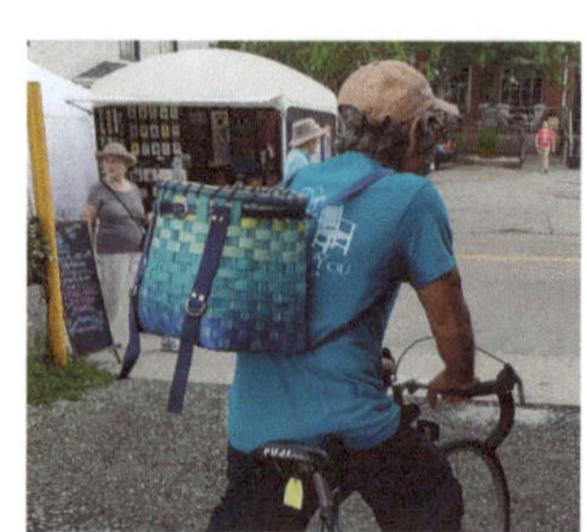